SET FREE

Other Neil Anderson titles published by Monarch Books:

The Bondage Breaker
Daily in Christ (New Edition)
Freedom from Fear
Higher Ground
Living Free
Radical Image
Righteous Pursuit
Steps to Freedom in Christ
Victory Over the Darkness

Available from Christian bookshops or, in case of difficulty, contact Monarch Books, Concorde House, Grenville Place, Mill Hill, London NW7 3SA.

CONTENTS

The Way of Escape

Appendix

FOREWORD

After an exhausting day of teaching a 'Living Free in Christ' conference in Bogotá, Colombia, I turned on the television set in my hotel room which carried Cable News Network. It was late in the evening when I heard the news about the death of Princess Diana. Like everyone else, I was shocked. Within a week, Mother Teresa died. Undoubtedly, they were two of the most recognisable women in the world, but they were as different as two people could be.

One was a princess; the other, a pauper. One held a position of royalty in an earthly kingdom; the other held a position of royalty in the Kingdom of God, as do all His children. One was physically beautiful, the other was quite homely. Both received a state funeral even though political protocol didn't call for it. One received the greatest outpouring of love and adoration that the modern world has ever seen; the other received the Nobel Peace Prize. Many longed to have the power, prestige, position and pleasures that one had, but few wanted what the other had (or didn't have).

Although people could debate the moral character of Princess Diana and the theology of Mother Teresa, that would only cause them to miss one of the greatest object lessons this world has ever seen. This incredible outpouring of love and admiration happened because the world perceived that these remarkable women *cared*.

The credibility of Christianity is at stake. Whether we like it or not, we are ambassadors for Christ with the vital ministry of reconciliation (2 Cor 5:17–21) and the world is watching. Consciously or unconsciously, people are asking two questions: 'Do we care?' and 'Is Christ really the answer for a sick world?' I wasn't in ministry very long before I realised that the world doesn't care how much we know until they know how much we care. We can't preach the good news and be the bad news. Jesus said, 'By this all men will know that you are my disciples, if you have love for one another' (Jn 13:35). 'The goal of our instruction is love from a pure heart and a good conscience and a sincere faith' (1 Tim 1:7). Having a good apologetic without love is to be a noisy gong and clanging cymbal (1 Cor 13:1). It makes a lot of noise, but accomplishes nothing.

I have never been more convinced that Christ is the only answer and that the truth of His Word, when ministered in love, will set people free. Freedom in Christ Ministries was birthed out of brokenness. God systematically brought me to the end of my resources so that I could discover God's. It was the greatest thing that ever happened to me. As long as we think we can do it ourselves, He will let us. During that period of brokenness, I got a glimpse of what compassion was all about. I now realise that it is the one essential prerequisite for ministry.

Beyond caring, however, there must be the biblical answer for people living in bondage to their past and to the sin that so easily entangles them. I wrote *Released from Bondage* (Part 1 of this book) to illustrate that freedom in Christ is a reality for even the most severe problems. Then I wrote *A Way of Escape* (Part 2 of this book) to show how people could be free from sexual strongholds. I was deeply pleased that Monarch wanted to combine these two books into this one single volume. It is my prayer that it will offer you some hope and encouragement in your Christian walk.

The discipleship/counselling tool that we use is 'The Steps to Freedom in Christ', which are explained in my book, *Helping Others Find Freedom in Christ*. May the Lord establish you alive and free in Christ.

Neil T. Anderson

Introduction
SETTING CAPTIVES FREE
Where are the hurting?
What is their hope?

When I graduated from seminary, I was looking forward to being the captain of a Gospel Ship. We would sail off into the eternal sunset, rescuing people from the watery abyss. We would have Bible classes, clubs for the children and sports for the athletically inclined (for the purpose of outreach, of course). Everybody would love one another.

Off I sailed on my first assignment and it wasn't long before I noticed a dark ship sailing alongside. On that ship were people with all kinds of problems. They were struggling with alcohol, sex, drugs and abuse of every conceivable kind. I suddenly realised that I was on the wrong ship. God had called me to be the captain of the dark ship. Through a series of life-transforming events, I ended up being that captain — and to my surprise I found out it was the same ship!

The needy are not only 'out there' somewhere. Our churches are filled with hurting people wearing masks, frightened that someone may find out what's really going on inside of them. They would love nothing more than to have some hope, affirmation and help.

This book is about being released from that kind of bondage. You will read actual accounts of courageous people who have agreed to tell their stories from their perspective. They were already committed evangelical Christians before our encounter together. Some are in full-time ministry. Only their names, occupations and geographical references have been changed to protect their identity. I assure you that what they share is true and they in no way represent a few isolated cases.

We have hundreds of similar stories from personal counselling and thousands that could be shared from conferences. What's at stake isn't my reputation or transient ministry, but the integrity of the church and countless millions who are counting on the church to take its rightful place in God's kingdom programme of setting captives free. I hope you will find great personal help in reading these pages, but beyond that, it is my earnest prayer that you will gain insights which will enable you to become a part of a captive-freeing movement of God which is beginning to grow in the church.

Hope for the hopeless

One day I received a call from a colleague in the ministry. We chatted about what God was doing in our respective lives. After recounting testimonies of marriages saved and people freed from bondage, he shifted to the real intent of his call. 'Neil,' he began, 'I recall you saying that a husband can get caught in a role conflict if he tries to counsel his own wife. I have had the privilege of helping others find freedom in Christ, but trying to help my own family is another matter. Could you possibly find time to see my wife, Mary? She is a wonderful lady, and people see her as composed, but she struggles inwardly on a daily basis.'

Mind you, this is the wife of a man in ministry. But then, why wouldn't Satan attack those in the front lines of the battle?

I met twice with Mary. The first day we just got acquainted. The second day I walked her through the Steps to Freedom in Christ, which address seven main areas where Satan could have an opportunity to gain a stronghold in our lives. (These Steps to Freedom are in the appendix.) A week later I received this letter from Mary:

Dear Neil:

How can I say thanks? The Lord allowed me to spend time with you just when I was concluding that there was no hope for me to ever break free from the downward spiral of continual defeat, depression and guilt. I did not know my place in Christ or recognise the enemy's accusations.

Having literally grown up in church and having been a pastor's wife for twenty-five years, everyone thought I was as put together on the inside as I was on the outside. On the contrary, I knew there was no infrastructure on the inside and often wondered when the weight of trying to hold myself together would cause my life to fall apart and come crumbling down. It seemed as if sheer determination was the only thing that kept me going.

When I left your office last Thursday it was a beautiful, crystal-clear day with snow visible on the mountains, and it felt like a film had been lifted from over my eyes. The cassette player was playing a piano arrangement of *It Is Well With My Soul*. The words of the song fairly exploded in my mind with the realisation that it was well in my soul...for the first time in years.

The next day at work my immediate response to 'How are you today?' was 'I'm doing great! How about you?' In the past I would have mumbled something about being almost alive. The next comment I heard was, 'Boy, something must have happened to you yesterday.'

I have heard the same songs and read the same Bible verses as before, but it is as if it's all totally new. There is underlying joy and peace in the midst of the same circumstances that used to bring defeat and discouragement. For the first time, I have wanted to read my Bible and pray. It is hard to contain myself — I want to shout from the rooftops what has taken place in my life, but my real desire is for my life itself to do the shouting.

Already the deceiver has tried to plant thoughts in my mind that this won't last, that it's just another gimmick that won't work. The difference is that now I know those are lies from Satan and not the truth. What a difference freedom in Christ makes!

With gratitude,

Mary

What a difference indeed! Is there something special about Neil Anderson that made this counselling session so effective? Do I have some unique gift from God or special anointing? No, I don't think so. In fact, there are people all over the world using the same truths that I do to help people find their freedom in Christ, with similar results. So how does one explain such results?

What is mental health?

Psychologists and mental health experts generally agree that people are mentally healthy if they are in touch with reality and relatively free of anxiety. From a secular view, then, every person in this book would be considered mentally ill, and so would anybody else under spiritual attack. Seen through the grid of our western culture, these people have either a neurological or psychological problem.

If someone hears voices or sees an apparition and the counsellor doesn't, the secular counsellor concludes that the person has lost touch with reality and he or she will be put on anti-psychotic medication to stop the voices. Yet I have counselled hundreds of people who are hearing voices, and to this day, every one has been demonic (or MPD — 'multiple personality disorder'). With the person's cooperation, it usually takes an average of two to three-and-a-half hours to free a Christian from that influence.

In 1 Timothy 4:1, we learn 'that in later times some will abandon the faith and follow deceiving spirits and things taught by demons' (NIV). It is easier for me to believe that these people who hear voices are under spiritual attack than to believe they are mentally ill and that their mind has somehow split apart and carries on a dialogue with the other half. After hearing their stories, I have told hundreds that they are not going crazy, but that there is a spiritual battle going on for their minds. You can't imagine the relief that brings to troubled people.

If they are mentally deranged, I can't offer them a very positive prognosis. But if there is a battle going on for their minds, we can win that war. I do believe, however, that the mind can dissociate during severe trauma as a defensive means to mentally survive. I will discuss that phenomenon in the last chapter of Part 1.

Satan paralyses his prey

Anyone under spiritual attack would also fail on the second criterion for mental health — relative freedom from anxiety. Fear is a given for those caught in bondage. Like a lion, Satan's deceptive roar (1 Peter 5:8) paralyses his prey in fear, but we are to remain firm in our faith (i.e., what we believe). Fear and faith are mutually exclusive. If fear of the unknown is governing one's life, then faith in God isn't. Only the fear of the Lord is compatible with biblical faith. In reality this lion named 'Satan' has no teeth, but he is, outrageously, getting away with gumming Christians to death!

A pastor friend called asking for my help. His wife was faced with what appeared to be a terminal illness and he called me because she was experiencing tremendous fear. As we talked, she proclaimed in tears that she may not be a

Christian. I was astonished. She was one of the most loving, pious examples of Christianity I had ever known. Yet here she was, facing the possibility of death without the assurance of salvation. I responded, 'Sweetheart, if you're not a Christian, I'm in deep trouble. Why would you think that?' She replied, 'Sometimes, when I go to church, I think these awful thoughts about God and dirty thoughts go through my mind.' 'That's not you,' I assured her. Half an hour later she understood the origin of those thoughts and Satan's tactics; the thoughts were gone and so was her fear.

If those thoughts had been her thoughts, then what could she have concluded about her nature? 'How can I be a Christian and have those kinds of thoughts?' she reasoned, and so do millions of other well-meaning Christians. Exposing the lie and understanding the battle for the mind is to win half the battle. The other half is having a true knowledge of God and knowing who you are as a child of God.

Where mental health begins

I believe mental health begins with a true knowledge of God and who we are as His children. If you know that God loves you, will never leave you nor forsake you, and has prepared a place for you for all eternity...if you know that your sins are forgiven, that God will supply all your needs and enable you to live a responsible life in Christ...if you have no fear of death because eternal life is something you possess now and forever...if you know that...if you deeply know and believe that...would you be mentally healthy? Surely, you would!

If that true knowledge of God and who we are is where mental health begins, let me quickly add that the greatest determinant of mental illness is a distorted knowledge of God — a pathetic understanding of your relationship with Him and ignorance of who you are as a child of God. That is why secular counsellors often hate religion. Most of their clients are very religious! Visit a 'psych' ward and you will observe some of the most religious people you have ever seen, but they are not people who have a true understanding of who they are in Christ. Since the secular counsellors are ignorant of the spiritual world, they wrongly blame pastors and churches for their clients' distress. (Although I must admit there are some pretty sick pastors and churches who do indeed create problems for people.)

The gospel in counselling

I pray for the day that Christian counselling can be identified on the basis of two definitive questions. First, *how does the gospel enter into the counselling procedure?* Are hurting people just a product of their past, or are they primarily a product of the work of Christ on the cross? Past experiences can and do have a profound effect on present day living and perspectives, but can we be free from our past — and how?

Various attempts are often made to fix the past. You can't fix the past; you cannot go back and undo what has been done. Much, much better is the truth that you can be a brand new creation in Christ and be set free from the past by establishing a new identity in Christ and forgiving those who offended you. The cross of Christ is the centre of human history and experience; without that there is no gospel and there is no forgiveness. (This is the subject of my first book, *Victory Over the Darkness*.)

The second definitive question that should identify Christian counselling relates to the issue of a biblical world view: *Does the pastoral counsellor take into account the reality of the spiritual world?* How does the fact that 'Our struggle is not against flesh and blood, but against the rulers, against the authorities, against the powers of this dark world and against the spiritual forces of evil in the heavenly realms' (Ephesians 6:12, NIV) enter into our counselling

procedure? How does a counsellor lead a person from
bondage to freedom? (This is the subject of my second
book, *The Bondage Breaker*. These two books provide the
theological basis for how the people, whose stories are told
in this book, found their freedom in Christ.)

Demon possession or demonisation?

Another issue concerns demon possession. Can a Christian
be demon possessed? No question polarises the Christian
community more than this one, and the tragedy is that there
is no absolutely biblical way to answer it. However, there are
two things worthy of note: In the English translations, the
term 'demon possession' is derived from only one Greek
word. Therefore, I prefer to use the word *demonised* instead.
Also, the word translated as 'demon possession' never
occurs in Scripture after the cross, so we are left with no
theological precision as to what demonisation would constitute in the Church Age.

However, the fact that a Christian can be influenced to
one degree or another by the 'god of this world' is a New
Testament given. If not, then why are we instructed to put
on the armour of God and stand firm (Ephesians 6:10), to
take every thought captive to the obedience of Christ (2
Corinthians 10:5), and to resist the devil (James 4:7)? And
what if we don't put on the armour of God, stand firm,
assume responsibility for what we think; and what if we fail
to resist the devil? Then what? We are easy prey for the
enemy of our souls.

So how can we tell if a problem is psychological or spiritual? I believe that question is basically false. Our problems
are never divorced from the psychological. There is no time
when previous experiences, personal relationships and our
own mind, will and emotions are not contributing to our
present problems or are the key to their resolution. But our
problems are also never not spiritual. There is no time when

God isn't here, nor is there a time when it is safe to take off the armour of God. The possibility of being tempted, accused and deceived by the evil one is a continuous reality. We must deal with the whole person, addressing both the spiritual and the psychological, or a counterfeit spirituality will take the place of true spirituality — such as the encroachment of New Age philosophy into twelve-step and other self-help recovery groups, secular psychology and education.

An encounter of truth or power?

Next I'd like to talk about a procedural issue. I advocate what I call a 'truth encounter' rather than a 'power encounter'. The classic model for deliverance is to summon the expert who will call up the demon, get its name and sometimes rank, and then cast it out. In a power encounter, the struggle is between an outside agent and the demonic stronghold. But it's not power that sets the captive free; it's truth (John 8:32). Living in defeat, believers often falsely conclude that they need power, so they look for some religious experience that promises them power. There isn't a verse in the Bible after Pentecost that encourages us to seek power, only the truth. That's because the power of the Christian lies in the truth; we already possess all the power we need because we are in Christ. The problem is that we don't see or believe it, and that is why the apostle Paul prays that we might come to this understanding (Ephesians 1:18,19). In contrast, the power of Satan is in the lie and once you expose the lie, you break his power.

In a truth encounter, I deal only with the person, and I do not bypass the person's mind. In that way people are free to make their own choices. There is never a loss of control as I facilitate the process of helping them assume their own responsibility before God. After all, it isn't what I say, do or believe that sets people free — it's what they renounce, confess, forsake, whom they forgive and the truth they affirm that sets them free. This 'truth procedure' requires me to work with the whole person, dealing with body, soul and spirit.

Medicine and the church

Treating the whole person includes the physical and inter-personal. Of course, there are glandular problems and chemical imbalances, and the church and the medical field should covet one another's contributions. The medical profession positions itself to heal the body, but only the church is in any position to resolve the spiritual conflicts. So let's not sit in judgement of the shortcomings of the secular world if we as the church are not assuming our responsibility for spiritual resolution.

In these last days we are going to see many spiritual counterfeits. In *Walking Through the Darkness*, I try to identify those counterfeits and establish parameters of divine guidance. We need that kind of spiritual discernment to stand against the New Age philosophies and false teachers who will rise among us (2 Peter 2:1*f*). The primary proponents of holistic medicine are New Agers, and the majority of health food stores are staffed by them. There is nothing wrong with the pills on the shelves; just don't read the literature on the racks.

Satan's greatest access

Also, our problems never originate, nor are they resolved, in isolation from relationships. We absolutely need God, but we also desperately need each other. In my experience, unforgiveness of others affords the greatest access Satan has to the church. When people forgive from the heart, they take a giant step toward freedom. And once they are free, good relationships help nurture them toward growth. That's why, for example, resolving a child's spiritual problem only to send him back into a dysfunctional family is not an adequate solution. (Steve Russo and I have dealt with this at length in our book, *The Seduction of Our Children*.)

No instant maturity

The last issue is distinguishing between freedom and maturity. I don't believe in instant maturity. It takes time to renew our minds, develop character and learn to live responsible lives. But a captive first needs to be set free, and then he needs to learn how to enjoy that freedom, for it was for freedom that Christ set us free (Galatians 5:1). In my experience, bound people don't grow and seldom, if ever, do they experience emotional healing. A bound person needs to be released and a wounded person needs to be treated with compassion so they can be healed over time.

Now, let me introduce you to some choice followers of Christ. As they share their life stories, I will add some insights about the nature of their problems and their resolutions. You will learn at least as much from their experiences as you will from my comments. It's my prayer that their testimonies will be a tremendous encouragement, both to those who are longing to be free and to those who desire to help them.

Part 1

RELEASED FROM BONDAGE

Acknowledgements to Part 1

There are no 'self-made' people. Only the 'God-made' exist spiritually and bear fruit. The true children of God are born from above. They mature as their minds are renewed by the Word of God, and by overcoming the harsh realities of a fallen world. God does not save us from the trials and tribulations of this world, but from a Godless eternity. We enter into this eternal life the moment we put our trust in Him. He sets us free from our past and works through the difficulties of life to produce godly character.

This book is about finding our freedom in Christ and surviving in a world whose god is roaring around like a lion seeking someone to devour. Jesus said, 'In Me you have peace. In the world you have tribulation, but take courage; I have overcome the world' (John 16:33).

I want to acknowledge the people from whom you will hear in this book. They have found their peace *in* Christ and have overcome the world. They have graciously allowed their stories to be told. In the process of working with us, it required them to relive the horror they went through. In my mind they are heroes of the faith. 'They overcame him [Satan] because of the blood of the Lamb, and because of the word of their testimony' (Revelation 12:11). Their only motive for sharing their stories is to help others.

I also want to acknowledge my dear friends, Ron and Carole Wormser, who made this book possible. They are responsible for much of the writing and editing, and they personally counselled some of the people in this book. They are a precious couple who have served the Lord in missionary service for more than thirty years.

1

MOLLY:
Freedom From the
Cycle of Abuse

I like to start a conference by asking the people, 'In the short time that I am here, if I really got to know you, would I like you? I mean, if I *really* got to know you?' I asked my seminary class that question and before I could go on, one of my students responded, 'You'd feel sorry for me!' It was said in humour, but it captured the perspective of many who live a life of quiet desperation. Lost in their loneliness and self-pity, they cling to a thin thread of hope that somehow God will break through the fog of despair surrounding their life.

The system has not been kind to them. The parents who were to provide the nurturing love and acceptance they needed were instead the cause of their plight. The church they clung to for hope didn't seem to have the answers.

Such is the case of our first story. I had never met Molly before I received a rather lengthy letter sharing her new-found freedom in Christ. Then, months later on a conference tour, I had the privilege to meet her. I expected to see a broken-down, dumpy human being. But instead, the person who had lunch with my wife and me was a thoroughly professional, intelligent and attractive woman.

You will form your own mental picture as you meet her yourself. Her story is important because I didn't personally counsel her. She found her freedom by watching the videos of our conference on 'Resolving Personal and Spiritual

Conflicts' in Sunday school. Her story is representative of those who suffer because of a dysfunctional family and an inept church. I believe that many who are in spiritual bondage would step into freedom today if they knew who they are in Christ and what is the nature of the spiritual battle going on for their mind. Jesus Christ is the deliverer, and He has come to give abundant life.

Molly's Story

I was born to the two meanest people
I have ever met.

My whole life has changed since I became involved in the video series on 'Resolving Personal and Spiritual Conflicts'. The source of my lifelong bondages became clear to me for the first time. I am forty years old, and I feel that I have just now reached the 'promised land'.

I was born in a rural area in the U.S.A. to the two meanest people I have ever met. My father was a farmer with very little education who married my mother very young. My father was one of fifteen children in a family plagued with mental illness. There is a lot of instability in my mother's family as well, but they simply deny there is a problem.

The bright spot among my relatives was my grandmother. I'm sure I would have gone over the edge long ago if it had not been for her. She was a saint and I knew she loved me.

I was the firstborn of my parents, but that was after they had been married for twelve years. My first memory of them together is that of my mum locking my dad outside at night. I can still see the fierce expression on his face as he looked at me through the door and yelled, 'Molly! Open the door and let me in.' My mum, who was standing directly behind me, screamed, 'Don't you dare open that door.'

My mother and father divorced when I was four and my mother moved us out of the house. Sometime before the divorce, I remember one evening when my mother and father were planning to go out. My one-year-old sister and I were in bed, probably waiting for a baby-sitter, when suddenly I saw an evil appearance that was *exactly* like the classic red devil, dancing at the end of the bed. I was petrified with fear and felt compelled not to tell anyone exactly what I was seeing.

I called for my mother, crying as I told her only that there was something in the room. She turned the light on and said, 'There's nothing here; there's nothing here.' I pulled up the covers so I couldn't see the end of the bed as she turned out the light and went out of the room. I stayed hidden under the bed covers for a long time, afraid to look out. When I did, the presence was still there, laughing.

After my mother and father divorced, I remember the two of them meeting on the street, stopping to chat, and my father asking my mother if he could have my sister. Those words felt like a knife going through my heart because they meant that my father did not want me.

The voices probably started right then: 'Your father doesn't even want you.' And it was true. He told me all through my life that I was 'just like my mother.' I knew what that meant; I knew he hated her. She was a 'rageaholic', and I was terrorised by her outbursts of anger.

One time when I was about six, I was at my dad's house and an aunt said to him, 'Molly looks exactly like you.' Instantly, his whole demeanour changed, and he stood up and screamed at her, 'She looks exactly like her mother! I lived with that woman for sixteen years and she looks like her mother!' With that, he stomped out of the house, and I felt a sharp pain shoot through my chest.

Members of our family thought my mother might harm us. One time when my mother was really bad, an aunt came to our home and stood outside one of our windows. She was watching over us because she worried about our safety. Mother cursed us a lot of the time and totally controlled our lives. She had no friends, no love or tenderness, and often said that her life would have been a lot better without me. I felt she resented us and we were a bother to her.

In the next couple of years, Mum became even more bitter and mean. For the remainder of my years with her, I feared for my life. Though I didn't know much about the spiritual world, I felt, even then, that Satan was involved in our home life.

Finally there came a time when I would not eat my food unless my mother ate hers first because I was so afraid she would poison us. I can't describe the terror of being a child and always living with a foreboding threat of danger. Though some of our relatives feared for us as well, they feared her more, so they never did anything about it.

Once when I was fourteen, my mother decided that I'd lost something and she refused to listen when I tried to tell her that I never had the thing. She beat and cursed me from six in the evening until one in the morning, making me go from room to room and even outside in the dark to go through the rubbish, searching over and over again for this item. I guess she finally got tired and went to bed. The thing I was looking for was the top to the toothpaste tube!

Right after that, my dad came for his monthly visit. He probably would have seen us more, but his wife ranted and raved the whole time they were with us, treating us much the same way our mother did. On the way home that day, my mind suddenly blanked out. I could not remember who I was or who all the people in the car were. A huge lump welled up in my throat, and I was so scared that I couldn't talk. Then just as suddenly, when Dad turned onto our street, my memory came flooding back. Oh, how I hated walking back into the 'hell' of my home, but there was nowhere else to go.

Through all of this, I desperately wanted the love of my father and mother. All the way into my thirties, I called my mum every day even though she would often slam the phone in my ear. I was still trying to get her to love me.

When I was quite young, one of my uncles, who had a number of children of his own, would come over to our house and take me out. Apparently, it never occurred to my mother to be cautious and question why he would do that. From the time I was four until I was seven, I remember him fondling me and threatening to tell my mother that I was smoking cigarettes if I told her what he did. I remember feeling tremendous guilt, thinking that I should have said 'no', but was afraid to do it.

After that I became addicted to masturbation, a problem that I never could control until I found my freedom in Christ. That sexual desire has tried to come back, but now I know what to do about it. I just proclaim aloud that I am a child of God and tell Satan and his evil emissaries to leave me. The compulsion is gone, instantly.

Recently I wanted to tell someone about that sexual addiction so that I would be accountable. When I did tell one of my friends who went to the Bible study I was attending, she said, 'I've always had that problem, too.' We cried together and I told her of my victory over that demonic influence and all of the violent sexual thoughts that went along with it. I rejoice now that I no longer have to be subject to the evil presence associated with that act and its overwhelming power. In Christ, I am free to choose not to sin in that way.

I was molested again at age nine by a business acquaintance of my mother. She let him take my sister and me for drives in his car and he would kiss me and put his tongue in my mouth. One time, I was so scared of what he might do that I crawled up in the back window of his car and begged him to take us home. After that, he stopped taking us out.

Things became worse as I grew older. I don't remember when, but I started to pray that God would not let me lose my mind and end up in an institution. I knew that I could very easily because I had been hearing voices as long as I can remember. I had seen movies like *The Three Faces of Eve* where people lost touch with reality, and I could see how that could happen to me.

We had no spiritual life. My mother totally rejected Christianity and wouldn't let me talk about it with her. My dad went to church every Sunday, but was extremely legalistic — a trap I later fell into.

I began to attend a neighbourhood church as a teenager and became very legalistic, doing everything they told me to do...everything...to make sure that I would be happy when I was older.

At the age of fourteen, I asked Jesus Christ to be my Saviour, and I was so thrilled I couldn't wait to learn all that I could about Him. The first time I went to a youth group, they distributed some books and gave us an assignment to do. By the next week, I had answered all of the questions and purchased a notebook. Someone saw that I had completed the work and yelled out, 'Look, everybody, she even answered the questions.' The whole group laughed and I never did an assignment again.

Sunday school was worse. There were a lot of girls in our church who were wealthy, and everyone in our Sunday school class was in a sorority except me and one other girl. We would call each other every Sunday morning to be sure we would both be there because the others didn't talk to us, and neither of us wanted to be there alone.

All during this time the voices were saying, 'You're ugly. You're disgusting. You're unworthy. God couldn't possibly love you.' My life seemed to have a way of making me believe that about myself.

The oppression, depression and condemning voices continued, but no one knew. There was no one I could talk to. I thought I deserved it. When I tried to tell people what my mother was like, they either didn't understand or responded inappropriately. Once I confided in a Sunday school teacher and she said, 'Let's go and talk to your mother.' That struck icy fear in my heart because I knew what I would get from my mother after the teacher left, so I wouldn't do it. I was too terrified.

I lived by a code of self-effort, trying to please my mother to keep her from becoming angry. I believed that God put me where I was, and if I could stand the suffering, be obedient, live a good life and not sin, then when I got married He would let me find happiness. My goal was to have a Christian home and a Christian husband so I could find happiness and a secure place where no one would abuse me.

The summer after my final school year I ran into a man I had met at school, and it was love at first sight. He was the man I would marry for happiness ten months later, when I was nineteen. We were in church every Sunday and every Wednesday night, and we went to everything else there was to attend. But we had no friends and were never invited to anyone's home.

They didn't offer pre-marital counselling at our church and marriage was a big shock. I had saved myself for marriage, but I hated sex. Within a week, my husband began staying away, sometimes for a weekend. We moved into an apartment, and with the boxes still unpacked he simply left to play golf and be with his friends.

That was the final straw after a lifetime of never having felt loved by anyone. My self-esteem was so low that when I realised my husband didn't care anymore, I just went to bed and sank into a deep depression. Three weeks later, I felt convicted and got up. I thought, *How could he love me? He couldn't respect someone who clung to him and tried to hold on for dear life to his every move.* So I tried to change and make our marriage work. Somehow, we managed to stay together for fifteen years...fifteen years of conflict, rejection and pain...vacillating between living a legalistic pretence of Christianity and completely turning our backs on God.

I hoped that having a child would bring happiness, and when I couldn't get pregnant I started seeing doctors. When my fifty-year-old doctor was kind and held my hand, I felt he was just being fatherly. But then he fondled me while I was on the examination table. Later, when I developed a lump in my breast, I went to another doctor, and he did something similar.

I wasn't the kind of woman who is flirty; I could hardly look another person in the eye. I believe that is just the way Satan works, using others to bring his evil into our lives when we are vulnerable. I felt so very uncomfortable while these things were happening, but then I was used to being uncomfortable.

Later, one of my friends who worked in a law firm called and told me that one of those doctors had done the same thing to someone else and was being sued. That's when I finally knew that it wasn't me and I was relieved of some of my many doubts about myself. Right was wrong and wrong was right. My thought processes were so wrong that I just didn't know what was right.

I finally got pregnant and was catapulted into motherhood. Not very long after that, my husband came home one night and said, 'All the guys at work talk about are girls and sex, so I spend most of my time with Linda. She goes to our church and she's a Christian and I go on breaks with her.' He asked if I minded, and I said, 'No, I don't mind.' Eventually he left me for Linda.

My friends had warned me that he was seeing other women, but I wouldn't believe it. I just said, 'He wouldn't do that.' That was my way of dealing with it, because I wanted to avoid the pain of knowing or finding out that he was unfaithful.

When my husband finally walked out and left me with two babies, I gave up on God, blaming Him for all the pain. I learned in church that the way to happiness for a single girl is to marry a Christian, and I had done that. Now I was angry at God, and for six years I lived ignoring Him.

My mother urged me to 'Do something. Don't just sit there with your life. Do something, even if it's wrong.'

The people from work wanted me to go to the bar with them, and though I had never been to a bar, I went and soon got into that lifestyle. I never intended to date seamy people, but the lowest class of people would make me feel better. I even went to bars where some of the people had no teeth! I guess that was the only place I felt okay about myself because they were worse off than I was.

I was still bound by legalism and sometimes would try to go to church, but it took a Herculean effort. On Friday evenings I would go to the bar, and when my children came home from visiting their father on Saturday, I would go back to being a good little mother. On Sunday I would try to take them to church, but when I did I felt like a nail was being driven into my temple. I had always had a lot of headaches, but this pain was excruciating. Sometimes I would get sick and have to leave, and once I threw up in the car, so I finally quit going to church.

I remember one of the last sermons I heard. The preacher said, 'There is a downward spiral. When it starts, the circle is really big and things are moving slow at the top. As it goes down, things are closer and closer together and go faster and faster until they are out of control. But you can stop the downward spiral by not taking that first step.'

I took that first step. Things did get out of control and I couldn't stop. When I got depressed, I would go to the bar and someone would say something nice to me. I would have a drink and, temporarily, I didn't feel so bad. There was acceptance at the bar when there was very little of it in the church. I was in church regularly since I was fourteen, but never had a close friend. I was so withdrawn and it seemed like people didn't reach out, so I just sat there miserable and alone.

I was in such a bad place in my life. In those bars, people would get into knife fights and sometimes somebody would pull a gun. But as time passed I got to the place where I would even go in to drink by myself and ignore the danger. I really didn't care anymore what happened to me.

I had a brush with cancer which frightened me, and I thought maybe God was stomping on me. So I quit the bars and went back to church. But after a year I forgot my cancer scare and slipped into the old lifestyle. I was living such a lie that it was inevitable. I had always had a strong conscience before, but at that time I remember thinking, *I don't even feel bad about this.*

I was unhappy and miserable and thought of suicide, but I was such a chicken I couldn't do it. My life was so out of control that when I met a man at a bar who wanted to marry me, I rushed headlong into it. I didn't ask God what He thought about it, because I knew what His answer would be and I didn't care. The man was still married when I met him and was a client where I worked. I was so afraid he would mention that he knew me from the bar — I wanted to keep that part of my life secret. I married him out of desperation to find happiness, but we were only together for two years.

Even before that marriage, I had slipped back into a legalistic cycle where I tried to control everything. We went to church, and I made sure my husband read everything I wanted him to read. But he was more sick than I was and very weak, with no sense of his own identity. In the beginning, I could control everything. But when his two daughters came to live with us, 'all hell broke loose'. Their mother had been in a mental hospital and was now living in a lesbian relationship. The girls were totally without discipline and I decided I was going to 'save' them, but my efforts blew up in my face.

I asked my husband to leave because I knew he was planning to leave me anyway, and I wanted to get the jump on him. I filed for divorce, but then I couldn't sleep nights and I stopped the proceedings. I knew it was wrong. I told him that he could get the divorce if he wanted to, but I never heard from him again.

My second husband and I did go to counselling, but no one was able to help us. They didn't deal with the reality of spiritual conflict, so how could they help us? They just patted us on the hand and said everything would be all right.

Finally my last counsellor did acknowledge that I was having a spiritual problem. I told him repeatedly about the fear of dying...about the suicide thoughts...about never being able to feel loved by God...about the cloud that overwhelmed me when I came home...but he didn't seem to know how to help me.

He asked me if I loved God, and I said, 'I don't know.' He responded, 'Well, I know you do.' I told him that the only God I knew was up in the heavens with a hammer waiting to beat me. He argued with me that God was not like that, but it didn't help.

I didn't tell him about the big black spider I saw as I woke up in the mornings, because after I started the day I forgot about it. It's incredible that this went on for about ten years and I never thought about it except while it was happening. Then I convinced myself I was having a nightmare with my eyes open.

Finally I couldn't stand pretending any more. I would cry all weekend and pray, 'God, I can't pretend any more that I'm okay.' I would get up when the kids came home from their weekend and put on my good-mother face. The truth was that all weekend I had laid on the couch in utter blackness. I didn't open the windows and I never went out. And I never talked to anybody because there were always the voices: 'They don't want to talk with you. They don't like you.' I never realised the negative things I heard in my head were put there by Satan.

I would do okay at work, but the second I walked in the door at night a cloud was waiting there to engulf me. I would usually just lay on the couch again, feeling miserable. Menial things like going to the store were really difficult because people were out there, and I felt they all hated me.

I kept going to the last counsellor because I was desperate and couldn't keep up the pretence any longer. I was even crying at work. I told the counsellor, 'I'm losing my mind. I'm miserable. I can't go on.'

He gave me a book to read, but it never got to the core of the problem. Although it spoke of Christ, there was no resolution; there was only hope if you could go to one of the clinics it described. However, the book did refer to malignant co-dependency and I knew that was me: no friends, totally isolated, living a lie, not knowing who I was. That petrified me.

After I read the book, I went to my counsellor and said, 'This is me...' I was on the verge of suicide, but he simply told me to come back in two weeks. I tried to get into the clinic but couldn't because I didn't have the money they required.

My sister was also going through serious problems at the time, but she couldn't go to the counsellor at our church because she wasn't a member. They were so overloaded they couldn't take non-members. My counsellor recommended a class for children of dysfunctional families at another church. I wanted to go too, but it was hard to start all over again with a new group of people.

When the weekend came, my children went away and I laid on the couch all Friday night and all day Saturday, totally depressed and eating nothing but popcorn. By Sunday the thought came that I should attend the class. Nothing in the world could have been harder to do, but somehow I gathered the courage to go. When I walked into that class, I felt completely at home. I attended regularly and it helped a lot. It was so good to have friends even though they were sick themselves.

One of my new friends invited me to a different class where they were showing the video series by Neil Anderson. As I viewed the video, my mouth fell open and I found myself saying repeatedly, 'This is the truth.' After that, I wouldn't have missed that class for anything. Once I went sick because nothing in my life had given me such hope.

When I heard Neil talk about people hearing voices, I was so excited because I'd finally found someone who knew what I was experiencing. Then he talked about Zechariah 3, where Satan is accusing the high priest and the Lord says, 'I rebuke you, Satan.' And that truth set me free. I thought, *I can do that*.

I realised then that I had been deceived by the father of lies, Satan. He has been accusing me all my life and I did not stand against him. I learned that because I am in the Lord Jesus Christ, I have authority to rebuke deceiving spirits and reject Satan's lies. I left that evening floating on air.

The depression is gone…the voices are gone…that huge spider-like object that I have been seeing in my room for the past ten years when I first wake up is gone!

My employer gave me the 'Resolving Personal and Spiritual Conflicts' tape series for Christmas, and I have been listening to them over and over again. There's light in my mind where there was darkness before. I love the light now and open the curtains and windows to let it shine in. I really am a new person! I have people into my home for a Bible study with the tapes, something I couldn't have done before.

As I look back over my life, I see that the messages I got from my family were negative. I can't remember really feeling love in my life until I heard the video tapes and realised God loves me just as I am.

Before I found my freedom in Christ, I was behaving just as my mother before me, going into rages with my children and then hating myself afterwards. That is so rare now, and my children feel comfortable with me.

I'm not like I was; I'm being healed. When I see myself falling back into old habits or thought patterns, I know what to do. I don't have to grovel in self-pity. At each point of conflict I can look for the particular lie Satan wants me to believe and then stand against it by deliberately choosing what I now know to be true.

My great goal now is to be the kind of parent God wants me to be, and I believe He will make up for all of the years the locusts have eaten (Joel 2:24,25).

How people live

Nobody can consistently behave in a way that is inconsistent with how they perceive themselves. Molly believed she wasn't any good, that nobody wanted her, that she wasn't worthy of love. She was living a distorted life, foisted on her by abused and abusive parents. The cycle of abuse would have continued except for the grace of God.

When I hear a story like this, and I hear a lot of them, I just wish people like Molly could be hugged by someone in a healthy way for every time they have been touched wrongly. I want to apologise to her for her parents. I want to see people have a chance. They are sitting in bars near your church. Some sneak in the back door of the chapel or church building and sit in the last row. Others become clinging pests whom we seek to avoid. They are children of God, but they don't know it and most have never been treated as such.

Stopping the abuse cycle

We Christians have all the power we need to live productive lives and the authority to resist the devil. People like Molly are not the problem; they are the victims — victimised by the god of this world, abusive parents, a cruel society and legalistic or liberal churches.

How do we stop this cycle of abuse? We lead them to Christ and help them establish their identity as children of God. We teach them the reality of the spiritual world, and encourage them to walk by faith in the power of the Holy Spirit. We care enough to confront them in love and stand by them when they fall. We do it by becoming the pastors, parents and friends that God wants us to be. We pay attention to the words of Christ in Matthew 9:12,13:

> It is not those who are healthy who need a physician, but those who are sick. But go and learn what this means, 'I desire compassion, and not sacrifice,' for I did not come to call the righteous, but sinners.

The Steps to Freedom in Christ that helped Molly as she viewed the video tapes are given in the appendix. They can also be found in *The Bondage Breaker*.

The path to God

In no way am I advocating a quick fix for difficult problems. Just going through seven simple steps or prayers may seem simplistic or easy, but I would beg to differ. There are a million ways to go wrong. The road to destruction is broad, the paths numerous and their explanation complex. But the path back to God is not so broad. Jesus is the way which is narrow, the truth which is simple, and the life which is transforming. No wonder Paul said, 'I am afraid, lest as the serpent deceived Eve by his craftiness, your minds should be led astray from the simplicity and purity of devotion to Christ' (2 Cor 11:3).

However, helping a person to recognise deception and counterfeit guidance and to choose the truth isn't simple. Knowing how to get a person in touch with the emotional pain of the past and work through forgiveness isn't easy. Confronting a person about pride, rebellion and sinful behaviour requires a lot of unconditional love and acceptance.

Some are able to process these steps on their own as Molly did. My son asked me once if people could effect their own freedom in Christ. Yes they can, because truth is what sets us free and Jesus is the deliverer. However, many are going to need the assistance of a godly person. Prerequisites for the pastor/counsellor are the character of Christ and the knowledge of His ways. This type of counselling requires the presence and leading of the Holy Spirit who is the 'Wonderful Counsellor'.

It seems as though the majority of the helping professions focus on the problem. We are suffering from a paralysis of analysis. If I were lost in a maze, I wouldn't want someone to explain to me all the intricacies of mazes and why people stumble into them. I certainly wouldn't need someone to tell me how daft I was for getting in there in the first place. I would need and want someone to give me a road map out of there. God sent his Son as our Saviour, provided the Scriptures as a road map and sent the Holy Spirit to guide us. People all around us are dying in the maze of life, for want of someone to gently show them the way.

2

ANNE:
Freedom Through
Stages of Growth

Molly has shared her life, and I hope it has impacted yours. In the following chapters we will benefit from the stories of other courageous people who have allowed their stories to be told.

However, this chapter will be a little different. Before we go on, I believe it is important to see God's growth and sanctification process, both explained from the Scriptures and illustrated in the life of another restored person, Anne. This will help you to better understand the spiritual journeys of the people you will be meeting here and how you can help heal the hurting lives of those who cross your path.

Born dead

Paul writes, 'As for you, you were dead in your transgressions and sins, in which you used to live when you followed the ways of this world and of the ruler of the kingdom of the air, the spirit who is now at work in those who are disobedient' (Eph 2:1,2, NIV). Since Adam, we are all born physically alive but spiritually dead (i.e., separated from God). During our formative years, we learned how to live our lives independent of God. We had neither the presence of God in our lives nor the knowledge of God's ways.

This learned independence from God is characteristic of the flesh or old nature. And one of the ways the flesh functions is to develop defence mechanisms whereby we learn how to cope, succeed, survive or win without God.

Eternally alive

When we come to Christ, we become spiritually alive, which means that we are now in union with God. Eternal life is not something we receive when we die; we possess eternal life right now because we are *in* Christ: 'The witness is this, that God has given us eternal life, and this life is in His Son. He who has the Son has the life; he who does not have the Son of God does not have the life' (1 Jn 5:11,12).

Reprogrammed

At the moment of conversion, all of God's resources are available to us. Unfortunately, nobody pushes the 'clear' button in our previously programmed minds. Until God's transformation process begins in our lives, we live in a state of being conformed to this world and regimented by it. That's why Paul writes, 'Do not conform any longer to the pattern of this world, but be transformed by the renewing of your mind. Then you will be able to test and approve what God's will is — His good, pleasing and perfect will' (Rom 12:2, NIV). Therefore —

- the major task of Christian education is to disciple previously programmed people, living independent of God, into a dependant relationship with Him.

- the major task of discipleship/counselling is to free people from their past and eradicate old defence mechanisms by substituting Christ as their only defence.

Becoming transformed

Truth and obedience are key issues in living a Christ dependent lifestyle. But truth can only be believed if it is understood, and commandments can only be obeyed if they are known. As the Holy Spirit leads us into all truth, we must respond by trusting and obeying: 'The one who says, "I have come to know Him," and does not keep His commandments, is a liar, and the truth is not in him' (1 Jn 2:4). Disobedience allows Satan to work in us. According to Ephesians 2:2, that spirit 'is now at work in those who are disobedient' (NIV).

'Sanctification' is the name applied to the process of our becoming conformed into the image and character of Christ. God is at work in this process, patiently and gently moving us along, because it takes time to renew our minds and develop character. But another god is also active — to see this process as taking place independent of 'the ruler of the kingdom of the air' (the god of this world, Satan) would be a disastrous oversight.

Diffusing the past

In many cases, traumatic childhood experiences continue to have a debilitating effect upon present living. It is very common to have many of these experiences blocked from memory. Secular psychologists are aware of this and attempt to get at hidden memories through hypnosis. Some try a hospitalisation programme using drugs to induce memories. While their sincerity is commendable, I am unequivocally opposed to both procedures for two reasons: One, I don't want to do anything to bypass the mind of a person; and two, I don't want to get ahead of God's timing.

You will find no instruction in Scripture to dwell on yourself or direct your thoughts inward. Scripture always argues for the active use of our minds and for our thoughts to be directed outward. We invite God to search our hearts (Ps 139:23,24). All occultic practices will try to induce a passive state of the mind, and Eastern religions will admonish us to bypass it. Scripture requires us to think and assume responsibility for taking every thought captive to the obedience of Christ (2 Cor 10:5).

If there are hurtful ways within us, and hidden memories of our past, God will wait until we reach enough maturity before He reveals them. Paul says:

> I care very little if I am judged by you or by any human court; indeed, I do not even judge myself. My conscience is clear, but that does not make me innocent. It is the Lord who judges me. Therefore judge nothing before the appointed time; wait till the Lord comes. He will bring to light what is hidden in darkness and will expose the motives of men's hearts. At that time each will receive his praise from God (1 Cor 4:3–5, NIV).

Pursuing God

What should we do if we know something in our past is still affecting us? I believe we should continue the pursuit of knowing God, learn to believe and obey that which is true, and commit ourselves to the sanctifying process of developing character. When we have reached enough security and maturity in Christ, He reveals a little more about who we really are. As Christ becomes the only defence we need, He weans us of our old means of defending ourselves.

Stripping off old defence mechanisms and revealing character deficiencies is like taking off layers of an onion. When one layer is off, we feel great. We have nothing against ourselves, and we are free from what others think about us, but we have not yet fully arrived. At the right time, He reveals more in order that we may share in His holiness.

Our next story is about this progressive process of sanctification. Anne wrote me the following letter and handed it to me halfway through a conference. She heard who she was as a child of God, learned how to walk by faith and saw the nature of the battle for her mind. She was so excited that she jumped ahead and processed the Steps to Freedom on her own.

Dear Neil:

Praise God, I think this is the answer I've been searching for. I'm not crazy! I don't have an overactive imagination as I have been told and believed for years. I'm just normal like everybody else.

I have struggled for my whole Christian experience with bizarre thoughts that were so embarrassing I usually never told anyone else. How could I admit to someone in the church what had crossed my mind? I tried once to honestly share part of what I was struggling with in a Christian group. People sucked in their breath, there was a stiff silence, then someone changed the subject. I could have died. I learned quickly that these things are not acceptable in the church, or at least they weren't at that time.

I didn't know what it meant to take every thought captive.[1] I tried to do this once, but I was unsuccessful because I blamed myself for all this stuff. I thought all those thoughts were mine and that I was the one who was doing it. There has always been a terrible cloud hanging over my head because of these issues. I never could accept the fact that I was really righteous because I didn't feel like it.

Praise God it was only Satan — not me. I have worth!! The problem is so easy to deal with when you know what it is.

I was abused as a child. My mother lied to me a lot and Satan used the things she said, like, 'You're lazy. You'll never amount to anything.' Over and over he has been feeding me so much junk — preying on my worst fears. At night I would have nightmares that the lies were true and in the morning I would be so depressed. I have had a difficult time shaking this stuff.

Being abused, I was taught not to think for myself. I did what I was told and never questioned anything for fear of being beaten. This set me up for Satan's mind games. I was conditioned to have someone lie to me about myself, primarily my mother. I feared taking control of my mind because I didn't know what would happen. I believed I would lose my identity because I wouldn't have anyone to tell me what to do.

In actuality, I have gained my identity for the first time. I am not a product of my mother's lies; I am not a product of the garbage Satan feeds me. Now I'm finally me, a child of God! Through all his junk, Satan has terrorised me. I have been living in fear of myself, but praise God I think it's over. I used to worry whether a thought came from Satan or myself. Now I realise that's not the issue. I just need to examine the thought according to the Word of God and then choose the truth.

I feel a little unsure writing this so soon. Maybe I should take a 'wait and see' attitude, but I am sensing such joy and peace that I feel in my gut it must be real. Praise God for the truth and answered prayer! I am free!

With a heart full of thanks,

Anne

One layer of the onion was exposed. The critical first part of the Epistles, which speaks of our identity in Christ, was made known to Anne. She is no longer just a product of her past; she is a new creation in Christ. With that foundation laid, she was able to face and repudiate the lies she had believed for so many years. When she had tried to share some of her struggles in the past, she had felt rejected, probably because others in the group were struggling in a similar fashion but were unable to reciprocate.

Oh, how I long for the day when our churches will help

people firmly establish their identity in Christ and provide an atmosphere where people like Anne could share the real nature of their struggle. Satan does everything in the dark. When issues like this arise, let's not suck in our breath and change the subject. We buy Satan's devious strategy by keeping everything hidden. Let's walk in the light, and have fellowship with one another in order that the blood of Jesus will cleanse us from all sin (1 Jn 1:7). God is light and in Him there is no darkness at all (1 Jn 1:5). Let's lay aside falsehood and speak the truth in love, for we are members of one another (Eph 4:15,25).

Now Anne knows who she is and understands the nature of the battle going on for her mind. She must be totally free, right? Wrong! She was free of what she processed, but God wasn't through with her yet. One layer doesn't constitute the whole onion. Two weeks after the conference she wrote a second letter.

Dear Neil:

Good night! Where do I start? Let me just say that I came to your conference for academic reasons. I could not have fathomed in advance what the Lord had in store for me. In fact, I probably wouldn't have believed it anyway. I guess I should start where I left off with you a few days ago.

I wrote you a letter explaining that I had been freed from obsessive thoughts. A few months ago, I had specifically asked the Lord to help me understand this problem. When I heard the information in the conference at the beginning of the week, I was thrilled. It was exactly what I had asked the Lord for. At home, I prayed through all of the prayers in the Steps to Freedom. It was a struggle, but the voices stopped. I felt free; thus, I thought I was done. Little did I know!

You talked to me one evening after a session and told me that I probably needed to forgive my mother. I didn't buy it very well because I had tried it once before and it didn't work. I now realise that I was pushed into it by some well-meaning Christians who said that my feelings didn't matter. In fact, they said I shouldn't even have any angry feelings. To them, the kind of rage I was feeling was very sinful. So I grudgingly went through the motions of saying that I forgave the people who had hurt me. As a result of that phony effort, I became very bitter and sarcastic. I tried not to be, but the truth is that I was. God showed me later that my bitterness resulted from denying that I was angry while going through the motions of forgiving.

A year ago, I attended a support group for abuse victims. The leader of the group told me that I was bitter because I had tried to forgive before I was ready. She said that I needed to work through all of my feelings I had about each incident. After that, I would be able to forgive.

When you talked to me that evening, I thought you were coercing me into another ritual prayer of forgiveness that would mean nothing. All I knew was that I couldn't return to the bitterness trail. I decided to just take the information that I received at the beginning of the conference as what God wanted me to receive and put the rest of the information on the academic shelf.

Thursday evening, when you spoke on forgiveness, I was miserable. I had a horrible time sitting through the meeting, feeling bored and angry. I felt very misunderstood and thought I was wasting my time. I knew I couldn't leave or everybody would think I was possessed or something, so I struggled with staying awake and couldn't wait to get out of there.

That night, I started working on an assignment for a class I was taking. I couldn't process anything because the forgiveness issue hit me square in the face again. I felt angry, but something in my gut told me that there had to be something more to what you were saying. I decided that I should be open and willing to try anything. I figured it couldn't hurt, although I really doubted that it would help since I had been trying to forgive my parents for years.

So I made a list of people and offences and worked through them as you had suggested that night. During that time, God showed me that I had been hanging onto their offences in anger because it was my way of protecting myself against further abuse. I didn't know how to scripturally set boundaries around myself to protect myself from them. I had been taught by the church that I must keep turning the other cheek and keep letting them slap it. When you spoke of what it really meant to honour your parents, I knew that was my ticket to freedom.

God showed me that it was okay to stick up for myself and that I didn't need an unforgiving attitude to protect myself. He showed me that the abuse support group was right in telling me to focus on my emotions; however, there was never any real closure because they never taught us to come to a decision about forgiveness. That was always down the road when you felt better. I see now that both Christians groups were emphasising one aspect about forgiveness, but not both.

After forgiving, I felt exhausted. Interestingly, though, I immediately had a real love-jump in my heart for you, Neil. It hadn't been there before. I went to sleep feeling pretty good.

An hour later, I woke up with cold sweats and my heart racing. I had just had another one of my awful nightmares. I hadn't had one in several months, so I was kind of surprised. For the first time in my life, it occurred to me that maybe this wasn't all a result of my abuse as I had been taught in the past. I prayed that the Lord would help me figure it out and went back to sleep. At 2:30 am, my room-mate woke me up with her screaming. I jumped out of bed and woke her up. We compared notes and realised we both had had similar dreams. After praying together and renouncing Satan,[2] we went back to bed and both slept fine the rest of the night.

In those early morning hours as I was drifting back to sleep, God showed me that I had been having similar dreams since third grade — dreams that I had met the devil and he had put a curse on me. I can't believe I forgot all that. I asked the Lord what happened in the third grade and remembered that I had started watching *Bewitched* at that time. It was my favourite television show and I watched it religiously.

Because of that show, I became very interested in spiritual powers. Along with many of my school friends, I read books on ghosts, E.S.P. (extra-sensory perception), palm reading, and even a book on spells and curses. It also was an 'in' thing to play with magic eight balls, ouija-boards and magic sets. Another television favourite was *Gilligan's Island*, where I got the idea to use my dolls as voodoo dolls to get back at my mother. I considered putting a curse on her. By the time I was in sixth grade, I was so depressed. I started reading Edgar Allan Poe and it became the only thing I craved. I can't believe I had forgotten all this.

In high school the dreams came back and I became suicidal. By the grace of God, I invited Jesus Christ into my life soon after that. The biggest thing God showed me was that I knew when I was very young that there was evil power out there, and I had desired to have it.

When Saturday came, you can bet I was all ears. This wasn't hocus-pocus to me any more. So as you led us through the Steps to Freedom, I prayed all the prayers again and renounced all of the lies that have been going on in my family for years. I acknowledged my own sin and lack of forgiveness.

The best way I can describe what happened to me this week is this: You know how it is when somebody has been in a cult for a long time, and they get taken in for deprogramming? That's the way it was for me. It was like God locked me in a room and said, 'Give me your brain. We're not leaving here until you do.' It's taken an intensive week to get me to see the lies I have been living in. I had no idea.

Since I have returned home, the lying thoughts — 'You're no good. You're stupid. No one likes you.' — have been coming out in great numbers. I told my husband everything, so every time I have a lying thought I tell him and we both laugh about it and talk about what's really true. Praise God! I was too embarrassed to tell him before.

Last night one of my nightmares started up again. I felt the oppression coming on as I was drifting off to sleep. I said 'Jesus' right away. Neil, I could feel the oppression lifting off my heart, quickly, almost like it had been torn away. Praise God!

Because of counselling through the years, I have quite a few notebooks filled with accounts of the pain from my past. This pain pile has been sitting in my drawer and has been an eyesore every time I have looked at it. I now know that my identity isn't in the past any more; it's in Christ. I burned all the notebooks.

Thank you for telling me the truth even if I didn't understand it at first. The joy I feel is the same joy I felt when I first received Christ! Finally I understand what it means to be a child of God.

Joyfully,

Anne

Three layers of the onion peeled off in a week is rather remarkable. Anne saw her identity in Christ, was able to forgive from her heart and learned to stand against Satan. she may have more going for her than most, having a Christian education and a loving, understanding and supportive husband to go home to. That is not to say that others can't resolve the same issues, but for some it may take longer.

Forgiveness brings freedom

Several issues need to be brought out. Every person in this book has had to face the need to forgive. It drives legitimate counsellors up a wall when well-meaning Christians suggest that somebody who expresses feelings like anger and bitterness shouldn't 'feel that way.' Bypassing feelings will never bring resolution to problems. If you want healing, you will have to get in touch with your emotional core. God will surface the emotional pain in order that it may be dealt with. Those who don't want to face reality will try to shove it down, but that will only result in increased bitterness.

Forgiveness is what sets us free from our past. We don't do it for the other person's sake; we do it for our sake. We are to forgive as Christ has forgiven us. There is no freedom without forgiveness. 'But you don't know how bad they hurt me,' says the victim. The point is, they're still hurting you, so how do you stop the pain? You need to forgive from the heart — acknowledge the hurt and the hate and then let it go. To not forgive from the heart is to give Satan an opportunity (Mt 18:34,35; 2 Cor 2:10,11).

Another error is to see forgiveness as a long-term

process. Many counsellors say, 'You will have to feel all the emotion, then you will be able to forgive.' Going over the past and reliving all the pain without forgiveness only reinforces it. The more you talk about it, the stronger the hold it has upon you. The assumption seems to be that you have to heal first, then you will be able to forgive. Not true! You forgive first, then the healing process can begin.

There is no way that you can read Scripture and come to the conclusion that forgiveness is a long-term process. The painful feelings may take time to heal, but forgiveness is a choice. It is a crisis of the will and the reward is freedom.

Stand against sin

Many, like Anne, see their anger as a means of protecting themselves from further abuse. Secular counsellors see Christian forgiveness as co-dependency and argue, 'Don't let that person shove you around anymore. Get mad!' I say, 'Don't let that person shove you around any more. Forgive!'

Then take a stand against sin. Forgiveness is not tolerating ways in which others may be sinning against you. God forgives, but He doesn't tolerate sin. It grieves me that some pastors will hear of abuse and tell the child or wife to just go home and submit, saying, 'Trust God to protect you.' I want to say to that pastor, 'You go home in the place of that person and get knocked around.' But doesn't the Bible say that wives and children are to be submissive? True, but it also says that God has established government to protect abused children and battered wives. Read Romans 13:1–7, and turn abusers in as the law even requires you to do.

If a man in your church abused another woman in your church, would you tolerate it? If a man or woman in your church abused another person's child, would you tolerate that? Why, then, would you allow in your own home what is so clearly an intolerable sin in others, just because you are the wife or child?

Parents are charged by God to love, protect and provide for their household. Never are they given a license to abuse, nor should it ever be tolerated. Turn them in, for everyone's sake. It isn't helping the abuser to let him or her continue in sin.

One mother of three shared with me in tears one evening that she knew exactly who it was that she needed to forgive. It was her mother. But if she forgave her that evening, what was she to do that Sunday when she had to go over to her house? 'She will just put me down all over again.' I said, 'Put a stop to it. Maybe you should say something like, "Listen Mum, you have been putting me down all my life. It isn't doing you any good and it certainly isn't doing me any good. I really can't be a part of that any more. If you have to treat me that way then I'm going to leave."'

Her response was typical: 'Doesn't the Bible say that I am supposed to honour my mother?' I explained that letting her mother systematically destroy her and her present family would certainly not honour her mother. Eventually it would dishonour her.

'Honour your mother and father' is better understood as taking care of them in their old age. The need to obey one's parents no longer applies to this woman since she had left her mother and father and was now under the authority of her husband.

Living with consequences

The major decision you are making in forgiveness is to bear the penalty of the other person's sin. All forgiveness is efficacious. If we are to forgive as Christ forgave us, how then did He forgive? He took the sins of the world on Himself; He suffered the consequences of our sin. When we forgive the sin of another, we are agreeing to live with the consequences of his or her sin. You say, 'That's not fair!' Well, the fact is that you will have to anyway, whether you forgive or not. Everybody is living with the consequences of somebody else's sin. We are all living with the consequences of Adam's sin. The only real choice is whether we will do it in the freedom of forgiveness or the bondage of bitterness.

You might ask, 'Why should I let them off my hook?' The point is that when you have them on your hook, you are also hooked to them through your unforgiveness. One man exclaimed, 'That's why moving away didn't resolve it.' When you let them off your hook, are they off God's? Never! God says, 'Vengeance is mine. I will repay' (Heb 10:30). God will deal justly with everyone in the final judgement.

Get God into the process

We need to get God into the process. Step Three in the Steps to Freedom addresses 'Bitterness versus Forgiveness', and begins with a prayer asking God to reveal 'to my mind those people I have not forgiven in order that I may do so.' I have had many look at me in all sincerity and say they don't think there is anyone they need to forgive. But I ask them to share with me names that are coming to their mind anyway. Within minutes, I often have a full page of names because the Lord is faithful to answer that kind of prayer. Then we spend the next hour (or sometimes hours) working through forgiveness.

I encourage them to pray, 'Lord, I forgive (name) for (what for)' and to go through every remembered pain and abuse. God will bring to their mind many painful memories in order for them to forgive from their heart. He probably has been trying to for years, but they have been suppressing them. One person said, 'I can't forgive my mother. I hate her!' 'Now you can,' I said. God never asks us to lie about how we feel. He only asks us to let it go from our hearts so He can free us from our past.

I encourage people to stay with the person they are forgiving until every painful memory has surfaced, and then go on to the next person. I have seen experiences surface that they have never talked about or remembered before. Some may respond, 'My list is so long, you don't have enough time.' I reply, 'Yes, I do. I'll stay here all night if I have to.' And I mean it. One man started to cry and said, 'You're the only person who has ever said that to me.'

This type of counselling cannot be done in fifty-minute segments. I am committed to staying with a person through all seven of the Steps to Freedom so he can deal with every area where Satan has had a foothold. Once you start the steps, finish them — don't divide them into separate sessions. A partial resolution gives Satan an opportunity and incentive for increased harassment.

Layers of the onion

Don't be surprised if people leave feeling free, only to struggle a few weeks or months later. They may conclude it didn't work, but if you check the issues they are dealing with now, they are probably working on another layer of the onion. In many cases, like the stories in this book, the freedom is maintained if they know who they are as children of God and understand the nature of the battle we are in. As long as we are on planet Earth, we will have to pick up our cross daily and follow Jesus. This means putting on the whole armour of God and resisting the world, the flesh and the devil.

In chapter 10, I will be dealing with the issue of severe childhood trauma such as Satanic ritual abuse (SRA). Memories for these people are much more deeply buried. Usually, recall doesn't happen until the victims are in their thirties and forties. The 'onion effect' is more pronounced, and always begins with early childhood and works forward. I believe that we are to help these people firmly establish their identity in Christ and then assist them in resolving the conflicts of their past as God slowly reveals it to them.

I have been saying all along that freedom is a prerequisite to growth. You can observe this by the rapid growth that will take place in a person's life when he gains a certain degree of freedom. However, these people will face, as Anne did, many other issues with which they will have to deal. For instance, she felt an oppression come on her one evening, but she had learned that all she had to do to stand against it was what she did — to express verbally the name of Jesus. She was depending on Him to defend her and she was announcing that to the enemy. As other schemes of Satan surface, she is learning to recognise and expose them in the light of the truth, and the truth continues to set her free.

NOTES

1. Anne gives a good description of what it means to 'take every thought captive,' when, later in her letter, she says, 'I just need to examine the thought according to the Word of God and then choose the truth.'

2. Renouncing Satan is verbally standing against him as we are taught in James 4:7: 'Resist the devil, and he will flee from you' (NIV).

3

SANDY:
Freedom From Cultic
and Occultic Bondage

When I first met Sandy, she was fleeing from a conference session in fear. She is a pretty lady in her early forties, usually with a bubbly personality and enough energy for two. She has a committed Christian husband, several children, and she lives in a beautiful suburban community.

Sandy had masked very well the battle that had been raging in her mind for most of her life. Few, if any, suspected the war going on inside until she mysteriously started dropping out of her world eighteen months before we met. Here is her story.

Sandy's Story

*I lived mostly in a very tiny corner
of my mind.*

At last I am able to believe I am a child of God. I am now sure of my place in my Father's heart. He loves me. My spirit bears witness with His Spirit that it is so. I no longer feel outside the family of God — I no longer feel like an orphan.

Since the time we spent together at the conference, the evil presence inside of me is gone, and the many voices that haunted me for thirty-five years are also gone. It feels clean, spacious and beautiful inside *all* of my mind.

Before I found my freedom in Christ, I lived mostly in a very tiny corner of my mind. Even then, I could never escape the commanding voices or the filthy language or the accusing anger. So I tried to separate myself from my mind altogether and live a life dissociated from it.

I became a Christian in 1979 and have struggled continually to believe that God actually accepted me, wanted me, cared about me. At last this lifelong struggle has come to an end. Before, I could never hear that still, small voice of God in my mind without being punished for it by the other voices. Today only the still, small voice is there.

It all started when I was very young. My father professed to be an atheist and my mother was very religious, so there was a lot of conflict and confusion in our home. I went to religious schools, but when I came home I heard from my father that religion was all a lot of nonsense for weak people. I actually hoped that he was correct and that there wasn't any God because I was afraid of my mother's religion. I was afraid that God would get me if I didn't behave correctly. But I was looking for spiritual answers, even though I rejected both of my parents' solutions.

My family, both parents and grandparents, was riddled with superstitious beliefs and good luck charms. I remember visiting my grandparents on my mother's side and feeling that their house was a quiet place to get away from the chaos of the home I was growing up in. She didn't have any toys for me to play with, only a black Crazy 8 ball. There was a window in the ball and little chips inside with probably a hundred different answers. I would ask the ball a question like 'Will it rain tomorrow?' And one of the answers would float up to the top such as 'Probably'.

I grew very attached to that ball and spent a lot of time at my grandmother's house playing with it and believing that it had magic power and answers for everything in my life. I would communicate with the ball about my parents and what was happening in my life, using it as a fortune-telling device. Over a period of time, I saw that many of the answers the ball gave me were correct, confirming my belief that the ball had power.

I suppose the grown-ups thought it was just a toy for the grandchildren to play with. When I had problems, though, I would store them up until I got to my grandmother's house and try to solve them with the magic ball.

When I visited my father's parents, they would take me to their very legalistic church and I became terrified of hell. Being fearful of God and religion, I turned to the magic ball to try predicting events. That way I could be prepared in advance for any disasters God was going to send my way.

By the time I was fourteen I had become very religious in the Catholic church where, for some reason, I felt safe. While at home, my dad's alcoholism and my parents' fighting intensified and there was no peace. My parents would probably say that I was the problem, that I was a problem child. My mother tried to keep my father and me separated because he was very abusive and I was not passive. I loved to fight and I would always get in between him and anyone he was angry with. He would throw me out of the house whenever he saw me, so eventually I only came home when he was away or asleep.

I was angry and rebellious and hated everyone in authority to the extent that people would walk carefully around me because of my explosive anger. What they didn't know was that inside I felt like a sad, lonely, scared little girl. I just wanted someone to take care of me, but I could never share this. When someone attempted to get close to me, I hid my insecurity by becoming argumentative.

I was a problem at school and in the community, and I became sexually promiscuous — basically doing anything I could that would break the Ten Commandments. Once I went into a Catholic church, looked at the crucifix and said, 'Everything You hate, I love; and everything You love, I hate.' I was daring God to strike me, and I wasn't even afraid that He might.

At nineteen, I went to a major city and lived with two others girls for two years. In a bar at 2 am, a bartender gave us a small calling card and asked, 'Why don't you girls go to my church? Maybe you'll find answers to some of your problems and won't have to be out here in the middle of the night.' I felt that I might as well try the 'church' one more time, believing that all churches were the same. I just wanted to be in a family and feel safe, so the next day we went to that church. I had no idea it was a cult…and for ten years, I was involved in it!

Initially, I felt loved; it was my 'family'. They took an interest in my life. No one had paid that much attention to me before. No one had taken enough notice of me to say, 'We want you to get nine hours of sleep. We want you to eat three meals a day. We want to know where you are.' They held me accountable for my lifestyle and I interpreted their interest in me as love and concern for my well-being. I would have died for them.

I accepted their philosophy that we are all gods. This fit in with my father's atheistic views that there really is no supreme God and that religion is just somebody's invention to control people. They also explained who Jesus Christ was and to me that seemed to satisfy my mother's religion. They said that He was just a good teacher like Mohammed or Buddha, but that He wasn't supreme or God, or else He would have prevented Himself from having to die on the cross.

The more I got involved, the more the cult consumed my life. I believed everything they said and that anything I read in the newspapers or heard on television was a lie. So I read nothing unless the cult wrote it, and I believed nothing unless their signature was on it. My whole world revolved around its teaching.

I went through a lot of personal instruction where they told me what to do to become a 'totally free spiritual being.' Because they taught reincarnation, I believed that I had hundreds of past lifetimes. I 'learned' previous names, how many children I had, even the colour of my hair. This included lives on other planets. Because I trusted them, I believed them; the reason no one else knew this 'truth' about themselves is because they weren't willing to know the truth.

I tried to live in two worlds. Ever since I was seven years old I have heard voices in my head and had invisible friends. I would live in one world at school but in another world at home. The voices in my head continued speaking to me. The cult leaders said the voices were from my past lifetimes. My ill-fated hope was that they would be put to rest and not bother me any more when I was fully instructed.

While this was happening, my family moved away and my mother was invited to a neighbourhood Bible study where she became a born-again Christian. She didn't tell anyone because my father was still an atheist and wouldn't have let her go to the study. But she asked her friends to pray for the conversion of her husband and her children. Had I known they were praying for me, I, too, would have tried to stop her.

When my mother became ill with cancer, I visited her on her deathbed with the idea from a cult member to convert her so that we could have her spirit to care for in the next lifetime. In the next lifetime, she would live in the cult and I could become aware of her. Then she would have a better life than the one she had with Dad.

While visiting her, I felt total hatred for her friends who came into her room and talked about Jesus and prayed for her healing. I ridiculed their attempts, but was astounded by the strength of my mother's convictions. It was a battle between her mind and mine, but one night she was in so much pain, and so worn down emotionally, that she went through a commitment prayer with me to give her spirit to my cult. Satisfied, I went home the next day, and she died several days later.

I remember playing Scrabble with a neighbour at three o'clock one afternoon when suddenly I sensed the presence of my mother in the room. I said, 'What are you doing here? You should go to headquarters where you are supposed to be.' Later that day, my brother called and told me that my mother had died around that time in the afternoon.

My friend in the cult told me that everything was fine — they had received my mother's spirit. Eventually they would call me when the baby was born who would receive my mother's spirit, so that I could go to see this baby.

About a week later, I received a letter from one of my mother's friends who had been with her when she died. She said that my mother had gone to be with Jesus. That made me so angry that I went to a local church and stole a Bible. I was going to highlight all of the lies and then send it to this lady to show her how confused she was and to convert her to the cult.

I opened the Bible to the middle and began reading in the book of Isaiah. Instead of highlighting the 'lies', I found myself highlighting words like 'Come let us reason together says the Lord…If you will turn to Me, I will turn to you.' I discovered the book is filled with passages about not getting involved with mediums and astrologers. By the time I was finished, I was confused about what the truth was.

I had never read a Bible before, much less owned one, so I turned to the back to see how it ended. When I read the Book of Revelation, I was scared because the cult teaches the Book of Revelation backwards. They say that people are really 'gods' who go back and take their rightful place in heaven.

I went to the church where I stole the Bible and tried to get in touch with my mother's spirit. I figured that if she was a Christian, then I should be able to go to a Christian place and contact her. When I got to the church, a middle-aged couple approached me and asked if they could help me in any way. When I told them I was trying to get in touch with my mother, they lovingly said that they didn't think I would find her there, but they invited me to have breakfast with them and talk about it. It turned out to be a Christian Fellowship Breakfast where, for the first time in my life, I was with a group of people whose lives seemed special because of their relationship to Jesus Christ.

The next several months my confusion continued as I went back and forth between reading my Bible and my cult books. I visited the church where I had met the couple, and they would come over to my house just to read Scripture with me. I consider them my spiritual mother and father. They never made me feel evil or bad; they just loved and accepted me. Every month they would pick me up and take me to their Christian breakfast and other church services.

During this time I remember praying and telling God that wherever my mother went is where I wanted to be. If I caused her to lose heaven because of what I did, then I didn't want to be a Christian. I wanted to be with her. But if she had really gone to be with Jesus, as her friend who wrote me said, then I wanted to be there too. I just couldn't choose.

One night I had a dream where I saw my mother walking toward me with another person in white, and she said, 'I forgive you for what you did and I want you to forgive yourself and to pray for your father.' That woke me like a shot. I awakened my husband and said, 'I know where she is.' I was angry that she had asked me to pray for my father, but that's how I know it was my mother. No one else would dare ask me to do that.[1]

The next week I went to church with that couple, gave my life to the Lord and renounced my cult involvement. I gave them all of my cult books and paraphernalia and they took it out of the house. For the next two years I was discipled by them and their fellowship group.

Six weeks after becoming a Christian I found out that I was pregnant. I was angry with the Lord. I had already had three abortions and decided that I shouldn't have to go through with the pregnancy just because I was a Christian. But my husband said, 'I thought you were a Christian and that Christians don't believe in abortions.' It angered me that God would speak to me through my husband who wasn't even a Christian, but God seemed to say to me, 'Listen, your home is big enough for a baby, how about your heart? Is it big enough?' That's when I decided to keep the baby.

Nine months after the baby was born my husband gave his life to the Lord. He said, 'When you decided against an abortion, I was impressed by God's intervention and impact in your life.'

I wondered if I should become a Catholic as my mother had been. My spiritual parents said it would be all right to go to the Catholic church, so I went to a charismatic Catholic prayer group. When the priest learned of my background he suggested that I probably needed deliverance, so I met with him. He started talking to whatever was inside of me, asking its name. The 'thing' would give him a name and become angry and violent; I became frightened and beat up the priest.

It scared me so much I decided to keep all of this a secret. I wanted to believe that if I were really a Christian, God would make that horrible presence go away. Because it didn't, I couldn't believe I had a relationship with God.

People would tell me I was saved since I had given my heart to the Lord, but no one could provide the assurance I was looking for. I felt half evil and half good, and I couldn't see how half of me could go to heaven.

We moved again, had more children, and got involved in a new church and Bible studies. I still had this separated life. I would go to church, but when I came home the voices tormented me. They were no longer my friends. They were accusing, screaming, angry and profane. They told me, 'You think that you're a Christian, but you're not. You're dirty and sinful.' And the more involved I became as a Christian, the worse the voices became.

I became legalistic, thinking that I had to go to every Bible study and church activity. I went Sunday morning and Sunday and Wednesday evenings, feeling that being present every time the church was open was the only way I could prove that I was a Christian.

I went on mission trips and taught Sunday school. When I taught Bible studies and shared the dangers of cults with others, everything inside me became intensified. Anger became rage, the pain became torment, the accusations made me feel suicidal. I thought, *Why don't I just kill myself? I can't ever be good enough to be a real Christian.*

When I went on a radio programme and talked about the dangers of cults, I was plagued with fear that my children would be killed. I became paranoid about even sending them to school so I dropped everything. When I withdrew, I temporarily felt better and the voices lessened, but I became a loner — not going anywhere or talking to anybody, just wanting to be by myself all the time. I felt more and more bound, and my internal life became a prison where no light could shine.

I went to Christian counselling and it did help me to sort out my abusive childhood and put some things together. I was diagnosed as having a dissociative disorder because of the voices and MPD (multiple personality disorder), because many times I would say, 'Well, we feel this way.' My counsellor would ask, 'Why are you saying "we"?' I would say, 'I don't know.'

This frightened me, but I was also relieved to know that someone believed there were voices inside me. I went to counselling two days a week trying to relieve the pain and the torment. If at any time there was an apparent look in the right direction, I was fearful, and then I felt the need to punish myself by doing anything dangerous or painful. Nothing quieted the rage inside me but worship and praise tapes. Only while listening to them did I feel that I wasn't going crazy, but I could only listen, never sing.

The counsellors loved me and were faithfully there for me every week. They prayed for me and promised to stay with me for the journey. They felt it would take a long time for me to become integrated. They gave me hope, assuring me that God wanted me to be whole and that He would bring it about. I vacillated between hope and despair like I was on a roller coaster. The Christian counsellors were a lifeline for me. I felt God's love and acceptance through their listening, understanding and caring.

However, when I was seven a traumatic event had occurred in my life which resulted in such tremendous fear that even in counselling I could never progress beyond that point. I would get to the age of seven and then be too afraid to go on. I reasoned, *If it's that bad, I don't want to know what it is.* A voice in my head told me that I would be harmed if I remembered.

My neighbour was my friend and knew about my struggle. One day she asked me if I would help her prepare for a 'Resolving Personal and Spiritual Conflicts Conference' that was coming to her church in about six weeks — visiting churches, putting up posters and selling the books. I didn't want to do it. I was sure the conference was just one more meeting like the ones I had already tried. Every time I had come home so lonely and discouraged, knowing my punishment waited for me for even trying to find a cure. I was afraid it would make my life more miserable, but I half-heartedly said that I would help.

My neighbour gave me videos of the conference to preview so that I would be able to answer questions about the materials. After watching only ten minutes of the first video, I decided that I hated Neil Anderson and that he didn't have anything to say. I felt like telling people not to go and said to my neighbour, 'I don't like him. Are you sure you want him to come and give this conference? I think there's something wrong with him.' She replied, 'Well, you're the only one who has told me that and I've talked to about thirty-five people.'

At the conference, my resistance increased and I didn't hear all of what was said. I couldn't remember the nights Neil talked about our identity in Christ, and I sat in the second row unable to sing any of the hymns. He would speak and a part of me would say, *That's not new. We all knew that anyway.* Another little voice inside of me would say, *I sure wish that everything he said is true and that this man could help me.* But I never revealed that hopeful part, only my critical part. Talking with others I would say, 'So what do you think of the conference? It's really not that great, is it?'

Near the end of the week a two-hour taped counselling session was shown. I could not watch the woman on the video finding her freedom. I felt fear and anger all at the same time. I started choking, felt sick and headed for my car to go home, determined not to show up again on Saturday. But Neil was in the hallway between me and my car.

We went into a side room and Neil walked me through some renunciations where I verbally repeated a series of statements, taking a stand against Satan and all of his influences in my life. I also prayed that God would reveal to me whatever it was that prevented me from sitting to watch the video, and that's when I remembered what happened when I was seven years old. It was like the clouds rolled away and I saw myself as a little girl, terrified of a dark, black presence.

I was playing with dolls in the back bedroom of our home. It was daytime and nothing frightening was happening and no one else was present in the room. But suddenly I felt total fear. I remember stopping my play and laying down, facing the ceiling and saying, 'What do you want?' to a huge, black presence that was over me. The presence said to me, 'Can I share your body with you?' And I said, 'If you promise not to kill me, you can.'

I actually felt that presence totally infiltrating me from head to toe. It was so oppressive to have this thing go into every pore of my body that I remember thinking, *I am going to die.* I was only seven, but it was so sexual and so dirty that I felt I had a big secret I had to hide and that I could never tell anyone. From that time on I felt that I had more than one personality, and it seemed natural to share my body with unseen others. Sometimes I would do things and not remember them when people would tell me. And I would think, *Well that wasn't me. That was my invisible 'friend' who did that.*

I never played with the black ball again. I only spoke with my invisible friend who would suggest things that I should do. Sometimes the suggestions were bad, but sometimes they were good. Because I needed companionship in my abusive childhood, I never thought the voice was anything other than a friend.

As Neil led me by giving me the words to speak, I specifically renounced all Satanic guardians that had been assigned to me. At that point I was startled by the presence of evil and afraid we would both be beaten up. It reminded me that I had played with that magic ball for years.

Neil told me not to be afraid and asked what the presence was saying to my mind. Whenever I told him what the voices were saying, he would say, 'That's a lie,' and he gently led me through the Steps to Freedom. I can remember the very second the presence wasn't there any more. I felt like the small, little person that was really me was being blown up like a balloon inside of me. Finally, after thirty-five years of fractured living, I was the only person inside. The place that evil presence vacated I have now dedicated to my new occupant: the clean, gentle, quiet Spirit of God.

Saturday morning I was afraid to wake up, thinking, *This isn't real.* I didn't want to open my eyes because usually the voice would say something like, 'Get up, you stupid little slut. You've got work to do.' So I would get up and do whatever it said. But that morning there were no voices and I laid in my bed thinking, *There's no one here but me.*

When I went back to the conference and walked in the door, people noticed that I looked different. I told them how I had always felt like an orphan in the body of Christ, but now I felt free and part of the family of God.

I thought that as soon as Neil left, this thing was going to come back. But the peace lasted, because Jesus Christ is the one who set me free. Whenever that fear would come I would go through the Steps to Freedom by myself, something I did at least four or five more times. I became convinced that God wanted it gone as much as I did, and it's never been there since.

A week later, we had a head-on car collision. I was afraid the voice would be there to say, 'I'm going to crush you because you think you're free.' Instead I sensed God saying, 'I am here to protect you and I'll always be here like this.'

When one of my girls asked me if the wreck was her fault, I wondered why she felt this way. I remembered that one of the Steps to Freedom is breaking the ancestral ties because demonic strongholds can be passed on from one generation to the next (Ex 20:4,5). As we talked, my ten-year-old told me, 'Sometimes I know things are going to happen before they happen. And sometimes I look out the window and see things that nobody else sees.'

Instantly, I knew that my daughter also needed to be released from bondage. So I took her through the steps, paraphrasing the big words into her language. She prayed to cancel out all demonic working that was passed on from her ancestors, rejecting any way in which Satan might be claiming ownership of her. She declared herself to be eternally and completely signed over and committed to the Lord Jesus Christ. Since then she has never again experienced that demonic presence.

My husband was away during the conference, and when he came home I told him everything that had happened. The next Sunday, in our adult Sunday school class, the leader asked if anyone wanted to share about the conference. My husband stood and said, 'I want to share even though I wasn't there, because the Lord gave me a new wife to come home to.'

Before, I didn't have a self-image. Every day I felt that God had a measure of mercy for me and that some day it would run out, that even God Himself must wonder why He made me. I just supposed that some day He was going to say, 'I've had enough of Sandy.' So every day I would pray, 'God, please don't let it be today. Let me get this one last thing done before You do it.'

It was so freeing when Neil taught that God and Satan are not co-equal, but that God is off the charts and Satan is way beneath Him, that we should not make the mistake of thinking he has divine attributes. I had always thought that God and Satan were co-equal, fighting it out for us, and that God was basically saying, 'You can have Sandy.'

I had cried to God constantly since my conversion:

Create a clean heart in me!
Renew a right spirit in me!
Please don't cast me out of Your presence!
Please don't take Your Holy Spirit from me!

Over and over I had prayed these prayers for myself, agonising to know the Lord in a warm and personal way, but feeling like I had a relationship with God's back. Now I feel His face toward me and sense His smile.

Now I don't live in a tiny corner of my mind or outside of my body. I live inside, sharing my mind with only my precious Lord. What a profound difference! There are no words to adequately describe the peacefulness and absence of pain and torment that I now experience daily. It's like being blind all these years and now I see. Everything is new, precious and treasured because it doesn't look black. I'm not afraid anymore that I'll be punished for every move I make. I'm able to make decisions now and have choices. I am free to make mistakes!

The last year and a half I had become unable to have anyone touch me without feeling pain or having horrible sexual thoughts. While having sex I would watch it from outside of my body. When that evil presence claimed to be my 'husband' I knew why I had always felt like a prostitute, even as a Christian.

After exposing that lie and renouncing it, I have since come to understand the meaning of 'bride' for the first time in my life, after twenty years of marriage, and I now also feel the love from the Bridegroom I shall some day see.

He has wiped away my tears, and answered the cry of my heart. At last, I sense a right spirit inside of me, and the presence cast out was not the presence of God, but of the evil one. I was fearful that God's presence would leave me. I now feel clean inside. I continue to go to Christian counselling, and I am making progress. I am learning to face and let go of the past abuse. I am learning to live in community and trust others again after feeling betrayed by my cult experience.

I believe God in His loving kindness met me at my point of need, and ordained the meeting that exposed and expelled the Satanic oppression in my life. Now I can continue growing in the family of God. I now am certain I belong to this family, and I'm loved by it. God has shown me that He is faithful and able, not just to call me from darkness to light, but also to keep me and sustain me until the journey ends when I shall see Him face to face. I still face trials, temptations and the pain of living in a fallen world, but I walk in it sensing the strong heartbeat of a loving Father within. The Satanic interference has been removed.

Praise the Lord.

———————

Parents must know Satan's strategies

The hideousness of Satan is revealed in Sandy's life story. Would he actually take advantage of a child with dysfunctional parents and grandparents who ignorantly provided occultic toys for their grandchildren? Satan would and does.

I have traced the origin of many adult problems to childhood fantasies, imaginary friends, games, the occult and abuses. It is not enough to warn our children about the stranger in the street. What about the one who may appear in their room? Our research indicates that half of our professing Christian teenagers have had some experience in their room that frightened them. That, more than anything, has prompted Steve Russo and me to write *The Seduction of Our Children*. We want to help parents know how to protect their children and defeat the influence of darkness. At the back of that book, I have written some simplified Steps to Freedom for children and early teens.

Truth, not power encounter

In the area of deliverance, the priest's noble but disastrous attempt at an exorcism is one reason why I don't advocate the power encounter approach where the counsellor deals directly with the demon. It can be like sticking a broom handle in a hornet's nest, rattling it around and proclaiming, 'Hey, there are demons here!' That experience left Sandy terrorised and reluctant to address the issue again. I interacted only with Sandy, not the demons.

The brain is the control centre, and as long as Sandy was willing to share with me what was going on inside we never lost control. Accusing and terrorising thoughts were bombarding her mind. When she revealed what she was hearing, I would simply expose the deception by saying, 'That's a lie,' or by asking Sandy to renounce it as a lie and tell it to go. The power of Satan is in the lie; when the lie is exposed the power is broken. God's truth sets people free. Occasionally I will have a person ask God to reveal what it is that is keeping him in bondage, and it's not uncommon for past events (often blocked memories) to be brought to mind so the person can confess and renounce them. In Sandy's case, she had no conscious memory of what happened when she was seven. (A biblical means of getting at those memories will be discussed in chapter 10.)

Exercising authority in Christ

Her concern about my leaving town is another reason I like to deal only with the person. When she asked me what she was going to do when I wasn't there, I responded, 'I didn't do anything. You did the renouncing and you exercised your authority in Christ by telling the evil presence to go. Jesus Christ is your deliverer and He will always be with you.' She renounced her invitation to let the demon share her body. Later she renounced all her cult and occult experiences. It cannot be overstated how important this step is; it's tied into the whole concept of repentance.

The church throughout its history has publicly declared, 'I renounce you Satan and *all* your works and *all* your ways.' Most Catholic, orthodox and liturgical churches still make that profession, but for some reason evangelical churches don't. That generic statement needs to be applied specifically for each individual. Any dabbling in the occult, brush with cults or seeking false guidance must be confessed and renounced. *All* his works and *all* his ways need to be renounced as God brings them to our memory. All lies and counterfeit ways must be replaced by 'the way and the truth and the life' (Jn 14:6, NIV). This is done in the first of the Steps to Freedom: Counterfeit versus Real.

Satan's bondages

Sandy had never had a 'normal' sexual relationship. She perceived herself as a prostitute because the evil presence claimed to be her husband. Freedom from that bondage allowed her to have a loving, intimate relationship with her husband. I will have much more to say about sexual bondages after other testimonies.

The mental battle she suffered is quite typical of those in bondage. Most people caught in a spiritual conflict will talk about their dysfunctional family background or other abuses, but seldom will they reveal the battle going on for their minds. They already fear they are going crazy, and they don't relish the thought of it being confirmed. Nor do they like the prospect of prescription drugs.

Sandy was relieved when her Christian counsellor believed her. The secular world has no other alternative than to look for a physical cure, since mental illness is the only possible diagnosis. The tragedy of anti-psychotic medications, when the problem is actually spiritual, is the drugged state in which it leaves the recipient. How is the truth going to set someone free who is so medicated that he or she can hardly talk, much less think?

Christian counsellors with whom I have dialogued are greatly appreciative of being made aware of spiritual conflict and how to resolve it. This makes their counselling practice much more holistic and effective.

One lady shared in the middle of a conference that I was describing her to a 'T'. She said she was going to a treatment centre for thirty days. I asked if I could see her first since I knew that the treatment centre she was going to was notorious in its use of drugs for therapy. She agreed and wrote the following:

> After meeting with you Monday night, I was absolutely euphoric, and so was my husband. He was so happy to see me happy. I was finally able to take my position with Christ and renounce the deceiver. The Lord has released me from my bondage.
>
> My big news is that I didn't wake up with nightmares or screams. Instead I woke up with my heart singing! The very first thought that entered my mind was 'even the stones will cry out' followed by 'Abba Father.' Neil, the Holy Spirit is alive in me! Praise the Lord! I can't begin to tell you how free I feel, but somehow I think you know!

Assuming responsibility

Nightmares and voices may have a spiritual explanation for their origin and the church bears the responsibility to check it out. I believe that every pastor and Christian counsellor should be able to help people like this.

You have nothing to lose by going through or taking someone through the Steps to Freedom. It's just old-fashioned house cleaning which takes into account the reality of the spiritual world. All we are doing is helping people assume responsibility for their relationship with God.

Nobody is accusing anybody of anything. If there is nothing demonic going on in someone's life, the worst thing that can happen is that the person will really be ready for communion the next time it is served!

Sandy's story brings out very well the two most sought-after goals we have with this type of counselling. First, that people will know who they are as children of God, that they are a part of God's forever family. Second, that they will have a peace and quietness in their mind, the peace that guards our hearts and our minds, the peace which transcends all understanding (Phil 4:7).

NOTE

1. In the parable of the rich man and Lazarus, we are clearly told of the great chasm that separates the living from the dead. I do not believe it was actually Sandy's mother who appeared in her dream. There is no way to know for sure, but perhaps God used Sandy's sensitivity toward her mother as a means of communicating with her and drawing her to Himself.

4

JENNIFER:
Freedom From Eating Disorders

I received a call from Jennifer asking if I would spend some time with her if she flew out. I set aside one Monday morning and had the privilege to walk her through the Steps to Freedom. A month later I received the following letter.

Dear Neil,

I just wanted to write and thank you for the time you spent with me. I guess I felt like nothing happened at the time we prayed and that maybe there wasn't a problem with the demonic. I was wrong. Something really did happen, and I have not had one more self-destructive thought or action or compulsion since that day.

I think the deliverance process began through my prayers of repentance in the months following my suicide attempt. I don't understand it all, but I know something is really different in my life and I feel free today. I haven't cut myself in a month and that is a true miracle.

I have a few questions I wish you would respond to if you have time. They have to do with my psychological problems. I was told that I have a chronic manic-depressive, schizo-affective disorder, and I am on Lithium and an anti-psychotic medication. Do I need these? Am I really chronic?

I always felt during my acting out periods, which is what they based my diagnosis on, that it was not me but rather some strong power outside myself that drove me to act self-destructive and crazy. The last three times I have quit my Lithium I have become suicidal and ended up in the hospital. I don't want that to happen again, but was that demonic? I also had a lot of mood swings even on the pills, but since my visit with you I have had none! This makes me wonder if I'm really okay and don't need the pills.

Also, ever since I was a little girl I have never been able to pray; there always seemed to be a wall between me and God. I was never very happy and always felt a sense of fear and uneasiness, like something was wrong.

Jennifer

Jennifer's story is important because it clarifies the need to know who we are as children of God and the nature of the spiritual battle we are in. That one morning we were able to process a lot, and she did achieve a sense of freedom. But does she know who she is as a child of God, and does she know how to stay free in Christ?

Within six months Jennifer was having difficulty again. Another year passed before she was desperate enough to call. She decided to fly out again, but this time she attended a whole conference. Here is her story.

Jennifer's Story

Everything seemed like a dream and everybody was just a character.

In seventh grade my eating disorder started — overeating, then starving. I would baby-sit and clean out the refrigerator, and then I wouldn't eat anything for three or four days. My focus became my weight; I was obsessed with the need to be thin.

Everything around me seemed like a dream and everybody was just a character. I thought, *Some day I will wake up, but I won't know the dreamer.* Nothing seemed real. I lived in a 'checked-out' state. I didn't think. When people talked I would look at them in bewilderment because I wasn't in touch with my mind.

During the day I appeared normal and functioned fairly well in school. Night-times were weird with a lot of bad dreams and terror. I wept often because of the voices in my head and the images and nonsense thoughts that often filled my mind. But I never said a word to anyone. I knew people would think I was crazy and I was terrified that nobody would believe me.

My college years were really hard, filled with routine binging and purging. I lost thirty pounds and began fainting and having chest pains. Because I was pathetically thin from anorexia, the skin literally hung on my bones. Finally I agreed to be hospitalised. I was totally exhausted physically, mentally and spiritually.

I nearly died. My pulse was forty when I was admitted, and they had trouble finding my blood pressure. My parents were very supportive. The hospital was good and I had Christian therapists, but they never touched on the spiritual. I was cutting myself, using razor blades and knives, and I still have scars on my hands from digging holes into them with my finger-nails.

The voices and night-times were bad, with demonic visitations and something raping me at night, holding me down so I couldn't move. Sometimes I crawled down the hall, trying to get away from things flying around my room. I was terrorised; thoughts of cutting my heart out dominated my mind. I did actually cut on my chest with knives because I thought my heart was poison and that I needed to get rid of it so that I would be clean.

When childhood memories started to surface, I lost it. I

was back in the hospital again and absolutely out of control. On some days it required five or six people to restrain me. I would be out of my body watching those people hold me down while I was fighting and kicking, until they would sedate me. I was diagnosed as manic-depressive. I took Lithium and continued with anti-depressants for the next six years and the drugs did quiet me somewhat.

While I was in the hospital a friend suggested that I talk with Neil Anderson, but I told her no. The thought of there being something demonic was terrifying to me and I told her, 'God said if two or more people pray He would listen. Why can't several people just pray with me here in the hospital? Why do I have to have some man come?' I talked with my Christian counsellors and they said, 'Your associates just want to make this spiritual because they don't want to deal with the pain in your life.' The counsellors had gained my trust that year, so I believed them and refused to see Neil. That's the first time I ever heard Neil's name. I did not meet him for three years. I was too afraid; the whole idea freaked me out.

Somehow, I graduated and started working. I would do a fantastic job at work, then get in my car, pull out my razor blades and live in a different world for the next sixteen hours. Then I would go back to work. I was talking with all of my 'friends' in my head and cutting ritualistically on myself for the blood. I just wanted to feel; I knew I was not in touch with reality.

At night I would often lie awake, hoping I would die before morning. I wrote suicide notes and knew every empty house around: houses that were for sale, where I could drive my car into the garage, leave the motor running and kill myself. I also knew the gun shops in town and their hours, so that if I needed a gun I could get one. I kept two or three hundred pills at home so I always had an 'out' for when I could bare it no longer. I had many plans to commit suicide.

I kept thinking, *The Lord has got to get me through this.* I knew He was my only hope and that there was a reason to live, so I kept crying out to Him. I remember crawling into a corner of my room at night and sleeping there on the floor. I was trying to get away from it all and praying to God that I could get through one more night. I prayed that He would give me strength and protect me from myself. I blamed myself for all of this.

I feared for my life and so did many of my friends. I went to see a pastor and told him I thought I had a spiritual problem and that I also felt I was going to die. He said, 'You have one of the best psychiatrists in town; I don't know why you're talking to me.' Then he asked, 'Are you taking your medicine?' He was scared of me and he didn't know how to help me.

Once I spent several hours talking with some caring friends. One suggested, 'Jennifer, you just need to go into the throne room of Jesus.' The voices inside me said, 'That's it!' To me, 'going into the throne room' meant to die. I drove to a hotel, went to a room and took two hundred pills. I laid down by my simple note that read, *I'm going home to be with Jesus. I just can't take it any more.*

I called someone because I didn't want to be alone when I died. I felt that if there was someone on the other end of the phone it would help. At first I wouldn't give the phone number to my friend, but later I was so sleepy and out of it that I gave in so I could go to sleep and my friend could call me back later. Two-and-a-half hours later they found me and took me to a hospital where my stomach was pumped. I was placed in the intensive care unit. I should have died, but by a miracle of God I didn't.

I was hospitalised again in a different Christian clinic. The possibility of my problem being spiritual was never addressed. I was diagnosed as being schizo-affective and bi-polar. They told me I didn't know reality and that I needed to base my confidence on what others said and not on what was going on in my head. They told me I would be dependent on medication for the rest of my life. The side effects of the anti-psychotics and anti-depressants were horrendous. The tremors were so bad that I had trouble even using my hand to write my name, and my vision was blurred. I was so drugged I couldn't even hold my mouth open.

In counselling I told them I was hearing voices, but they never explored the possibility of them being demonic. They did tell me that since I had a lot of therapy already, they wanted to deal with me on the spiritual level. They brought in a godly man who was good, but I couldn't hear or remember a word he said. As soon as he opened his Bible and started to talk, I began listening to other things and planning to kill myself. I felt that if I could just get out of there I would do it, and this time I would be successful.

One day a friend called me at the clinic and honestly addressed the sin in my life. He basically told me I was being manipulative, dishonest, hateful, attention-seeking and selfish. That was heavy stuff, but he spoke kindly and I was at a point where I was ready to hear it. I got on my knees and wrote a letter to God in my journal asking forgiveness. Those sins were a part of me that I was ashamed of and I had lived with the guilt of them all my life. I did experience some release and I know that was the beginning of my healing.

Friends invited me to California for a visit, and I decided I wanted to meet Neil Anderson. I went to his office and we talked for about two hours. He opened his Bible and was going through the Scriptures, but the voices were so loud I couldn't hear a word he said. It was like he was talking gibberish — his words were like another language. That's how it always was with me when people were using the Bible.

I got through the Steps to Freedom, but I didn't feel any different when I left. I wondered if the words just went straight from my eyes to my mouth without my internalising anything I was reading. But then two areas improved. The struggle with food was better, and I never cut myself again. The voices were also gone for a couple of weeks, but then they came back. I didn't remember Neil saying what to do when the voices and thoughts came back, and it never occurred to me that I didn't have to listen. I didn't know I had a choice, so I got hit worse than ever.

Six months later I was in the hospital again, both suicidal and psychotic. I was out of it and did everything the voices were telling me to do. I was encouraged to see Neil again, but if that didn't work I knew I was going to die. All of this had been going on for seven terrible years, and the side effects of the drugs were so bad that all I did was work four hours and then sit in front of the television or sleep. I couldn't carry on a meaningful conversation with anybody, and I really didn't care about anything any more. I felt hopeless, exhausted and discouraged.

I went to the conference on Resolving Personal and Spiritual Conflicts. I again met with Neil and at one point I got so sick that I threw up. He introduced me to a lady with a past similar to mine. She sat beside me and prayed for me, so I was more able to hear and comprehend what Neil was saying.

I learned a lot about the spiritual battle that was going on for my mind and what I needed to do to take a stand. Once that part became clear, I was set free. I knew what to do and how to do it. Previously, I didn't know how to stay free and walk in my freedom, although I was raised in a good Christian home. Even though I accepted Christ when I was four, I never knew who I was in Christ and I didn't understand the authority I had as a child of God.

I told my psychiatrist that I was free in Christ now and

wanted to get off my medication. He said, 'You've tried this before and look at your history.' I said, 'But it's different now. Will you support me in this?' When he said, 'No, I can't,' I replied, 'Well I'm going to do it anyway; I'll take responsibility for myself.'

He said he would see me in a month. I came back in a month and was functioning on half of the prescription, and in two months I was off completely. He asked how I felt and when I told him I was fine, he shook my hand and said I wouldn't need to come back any more. It was like I was discovering life for the first time, and I felt impressed to write the following letter to Neil:

> Dear Neil:
>
> I was reading back over my journals from years past and was harshly reminded of the darkness and evil in which I was engulfed for so many years. I often wrote about 'them' and the control they had of me. I often felt that rather than be torn between Satan and God, I would rather rest in the darkness. What I did not realise was that I was a child of God and *in* Christ, not hanging between two spirits. So often I felt that I was being controlled and was crazy, having lost all sense of self and reality. I think in a way I had learned to like the darkness. I felt safe there and was deceived by the lie that if I let go of the evil, I would die and God would not meet my needs or care for me the way I wanted.
>
> This is why I would not talk with you the first time. I didn't want you to take away the only thing I had, feeling sheer terror at the thought. I guess the evil one had something to do with those thoughts and fears. I was so deceived. I really tried to pray and read the Bible, but it all made little sense. Once I tried to read *The Adversary* by Mark Bubeck, and I literally could not make my hand pick it up. I just stared at it.

Psychiatrists tried many different medications and doses (including large doses of anti-psychotics) to make things better. I took up to fifteen pills a day just to remain in control and somewhat functional. I was so drugged I couldn't think or feel much at all. I felt like a walking dead person! The therapists and doctors all agreed I had a chronic mental illness that I would deal with for the rest of my life — a very defeating prognosis to hear!

At the conference, I saw the total picture. Just weeks before I had made the decision that I did not want to entertain the darkness any longer and that I really wanted to get well, but I had no idea how to take that step. Well…I learned, and once again my head became quiet. The voices stopped, the doubts and confusion lifted, and I was free. Now I know how to stand.

I feel like a small child who has been through a horrible and terrifying storm, lost in confusion and loneliness. I knew my loving Father was on the other side of the door and that He was my only hope and relief, but I could not get through that strong door. Then someone told me how to turn the knob and told me that because I was God's child, I had all the authority and right to open the door. I have reached up and opened the door and run to my Father and now I am resting in His safe and loving arms. I know and believe that 'neither death, nor life, neither angels, nor principalities, neither things present nor things to come, nor any powers, nor height, nor depth, nor any created thing, shall be able to separate us from the love of God' (Rom 8:38).

I am working in ministry now, taking tons of time to read and pray and be loved by the God I had heard so much about but never experienced. I am giving and sharing and serving in ways I have always dreamed of doing. In bondage, I could never reach beyond my desperate self. Now I feel peaceful and full inside, some-what childlike, with purpose and direction, joy and hope.

Now when I get accusing or negative thoughts, they just bounce off because I have learned to bind Satan with one quick sentence, ignore his lies and choose the truth. It works! Because of my strong Saviour, Satan leaves me alone almost instantly. I've had a few pretty down days, but then I choose to remember who I am and tell Satan and his demons to leave. It's a miracle... the cloud lifts!

My sadness has come when I realise I have lived most of my life in captivity, believing lies. I try to remember, 'For this purpose I have raised you up, that I may show My power in you, and that My name may be declared in all the earth' (Ex 9:16, NKJV). I know God will use my experiences mightily in my own life as well as in others. The chains have fallen off. I have chosen the light and life.

Because of the obvious changes in my counte-nance, people have been seeking me out for light and truth. I can't keep up with 'who has which' of your tapes. I have shared them a lot with others who find themselves in bondage and need.

I am still seeing a Christian counsellor and this has been very helpful. It's horrendous coming out of my past, and it's a struggle learning how to live. My biggest temptation is to be sick because I got a lot of strokes from that. I needed to see that the sick person is not who I am, but that I am a child of God and that He desires for me to be free. It was difficult for me to accept that new identity. A few times I have had 'crazy' days. But I realise that this is not what I want, and I call my friend to pray with me and renounce the darkness with her encouragement.

My biggest fight is to stay single-minded because my tendency is to let my mind split off. My prayer every day is that He will help me to stay focused and that I will love Him with all my heart and soul, not just a part of it.

Another important friend is a woman who was delivered five years ago from being a medium in New Age. She has been a tremendous help, but my main support is the friend I met at your conference. Our phone bills are huge and we see each other three or four times a year. I really don't think I would have made it and stayed free those first couple of months without her.

My family and the treatment I received were the best. They did everything they knew to love me, help me and save my life. I have been so loved throughout my life by so many friends and family members. I feel it is because of their prayers, consistent love and support that I am alive today.

I firmly believe that the prescription drugs were what kept me from being able to think or fight. They left me in such a passive, semi-alert state that I couldn't concentrate. I couldn't write because of horrible hand tremors...I couldn't see at times because of blurred vision...I couldn't pray because there was no concentration...and never did I have the energy to discern thoughts or remember truths in Scripture...and I couldn't follow conversation. It was like being on twelve to fifteen antihistamine tablets at one time, leaving me in a very helpless condition, with no quality of life.

I have written out a ton of truth verses on cards that I carry everywhere. There have been times when the dark cloud of oppression is so crushing. That's when I pull out my cards and read them aloud until the light dispels the darkness and I'm able to pray again. Then I can find the lie I've been believing, claim the truth, announce my position in Christ and renounce the devil.

The process has become so routine that I find myself claiming and renouncing under my breath, almost without thinking.

My friend and I have talked often of an active surrender. How do I acknowledge my total dependence upon God and fight at the same time? I don't totally understand it, but it is an active surrender that sets us free.

My most difficult struggle to this day is to want to be free. I'm tempted to use my dissociative 'alters' or friends. They occupied the places in my split-off self where I used to go to escape reality and find relief. Satan takes advantage of those mental escapes, playing havoc in my mind and life.

I actually buried stones in the ground representing each split-off piece of my mind that I had held on to. In one sense, it was a huge loss. In another, I knew I had to do that because those identities and psychotic-like splits were homes where Satan and his workers resided. I still am tempted, and even have returned to those states when I am under stress, but I fight it and I am able to bounce back. I'm grasping for God's love and strength in a way I'd never been able to before. I now desire to find my safety in Him.

I cannot express the difference in my heart and life. Where my heart used to reside in pieces, now it is whole. Where my mind was void, now there is a song and an intellect beyond anything I could have previously comprehended. Where there was a life of unreality and despair, now there is joy and freedom and light. To God be the glory because all I have done is to finally say 'yes' to His offer of freedom. I am grateful to be alive!

Jennifer

Getting and staying free

When Jennifer saw me the first time, I led her through the Steps to Freedom. The fact that there was some resolution was clear from the first letter she sent. However, in a short, three-hour counselling session neither I nor anyone else have enough time to educate sufficiently regarding identity in Christ, much less the nature of the spiritual battle. Plus, I didn't have the experience base then that I do now. Since Jennifer lacked this knowledge, she slipped back into her old habit patterns. In her second visit, she sat through a whole conference designed to give her the information she needed to get and stay free.

Most pastors can't afford the time to sit one-on-one with people for extended teaching sessions. I usually ask a person to at least read *Victory Over the Darkness* before we meet for our first session. If they struggle with reading, as Jennifer did (which is often a symptom of demonic harassment), then I take them through the Steps to Freedom first and follow up with assignments, such as reading the book or listening to the tapes on the same subject.

Let me emphasise again that I don't assume anything regarding spiritual conflicts. What is needed is a safe means to spiritually check it out. It is no different than going to a medical doctor and having your blood and urine checked. The church needs to assume the responsibility for spiritual diagnosis and resolution.

Seeing deliverance as something you do for a person will usually result in problems. You may effect a person's freedom by casting out a demon, but it is very possible that it will return and the final state will be even worse. When Jennifer did the confessing, renouncing, forgiving, etc., she learned the nature of the battle by going through the process. Instead of bypassing her mind where the real battle was, I appealed to her mind and helped her to assume responsibility for choosing truth.

Jennifer's comments on prescription drugs are appropriate. Using drugs to cure the body is commendable, but using drugs to cure the soul is deplorable. Her ability to think was so impaired that she couldn't process anything. I often see people in this condition and it is extremely frustrating. However, I never go against the advice of a medical doctor. I strongly caution people not to go off prescription drugs too fast, or serious side effects will occur. Jennifer did go off too quickly after her first visit with me and that may have contributed to her subsequent relapse.

Some don't want freedom

Spiritually healthy people will have a hard time understanding that others may not always want to get free from their lifestyle of bondage. I have come across many people who don't want to get rid of their 'friends'. Once, after walking through the Steps to Freedom with a pastor's wife, I sensed that her freedom wasn't complete. She looked at me and asked, 'Now what?' I paused for a moment and said, 'Tell it to go.' A quizzical look came on her face and she responded, 'In the name of the Lord Jesus Christ, I command you to leave my presence.' Instantly she was free. The next day she confided that the presence was saying to her mind, 'You're not going to just send me away after all the years we have been together, are you?' It was playing on her sympathy.

One young man said a voice was pleading not to make him go because he didn't want to go to hell. The demon wanted to stay so he could go to heaven with him. I asked the young man to pray, asking God to reveal the true nature of the voice. As soon as he had finished praying, he cried out in disgust. I really don't know what he saw or heard, but the evil nature of it was very obvious. These are not harmless spirit guides; they are counterfeit spirits seeking to discredit God and promote allegiance to Satan. They are destroyers who will tear apart a family, church or ministry.

Binging and purging

Eating disorders are a plight of our age. The sick philosophies of our society have given godlike status to the body. Young girls are often obsessed with appearance as the standard of self-worth. Instead of finding identity in the inner person, they find it in the outer person. Rather than focus on the development of character, they focus on appearance, performance and status. Satan capitalises on this wrong pursuit of happiness and self-esteem.

Compounding the problem is the rise of sexual abuse and rape. Many girls and young women who are addicted to eating disorders have been sexually victimised. Lacking a gospel, the secular agencies have no way to completely free these people from their past. Knowing who they are in Christ and the absolute necessity of forgiveness is what brings freedom, but they still have to deal with the lies Satan has been using on them.

One young lady was taking seventy-five laxatives a day. Being a graduate of an excellent Christian college, she wasn't dumb. Yet reasoning with her had proved futile. Eating disorder units had stemmed the tide of weight loss by using strong behavioural controls. When I talked with her I asked, 'This has nothing to do with eating, does it?' 'No,' she responded. Then I said, 'You're defecating to purge yourself from evil, aren't you?' She nodded in agreement. I asked her to repeat after me, 'I renounce defecating in order to purge myself of evil, and I announce that only the blood of Jesus cleanses me from all unrighteousness.' She stopped taking laxatives for a short time, but in this case as in Jennifer's, she didn't have the total picture and failed to take advantage of the support she needed.

Another woman said she had purged all her life, just as

her mother had. She said she did not consciously plan to do it, and that it was a little joke with her teen daughters that she could vomit into a paper cup while driving and never cross over the line on the road. When I asked her why she was throwing up, she said she felt cleansed afterward. I asked her to repeat after me, 'I renounce the lie that throwing up will cleanse me. I believe only in the cleansing work of Christ on the cross.' Afterward she immediately cried out, 'Oh my God, that's it, isn't it? Only Jesus can cleanse me from my sin.' She said that she saw in her mind a vision of the cross.

That is also why people cut themselves. They are trying to purge themselves of evil. It's a spiritual counterfeit, a lie of Satan, that we can be the god our lives and effect our own cleansing. Remember the 450 prophets of Baal who came up against Elijah? They cut themselves (1 Kings 18:28). Travel around the world and you will witness many pagan religions where they cut themselves during religious ceremonies. It is necessary to reveal that lie and renounce it. In many cases the person isn't aware of why he does it, so asking why may be counter-productive. Jennifer was trying to cut out her heart, believing that it was evil. She also shared that she was cutting herself to get in touch with reality, believing that live people bleed. The young woman taking laxatives immediately started crying after renouncing the lie. After she gained her composure, I asked what she was thinking. She said, 'I can't believe all the lies I have believed.'

It is important to note that not all of those who cut themselves have eating disorders, and many who have eating disorders don't cut themselves.

I received an insightful letter from a lady who found tremendous release from going through the Steps to Freedom, but the pastor had not addressed her eating disorder at that time. She wrote:

Dear Neil:

I just finished reading *The Seduction of Our Children*, which I found very eye opening in many areas. In chapter 13, I was reading through the steps for children when I noticed a separate section for eating disorders. As I was reading, my heart was pierced with a severe pain, yet there was also a sigh of relief. Your words described what my life has been like since grade school.

Earlier this year I went through the Steps to Freedom with a pastor, and I was a totally different person. Yet, the one thing that didn't seem right was the struggle I was continuing to have with my physical appearance. That subject hadn't come up during my counselling session.

As I read your description of a typical person with an eating disorder, I just wept before the Lord. It started for me by cutting myself, then I became anorexic, then bulimic, and eventually a mixture of all three.

I read through the renouncing and announcing that you stated and agreed with a friend in prayer about it. God is so good to me. For whatever reason it was overlooked, the enemy meant it for evil to keep me in bondage to an area that had run most of my life. God used your book to add this step of freedom in my life. Thank you so much.

The need to be believed

These people are desperately looking for someone who will believe them, who understands what is going on. They know enough not to share too much of the bizarre thoughts and images with people who don't understand. In Jennifer's case, when she finally did share part of her story, people didn't really believe her and some don't to this day. They see her wholeness as a fluke. Counsellors must recognise the reality of Satan's tactics, that we truly do not 'fight' against flesh and blood, 'but against the rulers, against the powers, against the world forces of this darkness, against the spiritual forces of wickedness in the heavenly places' (Eph 6:12).

After-care

Jennifer's thoughts on after-care are choice. The need to have a friend to call and be accountable to can't be stressed enough. We were never intended by God to live alone; we need each other. And Jennifer needed to continue with counselling to help her adjust to a new life. In many ways, she had not developed as others do and needs now to mature into wholeness. Freedom does not constitute maturity. People like Jennifer are developing new habit patterns of thought and it takes time to reprogramme their minds.

Her counsellors provided her with the support she needed to survive, and they are good people who would have done anything to help her. Nobody has all the answers. First and foremost, we need the Lord, but we also need each other.

Effective prayer for others

I think of the pastors who try to help people like Jennifer. Most pastors haven't had formal training in counselling, and few have had seminary training that equipped them to deal with the kingdom of darkness. Desperate people come with overwhelming needs, knowing that their only hope is the Lord. Sometimes the only pastoral weapon at their disposal is prayer, so they pray. But often they see very little happen in response to their prayer of faith. That can be very discouraging.

Most Christians are aware of the passage in James that instructs those who are sick to call the elders who are to pray and anoint with oil. I believe the church should be doing this, but I think we have overlooked some very important concepts and the order implied in James: 'Is anyone among you suffering? Let him pray' (5:13). The primary person who needs to pray is the sufferer. Hurting people who saw me when I was pastoring asked for prayer. Of course, I prayed for them, but the one who really needed to pray was the person who was seeing me.

After walking a social worker through the Steps to Freedom, the change in her countenance was so noticeable that I encouraged her to visit the ladies room and take a good look in the mirror. She was glowing when she returned to my office. As she reflected on the resolution of her spiritual conflicts, she said, 'I always thought somebody else had to pray for me.' That is a very common misconception. In the Steps to Freedom, the counsellee is the one doing most of the praying.

We can't have a secondary relationship with God. We may need a third party to facilitate the reconciliation of two personalities, but they won't be reconciled by what the facilitator does. They will only be reconciled by the concessions made by the principal parties. In spiritual resolution, God doesn't make concessions in order for us to be reconciled to Him. The Steps to Freedom lay out the 'concessions' that we have to make in order to assume our responsibility.

'Is anyone among you sick? Let him call for the elders of the church' (5:14). Again the responsibility to take the initiative is upon the one who is sick. The primary responsibility to get well is always placed on the sick person. I doubt that we will ever be effective in trying to heal a hurting humanity that doesn't want to get well. The Steps to Freedom only work if the person wants to be well and will assume his own responsibility.

Mark records the incident when Jesus sent His disciples on ahead of Him in a boat. The wind came up, and the disciples ended up in the middle of the sea, 'straining at the oars'. As Jesus walked on the sea, 'He intended to pass by them' (Mk 6:48). I believe that Jesus intends to pass by the self-sufficient. If we want to do it ourselves, He will let us. When the disciples called upon Jesus, He came to them. When the sick call the elders, they should also come.

James continues, 'Therefore, confess your sins to one another, and pray for one another, so that you may be healed. The effective prayer of a righteous man can accomplish much' (5:16). I believe the prayers of our pastors will be effective when the people are willing to confess their sins. The Steps to Freedom are a fierce moral inventory. I have heard people confess incredible atrocities as they go through the steps. My role is to give them the assurance that God answers prayer and forgives His repentant children.

I am most confident in prayer after I have taken a person through the Steps to Freedom. John writes, 'The one who practices sin is of the devil; for the devil has sinned from the beginning. The Son of God appeared for this purpose, that He might destroy the works of the devil' (1 Jn 3:8). I believe we are perfectly in God's will when we ask Him to restore a life damaged by Satan. That damage could be physical, emotional or spiritual.

The order is 'seek first the Kingdom of God', then all the other things will be added unto us. A young lady approached me in a conference with a cheerful 'Hi!' 'Hi,' I responded. She said, 'You don't recognise me, do you?' I didn't, and even after she reminded me that I had counselled with her a year earlier, I still didn't recognise her. She had changed that much. Like Jennifer, her appearance and countenance were totally different, a beautiful demonstration of change in a person 'seeking first the kingdom of God'. What a difference freedom in Christ makes!

5

NANCY:
Female Sexual Abuse and Freedom

The sin, confess, sin, confess, sin, 'I give up' cycle is most common in sexual bondages. Suppose the neighbour's dog got into your garden because you left the gate open. The dog's jaw is now clamped around the calf of your leg. Would you beat on yourself or the dog?

Painfully aware that we left the door open to sin, we cry out to God for forgiveness. Guess what God does? He forgives us! He said He would — but the dog is still there. Rather than the sin, confess routine, the complete biblical perspective is: sin, confess, *resist*: 'Submit therefore to God. Resist the devil and he will flee from you' (James 4:7).

In our western world, we operate as though the only players in the drama are ourselves and God. That isn't true. If it's only you and God, then either you or God are going to have to take the rap for an awful lot of havoc in this world. I believe that God is not the author of confusion and death, but of order and life. The god of this world is the chief architect of rebellion, sin, sickness and death. He is the father of lies (Jn 8:44).

However, 'the devil made me do it' is not a part of my theology or practice. It is our responsibility not to let sin reign in our mortal body (Rom 6:12). But treating those in bondage as the principal culprits, and throwing them out because they can't get their act together, is the height of Pharisaic judgement and human rejection.

If you witness a little girl being sexually molested because she left the door open and evil intruders took advantage of her carelessness, would you overlook the abusers and confront only the girl? If you did, the little girl will conclude that there is something evil about herself. That's what Nancy and many others like her have experienced. Let's learn from her story.

Nancy's Story

We looked like a normal, happy family.

Both of my parents were young and non-Christians. They had been married two years, and their marriage was rocky, when I was born. Later two brothers and a sister were added, and photos from that time showed that we looked like a normal, happy family. My dad was handsome and my mother was nice looking, too. Mostly the pictures are of the family all dressed up for church on Easter Sunday — we never went any other time.

We moved a lot, and I attended eight different schools before attending high school — two different high schools.

My father had a drug and alcohol problem and was in and out of jail for stealing to buy the things he needed in order to feed his addiction. He even broke open my piggy bank for whatever money I had and once sold all of the lamps in the house. He would leave for a couple of days at a time and then come home smashed and abusive, breaking furniture, pictures and glassware. This was not an uncommon thing; whenever my father got mad, things were destroyed.

My father told me when I was three that I could sleep in his room while my mother was at work. I remember lying in my parents' bed and my dad talking to me as though I was his wife. He told me that he loved me more than he did my mother and that I was his special girl. Then he would touch me sexually. I really had no idea what was going on, only that this made Daddy happy and then he would be nice to me. He told me that I should never tell my mother about this because she wouldn't understand. It was then that I started masturbating, usually several times a day.

This was a confusing time for me. Sometimes I was torn between my parents, but on other nights, when my mother was home, my father would beat me and throw me against the wall. One night he took a blanket and threw it over my entire body and then sat on the blanket. I couldn't breathe or see any light. At first my mother just laughed, but then she yelled at my dad and told him to get up. That experience was one of the first times I remember being outside of myself and watching what was going on.

Another time, my dad got my baby brother and me drunk. He would give us tastes of whatever he was drinking and then spin us around and watch us walk funny.

About every two or three months my mum would leave my dad and we would spend some time at my grandparents' home until my dad would say, 'I'm sorry; I won't ever do it again.' So we would move back with him. During those times of separation I would always be with my mum, and I was glad. I was so afraid of being totally alone with my father.

One time when I was about five, Dad came home and there was the usual broken furniture and pictures, but this time was different. It was late at night and mum and I were up, but we were not packing to leave as we often did. On this particular night we were crouched in a corner of their bedroom. The house was damaged beyond repair, worse than usual, and my dad was standing over us with a gun pointed at my mother's head. He said, 'This is it. I'm going to pull the trigger.' My mum hugged me tightly and pleaded with him not to kill her. I was crying, and I heard the trigger snap, but no explosion. Mum had thrown away the bullets and the gun that my dad thought was loaded was empty, although Mum wasn't sure whether he had got hold of more bullets or not.

At that, my dad became even more angry and picked up my mum and threw her across the room. Mum told me to run next door, so I did. The police came and took my dad away, and I stayed at the neighbours' house, sleeping in a strange bed all alone and crying like I had never cried before. I wanted my mum to hold me, but she wasn't there. I don't know where she went, but whenever things got really bad I always had to stay somewhere else without my mum. I still don't understand where she went and why she didn't want me with her.

Another time, my dad had a knife and my mother had a broken bottle and they were fighting. I remember battling in my mind about which one I wanted to win. I loved my mum, but I never felt that she loved me. I knew my dad loved me, but he scared me. That time, Dad did cut Mum's throat and beat her up, and a neighbour had to take her to the hospital where she stayed for several days. I was, of course, at a friend's house…again alone.

I thought my parents loved animals more than people. One time my dad brought home a dog that had been mistreated. My parents felt so bad for this dog — they loved him, fed him extra and talked about how awful his past owners had been. I remember being jealous of the dog, wishing that my parents would be good 'owners' of me.

By the time I was six, my dad had been in and out of jail several times and my mother finally left him. We moved in with my grandparents for a couple of years and then, later, into another house in the same town.

I talked to myself constantly, saying how much I needed to masturbate in order to feel better. I would dream of boys in class at school and pretend we were making love. One time I was masturbating while watching television, and my mother came into the room and watched. I didn't see her at first, but when I did, she just smiled at me and told me this was normal.

There were times in the bath when I would travel outside of myself and dream I was drowning myself. It felt both good and scary at the same time. I'd fill up the bath as high as I could, get in and see myself under the water, face up and dead.

I spent as much time as I could at my grandmother's house and saw strange things: shadows coming out of grandma's closet, voices and noises, and things moving around the room. Once my toy broom flew across my bedroom. These things startled me at first, but after awhile I enjoyed trying to make things move myself.

My grandmother gave me a ouija-board, and my brother and I played with it. It was about this time that I asked my brother to sleep with me, and we kissed and held hands. I loved him so much and felt there was no other way to really show him that I cared.

I was given a dog and would look at him and think, 'I love you truly.' I would let him lick me and for awhile it would feel good, but then I would get depressed. One day, I looked at him and wondered what it would be like for him to be dead. Only a few minutes later, he ran out in the road and was hit by a car and killed instantly. I remember having other dreams come true as well.

When I was about seven, I attended a neighbourhood church. I enjoyed the songs and the people seemed so nice, but I can't remember anyone ever asking who I was or why I was there by myself.

My grandmother and grandfather didn't sleep together. I learned later that my grandfather had an affair and my grandmother said that he could stay, but they never slept together again, so I would sleep with my grandmother. She wrote stories and would tell them to me, usually stories about friendly ghosts, so I thought the ghosts I was seeing in her house were good.

My grandfather loved me and told me I was his favourite grandchild. I slept with him, too, but he never touched me inappropriately or yelled at me or hurt me in any way. We would talk together at the dinner table and play games together, and he would play his guitar and sing for me. Even though there were strange things at their house, this was the closest thing to a happy family in my experience.

My mother remarried and we moved away. The first few years of their marriage seemed normal. We got spankings, but not beatings. I was in Brownies, tap dancing, gymnastics, and I did well at school. I still heard voices saying, 'You're ugly and stupid. This is going to end and your real father is going to come and get you.'

I started having dreams about dying and would lie in bed crying out to God for help, 'Please let there be something other than death, something beyond death.' I dreamed that my grandparents were going to die, that I would never see them again. I dreamed my mother would die. It became such an obsession that I couldn't get to sleep unless I thought of someone in my family dying, and then I would cry myself to sleep.

I went to a church with a Christian friend and went forward during the altar call, wanting so much for someone to love me and help me, but this was not the time or the place. The counsellor said that I needed to be 'slain under the cross' so that I could speak in another language. My friend said that I would fall over afterwards and that I shouldn't be afraid.

There were about thirty people around me who all started to pray, some in tongues and some not. It was hot and I just wanted to go home, so I thought I would talk some gibberish and fall over, which I did. Everyone was so excited that I was now a 'Christian'. I knew I had fooled them and was confused, wondering if Christians were fakes.

While in grade school, I had a baby-sitter only a few years older than me who would take off her clothes and my clothes and we would lay on each other on the living room floor. Sometimes I spent the night at her house and she would play with me, naked.

In the summers I visited my grandparents' home and the summer after I finished fifth grade, I took a friend with me. I had never had homosexual desires before, but that summer it was different. We played in the greenhouse and I told her she was my wife, or I hers, and we would hold hands and kiss. One thing led to another and we would end up on the floor rolling around together until I would end up masturbating. I don't think she ever did and she seemed scared, but she was always willing to play the game several times a day.

When we returned home, we went into the bushes and tried the game again, but this time it didn't seem right and we never did it again. We stayed friends throughout our school years but never again mentioned our summer together.

The next year I took another friend to Grandmother's house. This time we stayed in the bedroom and read magazines and acted out the stories in them.

By the time I was in junior high, my mum and stepdad were fighting more and more. I felt guilty about their fights, but mostly about my masturbation problem. I couldn't tell anyone or ask if this was normal, though I already knew it couldn't be. I tried my hardest to stop, but there was always that voice saying, 'No, it's all right. Everyone does it.' Then, afterwards, the same voice would say, 'You fool. You are so stupid and ugly, no one will want you.'

When I was in high school, lying became a big part of

my life. I wanted to have friends and fun, but I saw myself as stupid and inferior, so I would make up stories to make myself look and feel better.

I dated a lot and would let the boys do whatever they wanted with me, up to the point of actually having intercourse — I could finish that feeling at home. Of course, the guys didn't know that, so I became known as a big tease. Several told me that I drove them crazy for sex and that made me feel so down on myself: guilty, dirty inside and out, ugly, and again a failure.

Finally the inevitable happened. I did have intercourse with a boy in the front seat of his car. It wasn't really painful; it wasn't anything. We drove back to his house because his dad was an alcoholic and never at home. We took a shower together and I did sex dances for him.

When I got home, my stepdad was waiting up for me as he always did. We didn't talk much, just looked at each other, and I went to bed, feeling numb as I fell asleep thinking about all that had happened that night. The next morning I called the boy and told him I never wanted to see him again, and I told everyone at school what a loser he was.

Later I asked my mum if you could wear white to your wedding if you were not a virgin. She just said, 'You can wear whatever you want.' I felt so rejected — I wish she would have asked me what had happened.

After one of our family moves I rode the bus to my new school. I had decided I would not make friends with anyone because I hated it there and I hated my stepdad for making us move again. A blonde, bubbly cheerleader got on the bus and sat next to me, holding a trophy and smiling from ear to ear. I just glared at her. I was into cheerleading at the school I just moved from, and I didn't need her to remind me of what I had left behind.

She talked all the way to school and ended up inviting me to her church youth group. I had no idea what a church youth group was and I certainly wasn't going to make friends with her. However, we rode the bus together for several weeks and finally I agreed to go.

I was surprised to find a group of kids singing, laughing and reading Bibles. I remembered how good it felt in church when I was a child and felt that way again. My voices told me, 'No! These kids won't like you. You are stupid for being here.' But the girl I met on the bus continued to be my friend, and by the end of that school year I asked Christ to come into my life and was baptised.

I was so on fire for the Lord. I had finally found someone who would never leave me, hit me or make me do bad things — someone who would always love me. I told everyone about Jesus and walked around the house with my Bible, quoting verses. I began a Bible study with my brothers and we would pray together and talk about Christ's love.

Then when I was in my last year of school, my mum and stepdad had a very violent fight. I was frozen with fear and felt that I couldn't stand to see what had happened with my birth father re-enacted, so I took all the money I could find in the house and ran away. I drove to another part of the country and moved in with a boy I had met earlier. The voices within me started up again, saying, 'You slut! You call yourself a Christian?'

After awhile, my boyfriend and I broke up and I went back home, but my stepdad didn't want me to stay. One night I attended a ball game at a local Bible college. Through all that had been happening, I wore a façade and told people that I was a Christian and that God is great.

However, during the game, I was thinking about my situation: how I had been living with a boy, had come back from running away and now had no place to live. Just then, a girl next to me asked if I needed a place to live. I asked if she could read my mind and told her that I did. I moved in with her and two other girls and found out that she was a lesbian and thought I was cute. But that was one relationship I never did pursue.

One of the girls I lived with had a brother I liked, but she was trying to guard his innocence and really didn't want me to date him. However, we started to go out together, and it was a different relationship than I had ever had before. I knew Jim cared about me — really cared!

Shortly after we were engaged, I cheated on him. I felt so guilty that I gave back the engagement ring, but he wouldn't break off the relationship. I was all mixed up, still masturbating and not eating well. In my heart I wanted him to love me and stay with me, but I was mean to him.

I decided that the man I would marry would have to know the truth about me, so I shared my past with him. He had come from a very strict, sheltered Christian home, and some of the things in my life were hard for him to take, but he told me that he loved me anyway. Seven months later we were married.

We never slept together before we were married, but afterwards we had a very abnormal sexual relationship. I was addicted to sex, not only with my husband but also with masturbation. This created tension, so we fought and I began to feel dirty and alone again.

Our first ten years of marriage were turbulent. Jim attended Bible college, worked for a major company for seven years, and then officially went into ministry. I was excited to be a minister's wife and put high expectations on myself to be perfect and always available to help others.

We had two children, but I wasn't much of a mum. I hit them a lot and was depressed easily. I felt like my life was a waste; suicide was a daily thought. I would alternate between fits of rage and asking forgiveness. I wanted to be close to God but never felt that I was.

When I became pregnant a third time a big part of me wanted to have an abortion, but a small part of me said,

'Love this child.' My husband was excited about that pregnancy, but we fought even more and my mood swings went out of control. The baby came and I didn't know how I could possibly take care of another child. All I wanted was to be out of this life. I was depressed and bored, and felt ugly and stupid, unwanted and lonely.

Meanwhile, at church and in the meetings everyone seemed to like me. I was usually the life of the party, but that was a cover. No one really knew me.

I came very close to having an affair with one of the deacons who was married to my best friend. We never got beyond the talk stage, but I was very tempted and so confused. A voice inside of me said, 'Go for it. No one will ever know.' But another part of me said, 'Be faithful to your husband.' After that I became disinterested in sex with Jim, but still had the problem with masturbation.

My stepfather died and we brought his favourite chair home. When I sat in the chair and looked down our hallway, I could see shadows darting from the kids' rooms to the bedroom across the hall. At first I thought I was just tired, but then I learned my husband and others saw them too.

One night a figure stood at the end of my bed and stared at me. It was tall and dark with a short-looking child standing beside it. These apparitions occurred off and on for several months. I got more and more depressed and tried to kill myself several times with pills. I talked about death and sang songs about dying. I told my husband that was the only way I would ever have peace — then things would be quiet and I would be with God.

As I became increasingly morose, Jim began staying away at night and would take the kids away for the weekend. He didn't know what to do, so he ran and hid from it all. I would stay in bed for two or three days at a time with the door locked and a sign on the door telling everyone to go away. Meanwhile, Jim would make excuses for me at church, telling everyone I was sick.

Several times our oldest child called for an ambulance thinking that I was dying. They would take me to the emergency room, run some tests, tell me I was fine and send me home again.

Once a minister's name came to mind and I cried out in desperation for someone to get him to help me. Jim wasn't home, but our baby-sitter was there and she called him. He prayed with me and referred me to a Christian counsellor whom I saw for three months.

The counsellor began by saying I was a Christian and he was a Christian, but that this was not a spiritual problem. He said I had been abused by several men in my life, I was too busy, and I wasn't facing the child inside me. A small voice inside of me said, 'But where is Christ in all of this?' I knew the answers must be in Him, but I just couldn't get there. I finally stopped going to the counsellor.

One day I decided it was time for action, so I sold my father's chair. After that, we all stopped seeing ghosts in our home. I quit my job because I had been seeing ghosts there, too. At this point I started having a daily Bible study.

Jim and I started to get along better and things became nearer normal, though I still really wanted to die so he could find a better wife and our children could have a good mum who didn't cringe when they said 'I love you, Mum.' Then Jim was offered another job and we moved, desperately hoping this fresh start would help us.

In our new location, one of our children began seeing 'things' and having terrible dreams. He wouldn't be left alone. He would see a blond man run through his room and out the door. One night when he was four, he said, 'I need the Lord to live in me.' He asked Christ into his life and not only did the apparitions and dreams go away, he was also instantly healed of serious asthma attacks and went off all of his medicines and a breathing machine! If you ask him about that today, he will say, 'God healed me.'

After that brief time of near normalcy, the new job turned into a disaster. I started masturbating again, fighting and lying. My husband was fired and we moved to another location where God wonderfully provided a home and another job on the staff of a church. With the excitement of the new situation we were fine for awhile, but then depression set in again. I couldn't function and again I just wanted to die. I had no friends; there was no one I could talk to. Who would understand voices, ghosts, deep depression and an obsession with dying? I lived a double life — trying to help at church, even introducing some to the Lord, while at home I was a hysterical, raging person. I was fooling everyone but my family. I felt like I was going crazy.

A doctor diagnosed my problem as PMS and said there was a new pill that would help. I believed that a Christian could have physical problems, but in my case the problem was in my mind and I knew that somehow I needed to end this mental torment.

I was afraid…afraid to take a shower for fear that the shower curtain would wrap itself around me and kill me… afraid to answer the phone, not wanting to talk with anyone…afraid to take responsibility, no longer being the person who loved to plan and organise and conduct big events…afraid of the faces in the mirror in my bedroom… and afraid to drive at night because figures and snakes would appear in the headlights.

At a Bible bookstore, I found a prayer notebook and Jim bought it for me. He was so desperate for me to get better that he would do anything. All through this time, he was telling me that God would bring us through this, was praying for me constantly and, this time, not running away into his work.

I brought the prayer binder home and began to have

daily morning Bible studies. I had preached having daily Bible study to others, but had never been able to keep it up myself. I began a regular time with God and it was wonderful. The negative voices stopped, for awhile I stopped masturbating, prayers were being answers and our ministry at the church was growing.

In preparation for a 'Resolving Personal and Spiritual Conflicts Conference' at our church, a film was shown where Neil spoke and some people gave testimonies. As I watched, I started getting sick and wanted to run out, but I stayed because of what people would think. On the way home that night I told Jim that I didn't want to go to the conference and that I was better now. I felt that as long as I studied and prayed every morning I would be fine. We talked about it and then dropped the subject. Since the conference was still two months away, I felt safe.

In the weeks before the conference there was a lot of excitement at church. Everyone was talking about how great it sounded and they were inviting friends. I decided that I would go just to learn how to help others and to support Jim. Then the turmoil started again — I couldn't pray, I became angry easily and I started masturbating again. I felt so scared and sick that I wished Neil would cancel.

The first night of the conference I sat there acting cool, taking notes and pretending it didn't affect me. But by the third night I couldn't concentrate and nothing made sense. I felt that I would either throw up or dissolve in tears. I heard voices, had terrible thoughts and was going downhill fast, especially when Neil talked about rape.

Jim made an appointment for me with Neil, and when he told me about it I started shaking. When the morning of the appointment came, I told Jim there was no way I was going to see some conceited speaker who would just say that I am lying and needed to snap out of it.

Jim prayed a lot and convinced me to go with him to the

conference and then to the appointment. That morning I cried through the sessions. Finally I could take it no longer and went out to sit in the car. This was by far the worst internal struggle of my entire life. I found myself saying, 'Why did he come? Doesn't he know that I don't need his help? I like being this way. I'm just fine. Why can't he go away? He will ruin everything.' I especially kept hearing that last thought, *He will ruin everything*.

Then another part of me said, 'What could he ruin?' I felt such fear that I thought of driving my car right through the fence in front of me and escaping, but I didn't. I had no place to hide. I wanted help so badly but doubted that Neil would have any answers. Then I got mad. I hated Neil; he was the enemy. I would go to this stupid appointment, but I would win.

Jim found me in the car and we went to lunch with a friend. Then we went back to the conference and before I knew it, I was sitting in a room with Neil and a couple from his staff. What happened during the next two hours I will never forget, and I will never be the same.

First I told Neil that I didn't like him and that this wasn't going to work. I told him some of the things about my family in a very matter-of-fact way. Then I went through the first prayer in the Steps to Freedom with no problem, even though I didn't know what I read. But when it came time to renounce all my cultic, occultic and non-Christian experiences, I couldn't pray. I felt like throwing up, my vision went in and out, and I felt like I was choking and couldn't breathe. I remember Neil quietly telling Satan to release me, affirming that I was a child of God. I felt calmed and continued to go through the prayers.

When we came to the forgiveness part, I told Neil I had no one to forgive, that I loved everyone except him right now. He told me to pray and ask God to bring to mind people I needed to forgive. Names came to mind I hadn't thought about in years. When I started praying to forgive them, I cried and cried, and this time the tears felt good. I felt like a heavy block was being lifted from my chest and head.

We went through the other prayers and I felt progressively better. I could breathe and I felt loved. When we had finished, Neil suggested that I go into the ladies room and take a good look at myself in the mirror. I did, and for the first time in my life, I liked what I saw! I said, 'I like you, Nancy. In fact, I love you.' I looked into my eyes and was happy. I felt that because of Jesus, there was a truly good person there. That was the first time I have ever looked in the mirror without feeling disgust for myself.

That night I had to drive a three-hour distance to a brother's graduation. Jim couldn't join me because of his responsibilities at the conference.

I had not driven much in the dark because of the images I would see, usually white snakes jumping up at the car. One time I saw a burning car engulfed in flames, but when I got to the spot there was nothing. I have seen people hitch-hiking and then suddenly there was no one there. So driving at night brought great fear. But that night, during the entire three-hour drive, I saw nothing. Praise God!

The next day, along with 28,000 others, I attended the graduation ceremony. Before this, crowds would cause me to panic. I would feel like I was trapped and couldn't get out, like I was choking, like I couldn't breathe, and it was as though the sky was falling around me. That day, however, I felt none of those symptoms. In fact, it wasn't until I was walking out of the stadium with people all around me that I realised the fear was gone. I looked at the sky and said, 'Praise God, I really am free!'

When I was praying with Neil, what I appreciated most is that it wasn't a typical counselling appointment — it was a time with God. Neil guided me through the prayers and kept me going, but it was God who delivered me from Satan's clutches; it was God who cleaned the house of my mind.

The first morning in our home after the conference, I looked around our bedroom and listened. It was quiet, really quiet…no voices, and they haven't come back! Occasionally I have felt frustrated, but now I know how to deal with it.

Since then, our youngest child had some fears and bad dreams. Instead of praying in fear, we talked about who he is in Christ. Our son said, 'Hey! Satan's afraid of me. He had just better watch out because I'm a child of God.'

A few months later some missionary friends stayed with us for a week. The wife had been harassed in various ways including depression and thoughts of suicide. Jim and I took them through the Steps to Freedom and they, too, are free!

Since I found my freedom in Christ, I can say 'I love you' to my husband and not hear thoughts of *No you don't*, or *This marriage will never last.* For a long time now, I have not had depression. I haven't yelled uncontrollably at my children. I'm not afraid of the shower curtain. And masturbation is no longer a problem. Jim and I have been able to lead many of our friends at church through the Steps to Freedom, and we are enjoying seeing freedom spread. Praise God, I really am free!

Do they hate you?

You may be wondering why Nancy, Sandy and others expressed hatred toward me. I'm happy to share that's not their true feeling because that's not really them. Satan isn't pleased with what I'm saying and the fact that I am helping people take back ground where he has had a stronghold. If this happens when you're helping someone, just ignore those comments and continue. After they complete the steps and are free, they often express a great love toward you. Remember Anne's comment in chapter 2? She said, 'I immediately had a great love-jump in my heart toward you, Neil.'

Demonic transference

If demonic influence can be passed from one person to another, it will take place during illicit sex more than any other time that I am aware of. Every sexually abused person that I have worked with has had major spiritual difficulties. Compulsive masturbation from the age of three is not 'normal' sexual development, especially for girls. But it is a common stronghold for those who have been sexually violated. These women are often in deep condemnation, both from the enemy and themselves, and gladly turn from masturbation when they understand how to renounce its entrance point and stand against Satan.

The stronghold is greater if the sexual abuser is a parent. Parents are the authority in the home. They are supposed to provide the spiritual protection that every child needs in order to develop spiritually, socially, mentally and physically. Parents who are in bondage will pass on their iniquity to the next generation. When they become the abuser, they directly open the gate for spiritual assault in their child. Instead of being the spiritual umbrella of protection they are opening the floodgates of devastation.

Guarding what God entrusts to you

The underlying principle is stewardship. We are to be good stewards of whatever God entrusts to us (1 Cor 4:1-3). In *The Seduction of Our Children*, I develop this concept much further. Every parent should know what it means to dedicate their children to the Lord and how to pray for their spiritual protection. As parents we have no greater steward-ship than the lives of the little children God has entrusted to us.

Sexual union/spiritual bond

Every church has a story of a lovely young lady who gets involved with the wrong man. After having sex with him, she can't seem to break away. Everybody tries to convince her that he isn't any good for her. Sometimes even her close friends side with her parents and she really knows the rela-tionship is sick since he treats her like mud. Why doesn't she just tell him to take a hike? Because the sexual union has created a 'spiritual' bond. Unless she breaks that, she will always feel bound to him by something she doesn't even understand.

A pastor called me one day and said, 'If you can't help this young girl I've been counselling, she will be hospitalised in a psychiatric ward.' For two years she had a sick rela-tionship with a boy who was dealing drugs and generally treating her as a sex object. The mental assault she was experiencing was so vivid that she couldn't understand why others couldn't hear the voices she was hearing. After hear-ing her story, I asked her what she would do if I required her to leave this guy and never have anything to do with him again. She started to shake and said, 'I would probably have to leave this session.'

I took her through the Steps to Freedom, encouraging her to: ask forgiveness for using her body as an instrument of unrighteousness, renounce all sexual experiences that God revealed to her, and acknowledge that her body is the temple of the Holy Spirit. Her new-found freedom was immediately evident to me and my prayer partners in the room. Without any coaching she said she was also free from the boy, and to my knowledge she never saw him again.

God wants his children free

I have found it necessary for all sexual sins to be renounced. I usually have such people pray, asking the Lord to reveal to their minds all the sexual sins and partners with whom they have been involved, whether they were the victim or the perpetrator. It is amazing how experiences will come flooding back to their minds. God wants His children free. When they renounce the experience, they are specifically renouncing Satan and all his works and all his ways, and breaking those ties. When they ask forgiveness, they are choosing to walk in the light with God. The power of Satan and sin has then been broken and fellowship with the Lord is beautifully restored.

6

DOUG:
Male Sexual Abuse and Freedom

Feelings of disgust rise rapidly to the average mind when images of sexual perversion are entertained. Suppose that was your own self-perception, and you were in full-time ministry. To add insult to injury, add the self-concept of being illegitimately conceived raised in a racially mixed home with all the social rejection that unfortunately follows.

How would you feel toward yourself? Would you readily accept the fact that you are a saint who sins, or would you see yourself as a wretched sinner? Would you walk in the light, have fellowship with other believers, and speak the truth in love? Or would you live a lonely life, frightened to death that someone may somehow find out what is really going on inside? Such is the case of our next story.

Doug's Story

Dad never called me 'son'.

My mother wasn't married when I was born, but when I was two years old she married a black man. He was a decent person, but he never called me 'son', and never said he loved me. Whenever I would go somewhere with both of my parents, it was obvious I was not a product of their marriage, and sometimes I was called 'Sambo's little kid.'

While I was pre-school age, a woman babysitter took me to her apartment and played sexual games with me. In the ensuing years I did sexual experimentation with other children, was sexually exploited by older girls and boys, and eventually was raped by young men.

I understood my identity to be a 'bastard': unplanned, unwanted, an accident. Early on I perceived that my craving for love and acceptance might possibly be met through sex, and that by giving fulfilment to others through sex I could show that my love was not selfish. Thus sex became an obsession and eventually led to perversion.

I tried very hard to gain praise and approval in the 'straight' world also, and won many awards and honours at school. But my self-image was at zero, and no one or nothing seemed to help. At age sixteen I became suicidal.

Then one summer I went to camp and met people who genuinely seemed to care. It was there I learned of Jesus' love for me. The promise of that love, combined with a disgust for myself, drew me to receive Him as my Saviour. I then knew that my lifestyle was wrong and that I should turn from it, but I had been programmed to it for years and I seemed powerless to change.

Nevertheless, I purposed to follow Christ, praying that somehow, by some miracle, I would become the person I longed to be. I trained for the ministry, graduated from school and threw myself into my work. I think part of my motivation for going into ministry was to give myself to others so they could love me back.

After a few years I married a wonderful woman. Our relationship was doomed from the start because invading thoughts of male images and my own past perversion destroyed any possibility of a healthy sexual life. I continually struggled against going back to previous forms of wrongful sex. I turned to masturbation, which I considered 'safe' sex because I could control my environment.

My wife was always loyal to me, yet she sensed something was definitely wrong. It wasn't until we were married for ten years that I finally told her a little about my problem. That news was very painful for her, but at the same time she felt relief at finally knowing the truth.

I heard speaker after speaker talk about victory in Jesus and I thought, *That's fine for someone who doesn't have my background. That will work for others, but not for me. I will just have to live with my sin. I'll have heaven later, but for now I'll have to deal with the realities of my past.* I felt locked into a horrible identity; it was a heavy bondage.

I developed a contingency plan in the event that anyone ever found out I had been gay or bisexual. I would drive my car into an oncoming lorry. I prepared for that through the years by telling people how I would get very sleepy at the wheel and have to eat snacks to stay awake. If I ever committed suicide, I hoped it would look like an accident and there would be insurance money for my family.

One night in a therapy group, I was hypnotised and told some of my problem — more than I should have. I left with the group's encouragement, but did not feel good about what I had shared with them. I looked for lorries on the lonely road home, determined to end my life, but there were none. As I drove into the driveway my children came running to me, and their acceptance and love was so wonderful that I clicked back into reality.

After some defeats in ministry, I asked counsel from some older Christian brothers. One of them said, 'I hear you saying you are trying very hard to prove you are worthy.' That was hard truth, and I immediately went into my pattern of 'pity-partying', saying, 'Lord, there has never been a person so rejected as me.' Then it was as though God spoke aloud to my mind and said, 'The only one I ever turned my back on was My own Son who bore your sins on the cross.' That was a step toward recovery, of moving away from my prison of self-pity.

Little by little there was growth. God was helping me to see things from a different perspective and I wasn't so controlled by my passions. But the reality that our marriage relationship wasn't all that it should be continued to haunt me.

I had an opportunity to sit under Neil's teaching and heard him speak on spiritual conflict. There I learned some new dimensions of resisting Satan and, on a scale of ten, temptations in my thought life went down to a two. My prayer life became more vibrant and intense. My need for sexual self-gratification diminished until that addiction of a quarter-of-a-century stopped altogether.

Finally I found that I could have a normal relationship with my wife without a video-tape playing in my mind of others imposing themselves upon me sexually. It was a wholesome, beautiful thing. All of these changes were taking place without my pursuing them. I happened to sit under Neil's teaching, and the Lord did the rest.

Then some difficulties arose, and I realised that I was under attack and needed to go back and reinforce what I had learned. The truth that had helped me in such a variety of ways was the truth of who I am in Christ, defined by my Saviour and not by my sin. In Romans, I saw the difference between who I am and my activity: 'If I am doing the very thing I do not wish, I am no longer the one doing it, but sin which dwells in me' (Rom 7:20). I was finally able to separate the real me from my actions. The reason I was suicidal all those years was because I had thought the only way to destroy the sin was to destroy the sinner. There was still an ongoing battle between the authority of my experiences versus the authority of Scripture, but I began to be able to live out my true identity by choosing truth and standing against Satan's lies.

I was able to use the help given to me by Neil when I spoke at a weekend church conference. After the last session, there was a testimony time where people began confessing their faults to one another, like a mini-revival. I had never seen anything like it before; it was beautiful to experience.

But even as I spoke at that conference on spiritual conflict, my wife, who was hundreds of miles away, was startled with demonic manifestations in our home. She had to call in friends to support her and pray for her. And that became a pattern for a period of time.

On the plus side: People were being set free through our ministry from bondages that had enslaved them for years. Victims of abuse who had been dysfunctional in their relationships were having their marriages restored; pastors were being freed from problems paralysing their ministries. At the same time, we found ourselves harassed by Satan and being run ragged by a busy schedule.

As I reflect back to the time when I had planned on taking my life but had come home and met my children in the driveway, I realise that many of my memories from the past had been graciously blocked out. But during the demonic oppression that came later, there were flashbacks to perverted behaviour and tidal wave after tidal wave of perverse thoughts. Then there would be an onslaught of self-destructive thoughts — that suicide was again the easiest way to get out of all the pressure we were experiencing.

I went in and out of reality, not being able to control it. I became afraid of losing my mind. In the middle of the night, I would awake in a sweat, having dreamed of incredible horror, of killing loved ones and placing their bodies in transparent body bags.

I shared this attack with my brothers in Christ, and a massive amount of prayer went up. I was so weak and vulnerable and I needed the prayer support of God's people to lift that onslaught of demonic depression. Finally it did lift, and I was again able to think objectively and spiritually about the issues.

From experience, I am convinced that no one is ever so strong that he can stand alone. I have a wife who prays for me, a support group of men with whom I meet once a week, a Bible study group at church, and concerned friends and loved ones. We all need a body of believers for encouragement, people who will stand with us against the attacks of the enemy.

I'm looking forward to the challenges ahead. Our ministry continues. My wife and I are still working on some issues in our marriage which haven't been totally resolved, but there is nothing there that God cannot heal. My acceptance in Him is my greatest strength. Because of His unconditional love, I don't have to prove myself worthy. There is nothing I can do to increase His already proven love for me.

Whereas I used to wear the label of 'bastard', Colossians talks about the fact that, in Christ, we are chosen, beloved and holy. Those are the new labels I now wear, and they establish my identity.

When I was a boy and the others would pick sides for a baseball game, it seemed everyone was chosen before me. It was as though I was a handicap to the team who chose me. But God says that He chose me, and not as the last of the group.

Recently I took my dad's hand and told him that there has never been a time when I loved him more or have been more proud of him than now. Tears came to his eyes and he said, 'I never knew you cared. I never knew I was that important to you.' He reached over and gave me a hug, and for the first time he said, 'Son, I love you.' How that penetrated the depths of my heart!

God is in the ministry of repairing our lives. He is changing us into His likeness, His image. He is putting all the pieces back together, touching all the relationships between father and son, husband and wife, parent and child. He has begun the good work and will continue it until we stand before Him, complete in Christ.

Where is your identity?

There are a lot of sick ways to identify ourselves, and doing so by the colour of our skin or the stigma connected to our birth are some of the sickest. If we had only a physical heritage, it would make sense that we get our identity from the natural world. But we have a spiritual heritage as well.

Paul repeatedly admonishes the church to put off the old man and put on the new man, 'who is being renewed to a true knowledge according to the image of the One who created him — a renewal in which there is no distinction between Greek and Jew, circumcised and uncircumcised, barbarian, Scythian, slave, and freeman, but Christ is all, and in all' (Col 3:10,11). In other words, stop identifying yourself along racial, religious, cultural and social lines. Find your common identity in Christ!

Bondage to sin

Anybody who would heap more condemnation on this pastor or anyone else who struggles in this way is assisting the devil, not God. The devil is the adversary; Jesus is our advocate. People trapped by sexual sin would love nothing more than to be free.

No pastor in his rational mind would throw away his ministry for a one night stand, and yet many do. Why is that? Can we be a bond servant of Christ and at the same time be in bondage to sin? Sadly, many who have been delivered out of the kingdom of darkness and into the kingdom of God's beloved Son are living as bondservants to both kingdoms. Even though we are no longer in the flesh because we are in Christ, we can still walk (live) *according to* the flesh if we choose to. And the first deed of the flesh listed in Galatians 5:19 is immorality (fornication).

I surveyed a seminary student body and found out that 60 per cent were feeling convicted about their sexual morality. The other 40 per cent were probably in various stages of denial. Every legitimate Christian would love to be sexually free. The problem is that sexual sins are so uniquely resistant to conventional treatment. Nevertheless, freedom is attainable. Let me establish a theological basis for freedom and then suggest some practical steps that we need to take.

Two essentials

If I had to summarise the two essential functions that must take place in order for a believer to become free and stay free, I would say, 'First, take action. Do something about the neutral disposition of your physical body by giving it to God. And second, win the battle for your mind by reprogramming it with the truth of God's Word.' Paul summarised both in Romans 12:1,2:

> I urge you therefore, brethren, by the mercies of God, to present your bodies a living, and holy sacrifice, acceptable to God, which is your spiritual service of worship. And do not be conformed to this world, but be transformed by the renewing of your mind, that you may prove what the will of God is, that which is good and acceptable and perfect.

In this chapter I want to address the issue of habitual sexual sin as it relates to the physical body. In the next chapter I will deal with the battle for our mind as it relates to sexual bondage.

In Romans 6:12, we are admonished not to let sin reign in our mortal body that we should obey its lusts. That's our responsibility: not to let sin rule in our members. The difficulty is that the source of the conflicts is 'your pleasures that wage war in your members' (James 4:1).

Dead to sin

In Romans 6:6,7, you will find the basic understanding we need in order to *not* let sin reign in our bodies: 'Knowing this, that our old self was crucified with Him, that our body of sin might be done away with, that we should no longer be slaves to sin; for he who has died is freed from sin.' I often ask in a conference, 'How many have died with Christ?' Everybody will raise their hands. Then I will ask, 'How many are free from sin?' It had better be the same hands, or these people have a problem with Scripture.

When we fail in our Christian walk we often reason, 'What experience must I have in order for me to live as though I have really died with Christ?' The only experience necessary was the experience that Christ had on the cross. Many try and try to put the old self (the old man) to death and can't. Why not? Because the old self has already died! You cannot do what has already been done for you by Christ. Most Christians are desperately trying to become what they already are. We receive Christ by faith...we walk by faith...we are justified by faith...and we are also sanctified by faith.

In my experience, however, I often don't feel dead to sin. I often *feel* alive to sin and dead to Christ, even though we are admonished to 'consider yourselves to be dead to sin, but alive to God *in* Christ Jesus' (Rom 6:11). It is important to recognise that considering this to be so isn't what makes it so. We consider it so because it *is* so. Believing something doesn't make it true. It's true; therefore, I believe it. And when we choose to walk by faith according to what Scripture affirms is true, it works out in our experience. So to summarise: You can't die to sin because you have already died to sin. You choose to believe that truth and walk in it by faith, and then the result of being dead to sin works out in your experience.

In a similar fashion, I don't serve the Lord in order to gain His approval. I am approved by God; therefore, I serve Him. I don't try to live a righteous life in the hopes that some day He will love me. I live a righteous life because He already loves me. I don't labour in the vineyard trying to gain His acceptance. I am accepted in the beloved; therefore, I gladly serve Him.

Living free

When sin makes its appeal, I say, 'I don't have to sin because I have been delivered out of darkness and I am now alive in Christ. Satan, you have no relationship to me, and I am no longer under your authority.' Sin hasn't died. It's still strong and appealing, but I am no longer under its authority and I have no relationship to the kingdom of darkness. Romans 8:1,2 helps to clarify the issue: 'There is therefore now no condemnation for those who are in Christ Jesus. For the law of the Spirit of life in Christ Jesus has set you free from the law of sin and death.'

Is the law of sin and death still operative? Yes, and it applies for everyone who isn't in Christ, those who have not received Him into their lives as Saviour. It is also in effect for those who are Christians but who choose to live according to the flesh. In the natural world, we can fly if we overcome the law of gravity by a greater law. But the moment we disconnect that greater power we will lose altitude.

That's the way it is in our Christian life. The law of sin and death has been superseded by a higher power — the resurrection life of Christ. But we will fall the moment we stop walking in the Spirit and living by faith. So we need to 'put on the Lord Jesus Christ, and make no provision for the flesh in regard to its lusts' (Rom 13:14). Satan can't do anything about our position in Christ, but if he can get us to believe it isn't true, we will live as though it's not, even though it is true.

Our mortal bodies

In Romans 6:12 we're told not to let sin reign in our mortal bodies, and then verse 13 gives insight on how to accomplish that: 'Do not go on presenting the members of your body to sin as instruments of unrighteousness but present yourselves to God as those alive from the dead, and your members as instruments of righteousness to God.' Our bodies are like an instrument that can be used for good or evil. They are not evil, but they are mortal, and whatever is mortal is corruptible.

But for the Christian, there is the wonderful anticipation of the resurrection when we shall receive an imperishable body like that of our Lord (1 Cor 15:35*ff*). Until then, we have a mortal body that can be used in the service of sin as an instrument of unrighteousness, or in the service of God as an instrument of righteousness.

Obviously, it's impossible to commit a sexual sin without using our body as an instrument of unrighteousness. When we do, we allow sin to reign in our mortal body and are being obedient to the lusts of the flesh instead of being obedient to God.

I personally believe that the word *sin* in Romans 6:12 is personified, referring to the person of Satan: 'Therefore do not let sin reign in your mortal body that you should obey its lusts.' Satan is sin: the epitome of evil, the prince of darkness, the father of lies. I would have a hard time understanding how only a principle (as opposed to an evil personal influence) would reign in my mortal body in such a way that I would have no control over it.

Even more difficult to understand is how I could get a principle out of my body. Paul says, 'I find then the principle that *evil* is present in me, *the one* who wishes to do good' (Rom 7:21). What is present in me is evil — the person, not the principle — and it is present in me because at some time I used my body as an instrument of unrighteousness.

Paul concludes with the victorious promise that we do not have to remain in that unrighteous state: 'Who will set me free from the body of this death? Thanks be to God through Jesus Christ our Lord!' (Rom 7:24,25) Jesus will set us free!

Sinning with our bodies

First Corinthians 6:15–20 shows the vital connection between sexual sin and the use of our bodies:

> Do you not know that your bodies are members of Christ? Shall I then take away the members of Christ and make them members of a harlot? May it never be! Or do you not know that the one who joins himself to a harlot is one body with her? For He says, 'The two shall become one flesh.' But the one who joins himself to the Lord is one spirit with Him. Flee immorality [fornication]. Every other sin that a man commits is outside the body, but the immoral man sins against his own body. Or do you not know that your body is a temple of the Holy Spirit who is in you, whom you have from God, and that you are not your own? For you have been bought with a price: therefore glorify God in your body.

Every believer is in Christ and is a member of His body. For me to join my body with a harlot would be to use my body to sin, as opposed to using it as a member of Christ's body, the church. 'Yet the body is not for immorality, but for the Lord; and the Lord is for the body' (1 Cor 6:13). If you are united to the Lord *in* Christ, can you imagine the inner turmoil that will result if you are at the same time united physically to a harlot? That union creates an unholy bond that is in opposition to the spiritual union that we have in Christ. The resulting bondage is so great that Paul warns us to 'flee immorality.' Run from it!

Sexual sins are in a category all by themselves, since every other sin is outside the body. We can be creative in how we arrange, organise or otherwise use what God has created, but we don't spontaneously create something out of nothing as only God can do. Procreation is the only creative act that the Creator allows man to participate in, and God provides careful instruction as to how we are to oversee the process of bringing life into this world. He confines sex to an intimate act of marriage, requires the marriage bond to last until death separates, and charges parents to provide a nurturing atmosphere where children can be brought up in the Lord.

Satanic perversion

Anybody who has helped victims get out of Satanic ritual abuse knows how profoundly Satan violates God's standards. Those rituals are the most disgusting sexual orgies your mind would ever dare entertain. It isn't sex as a normal human would understand it. Instead it is the most ripping, obscene, violent exploitation of another human being you can imagine. Little children are raped and tortured. The Satanist's ultimate 'high' is to sacrifice some innocent victim at the point of orgasm. The word 'sick' doesn't do justice to the abuse. 'Total wickedness' and 'absolute evil' better epitomise the utter degradation of Satan and his legions of demons. If Satan appeared in our presence as he really is, I believe he would be 90 per cent sex organ!

Satanists have certain breeders who are selected for the development of a Satanic 'super' race whom, they say, will rule this world. Other breeders are required to bring their offspring or aborted foetuses for sacrifice. Satan will do everything he can to establish his kingdom while, at the same time, trying to pervert the offspring of God's people.

No wonder sexual sins are so repugnant to God. Using our bodies as an instrument of unrighteousness permits Satan to reign in our mortal bodies. We have been bought with a price and we are to glorify God in our bodies. In other words, we are to manifest the presence of God in our lives as we bear fruit for His glory.

Homosexual behaviour

While homosexuality is a growing stronghold in our culture, there is no such thing as a homosexual. Considering oneself to be a homosexual is to believe a lie because God created us male and female. There is only homosexual *behaviour*, and usually that behaviour was developed in early childhood and was reinforced by the father of lies. Every person I have counselled who struggles with homosexual tendencies has had a major spiritual stronghold — some area of life where Satan has control.

But I don't believe in a specific demon of homosexuality. That mentality would have us cast out the demon and then the person would be completely delivered from any further thoughts or problems. I know of no such cases, although I would not presume to limit God from performing such a miracle. However, I have helped many people bound in homosexuality to find their freedom in Christ, and steered them to a new identity in Him and to an understanding of how they can resist Satan in this area.

Those caught up in homosexual behaviour struggle with a lifetime of bad relationships, dysfunctional homes and role confusions. Their emotions have been tied into their past and it takes time for them to establish a new identity in Christ. They will typically go through an arduous process of renewing their minds, thoughts and experiences. As they do, their emotions will eventually conform to the truth they have now come to believe.

Thundering from the pulpit that homosexuals are destined for hell will only drive the people who struggle into greater despair. Authoritarian parents who don't know how to love contribute to a child's wrong orientation, and judgemental messages reinforce an already damaged self-image.

Don't get me wrong. The Scriptures clearly condemn the practice of homosexuality as well as all other forms of fornication. But imagine what it must be like to suffer with homosexual feelings that you didn't ask for, and then hear that God condemns you for it. As a result, many want to believe that God created them that way, while militant homosexuals are trying to prove that their lifestyle is a legitimate alternative to heterosexuality and violently oppose conservative Christians who would say otherwise.

We must help those who struggle with homosexual tendencies to establish a new identity in Christ. Even secular counsellors know that identity is a critical issue in recovery. How much greater is the Christian's potential to help these people since we have a gospel that sets us free from our past and establishes us in Christ! So as I counsel, I have people trapped by homosexuality profess their identity in Christ. I also have them renounce the lie that they are a homosexual and announce the truth that they are men and women. Some may not have immediate transformation, but their public declaration starts them on a path of truth that they can choose to continue.

The path from sexual bondage

If you are in sexual bondage, what can you do? First, know that there is no condemnation for those who are in Christ Jesus. Putting yourself or others down is not going to resolve this bondage. Accusation is one of Satan's tactics. And most definitely, suicide is not God's means to set you free.

Second, get alone or with a trusted friend, and ask the Lord to reveal to your mind every time you used your body as an instrument of unrighteousness, including all sexual sins.

Third, verbally respond to each offence as it is recalled by saying, 'I confess (whatever the sin was), and I renounce that use of my body.' A pastor told me he spent three hours by himself one afternoon and was totally cleansed afterwards. Temptations still come, but the power has been broken. He is now able to say 'no' to sin. If you think this process might take too long, try not doing it and see how long the rest of your life will seem as you drag on in defeat! Take a day, two days or a week if necessary.

Fourth, when you have finished confessing and renouncing, express the following: 'I now commit myself to the Lord, and my body as an instrument of righteousness. I submit my body as a living and holy sacrifice to God. I command you, Satan, to leave my presence, and I ask You, Heavenly Father, to fill me with Your Holy Spirit.' If you are married, also say, 'For the purpose of sex, I reserve my body to be used only with my spouse according to 1 Corinthians 7:1–5.'

Lastly, choose to believe the truth that you are alive in Christ and dead to sin. There will be many times when temptation will seem to be overwhelming, but you must declare your position in Christ at the moment you are first aware of danger. Say, with authority, that you no longer have to sin because you are in Christ. Then live by faith according to what God says is true.

Getting sin out of my body is half the battle. Renewing my mind is the other half. Sexual sins and pornographic viewing have a way of staying in the memory bank far longer than other images. Getting free is one thing; staying free is another. I will deal with that in response to the story in the next chapter.

7
CHARLES:
Freeing
the Abuser

I received a call from a pastor one day that started with, 'Are you required by law to divulge confidential communication?' What he was really saying was, 'If I came to see you, could I tell you that I am molesting my child or other children without being turned in to the authorities?' I reminded him that most states of America still protect clergy confidentiality, but do require licensed professionals and public officials, including teachers, to report any suspected abuse. I said that even though I'm not required to do it by the law in our state, I had a moral responsibility to protect another person in danger.

He took the chance anyway and shared his story with me. It all started with back rubs on his daughter to get her awake in the morning, but it soon led to inappropriate fondling, though no intercourse was ever attempted. 'Neil,' he said, 'I didn't have a great battle with sexual temptation before this, but now as soon as I walk through the door of her room it is as though I have no control.' When I talked with his daughter, I understood why.

What was happening reminded me of Homer's ninth century BC depiction of the sirens (sea nymphs) whose singing lured sailors to their death on rocky coasts. Every ship that sailed too close suffered the same disastrous end. In the story, Ulysses ties himself to the mast of the ship and orders the crew to wear ear plugs and ignore any pleas he might make. The mental torment of trying to resist the sirens' call was unbearable.

I'm not excusing this pastor, but there is a line in temptation which, when stepped over, will result in losing rational control. This pastor crossed that line when he stepped through the door of his daughter's room. As I learned later, the daughter had major spiritual problems stemming from having been molested by a youth pastor in a former ministry, and this abuse was never resolved spiritually. It wasn't the daughter who was actually sexually enticing this father; it was the demonic stronghold in her life. The 'sirens' lured the father to do the unspeakable. When I met with the daughter, she couldn't even read through a prayer of commitment to stand against Satan and his attacks, which is a definite signal of enemy oppression. The father shared his struggle with his wife and, together, they sought the help they needed and worked toward resolution.

The story that follows is different from this in at least one respect. Charles's daughter had never been molested; she was never seductive and there was no apparent demonic stronghold in her life. But at some point in the pursuit of sexual gratification Charles crossed a line beyond which he lost control. His life became dominated by a power that led him to his daughter's bedroom and caused his world to disintegrate around him. Eventually he almost lost his life.

Charles is a successful professional who was abused as a child and who then became an abuser. Thankfully his story doesn't end there, for after the shipwreck there was recovery.

Charles's Story

God moulds those He chooses.

My story is one of God's redemption and the freedom that comes from resting in His grace, a story of being chosen for His work in spite of the opposition of His adversary, Satan. As I write this, I marvel at how little of me and how much of God is revealed in what has happened. I can only praise Him for His transforming work.

I am free from bondage to a vicious assortment of sinful attitudes and habits that cost me the respect of my family, my co-workers and my church. This bondage had me on a relentless path of personal destruction that, if left unchecked, would have taken my life as well. This freedom was bought at a terrible price that I did not pay. The suffering, death and resurrection of my Lord Jesus Christ were what bought my freedom, not my own efforts or my suffering. The life I live is Christ's life, God's Son in me, not my own. And I rejoice that I am able with the help of the Holy Spirit to bring my emotions in line with what I know to be true about myself in Christ. However, this has not happened instantly, and the story of how God moulds those He chooses is one of struggle and defeat as well as victory.

'Put down your gun! Don't do it! Jesus, help me! Jesus, help me!' My wife's anguished screams echoed in my ears as I ran for my life while my son loaded his pistol, preparing to hunt me down and kill me. I reached my car in the driveway, fumbled with the keys (he's coming to shoot me!) and opened the car door. Throwing my briefcase into the car, I slid behind the wheel and started the engine. I backed out of the driveway and sped down the hill, leaving my wife to struggle with my enraged son, not knowing whether he might shoot her instead, not caring enough to stay and face his wrath.

I raced down the street imagining my son pursuing me in his car, ready to run me off the road and finish the job. The side streets beckoned as a way to evade pursuit; I made several turns, finally coming to a stop under a grove of trees. My pounding heart was so loud I was sure everyone in the quiet neighbourhood could hear it. My shame was so immense that I thought the end of life as I had known it was imminent. I prayed, but all that would come out were groans and hot tears, and they were all for me. I had lost my family in an instant; I was sure my career, my freedom and perhaps my life would follow in rapid succession.

What had happened to me and to my family? What terrible fate had intervened in our affairs, threatening life itself? Where was God when I needed Him most? In my despair there were no answers, just questions and accusations. Thoughts of suicide fleetingly intruded, overcome quickly by my instinct for survival. After the initial fear of pursuit faded, I called a psychiatrist I had just met a couple of weeks before. Tearfully, I explained the situation.

'Do you remember my telling you I felt depressed about my daughter being in the psychiatric ward for the last month?' I began. 'She was committed for observation after she ran away and tried to commit suicide. Well, tonight I told my wife why our daughter was depressed; I had sexually molested her. While my wife was still reeling from the revelation, our adult son came in from work and she told him as he walked through the door. He became like a wild man, striking the walls, calling me a monster, and then he went for his gun. I ran for my life. When I left, my wife was struggling with him to keep him from shooting me. I don't know what happened after I left.' I finished my confession and broke down and wept.

'Find yourself a place to stay for a few days while we work this out,' my counsellor said. 'Obviously, you can't go back there just now. And call me when you get settled in so we can talk.'

For hours I drove aimlessly, tortured by thoughts of failure, of gross sin, of condemnation and rejection. I felt utterly dejected, despised by everyone — especially by God. I prayed and prayed but there was no answer. I phoned my supervisor at work, telling him I wouldn't be in the next day because of a family emergency. Then I started looking at rock-bottom motels which seemed to fit my current status. Each flea trap reminded me of how low my life had fallen, but my pride kept me from turning in to one of these and registering.

Finally I settled on a 'respectable' motel, as if to deny the power of the events that had turned my world on its head. The desk clerk asked no questions, but I was sure that the disgust must have been lurking behind his calm façade. Once inside the room, fear ran through me, unchecked, drenching me with sweat. I had lost my family, my self-respect, my cockiness, and there was nothing to replace it. I sensed only anger, rejection, condemnation; there was no hint of hope. I prayed, weeping bitterly over my loss but not facing the sins that had led to this moment. I wanted to read the Bible, but it hadn't been included in the things I grabbed when I fled my home. The motel didn't have a Gideon Bible and I didn't think to ask the desk clerk.

There was very little sleep for me that night. I kept waking, reliving the night before, trying to figure out what I had done wrong, how I could have protected myself better. I was focused on my own feelings of rejection and unworthiness, but not on my hurting family.

What events had led to such feelings of remorse and despair? Nothing mitigates the terrible fact that sin results from the decision to disobey God. You and I are both responsible for our own decisions and actions. Sometimes it's easier to learn from other's mistakes, though. Some background may be helpful in understanding how Satan established beach-heads in my life through my responses to life situations.

I was the first child, followed by a brother and two sisters, in a non-religious family. My parents were married almost forty years until my father's premature death. Ours was a traditional family according to external appearances. My father held a succession of occupations but we didn't move very often, and material needs were always taken care of. In later years my parents were well-to-do and many luxuries were provided for us children. I felt loved and cared for (by the criteria I knew), but I really didn't know much about other children's home life, so comparisons were infrequent. One of the characteristics of our family was that we didn't discuss how we got along, how the family was running, or our emotional response to anything. My siblings and I didn't discuss our personal lives with one another, much less with the outside world.

One of my earliest memories was of being spanked for having a toilet-training accident on the bathroom floor. Something I had regarded with childish amusement was suddenly transformed into a time of shaming, scolding and intense pain. I didn't know what I had done to call down such wrath; at that young age I was only aware of shame because I had disappointed my mother.

This episode was followed by many others in which accidents, careless or not, were met with punishment and shaming. Things didn't 'just happen'; someone had to be caught, blamed, shamed and punished in order for everyone else in the family to feel worthwhile. I only recently learned that this pattern of attitudes had been passed down through both sides of the family for generations.

I was never sure I was valued for being myself. Value seemed to be placed on what I did. In our family we constantly jockeyed for position, trying to earn approval or denigrating someone else in order to look better by comparison. At a very early age I started to make choices based on how I would appear to my parents and any other authority figures who were in a position to judge me.

My parents were not religious. My dad, in particular, was actively hostile to all kinds of religion and rarely passed up a chance to make a disparaging remark about those who loved God. We never went to church (I was sent to Sunday school once, never to be repeated), and the Bible was not part of our family.

When I was a teenager, my grandfather gave me a Bible that his mother had given him. Its almost-new condition indicated that my grandfather couldn't have given me a tour through it after he gave it to me. He seemed to regard it as a kind of talisman to be passed from one generation to the other, but he never discussed its contents or his relationship to God (if any). So it sat on my shelf next to Bertrand Russell's *Why I Am Not a Christian*, and I got as much use out of it as my grandfather apparently had.

My father's career choices meant prolonged absences from home while he tried out new businesses in another country, leaving my mother to contend with raising us the best she could. When he was home, he was capricious and wrathful and the spankings we received were brutal and inappropriate to the offence. There was no warmth at any time, and I remember being told, 'Get out of my sight! You make me sick!' on more than one occasion. My mother had her own emotional problems with my father and she was unable to communicate her emotions to anyone, much less her children. So we were on our own, coping in our unique ways with Dad's anger and rejection of us.

When I was about eleven or so I was introduced to masturbation by a classmate. Confused and fascinated, I found that I could feel better and have pleasure, if only for a few moments at a time. Lacking joy in my relationships, I found myself increasingly drawn to self-gratification as a way of getting solace and comfort when I was lonely or frightened or feeling rejected or inadequate.

The isolation bred by my solitary practice would have been bad enough, but along the way I discovered the power of fantasy to enhance the experience and heighten the stimulation. Beginning with the lingerie illustrations in the catalogue at my grandmother's house, I soon found out about pornography through a copy of *Playboy* magazine that my grandmother bought me (thinking, I suppose, that it had something to do with giving young boys suggestions for play activities). When she saw the contents later that day, she quickly confiscated it. But not before my impressionable mind had its contents seared into my brain.

Finding my father's private stash of hard-core pornography on an upper shelf of his study gave further impetus to my lustful fantasies. He apparently had mail-ordered materials that were illegal at that time; similar items can be bought legally in neighbourhood porno parlours in most communities today. I quickly learned to regard women as objects meant to satisfy my lust and stimulate me. Overwhelmed by the boundless promises of lust, I began attempting to make sexual contact with the girls my own age. I was rebuffed, learning very quickly that sexuality was something shameful. It was to be hidden, to be snickered at in locker rooms, but not to be discussed seriously with anyone.

I was adrift on the sea of lust, with no spiritual input and no sense of God's judgement at all. Each episode brought shame that could not be discussed with any friend, and certainly not with my parents. I felt more and more worthless. Throwing myself into academic pursuits, I became further alienated from my peers.

During all of this, I had the additional misfortune to be seduced by a man in a position of authority. He was a man whom I trusted and liked and whose prominence was such that I feared to tell anyone. Disgusted by the experience, confused by the attention and the sensuality, I felt violated but couldn't admit to my own rage about this until many years later. With my sexuality thoroughly confused, I continued to lust after any sensual experience I could read about or imagine. To satisfy my lust I seduced my younger brother for a period of several years, abusing his natural affections without compassion, pity or guilt.

At the same time I continued to seek out other sensual experiences and pornography. I gravitated toward those that were heterosexual, but the more perversely sexuality was depicted, the more stimulated I became. The transient 'adrenalin high' was mixed with shame, the fear of getting caught and the thrill of avoiding detection. The more I was involved with pornography, the easier it became to use it to relieve tension, escape the pressure of social relationships and avoid unpleasant responsibilities. Pictures on a printed page could promise thrills, ready acceptance, no conflicts — things that real women and girls my age couldn't offer. Each time I used the pornography I was driven into a depression that followed the exhilaration, and I swore that this time was the last time. I reflected on what worthless scum I was. I became more and more isolated from people, rationalising that if people really knew what I was like they wouldn't want any part of me.

After I began dating, my primary objective was to get the women I dated to meet what I perceived as being my sexual needs. Inflamed with passion by the pornography, I spent hours each day possessed by sexual thoughts and activities, missing assignments because of masturbation, fearful of reaching out socially for fear of rejection, and too stubborn to admit my life was out of control. There were interludes, of course, when my activities were more nearly 'normal' because of involvement with organisations, studies and occasional 'friends'. Yet even these were kept away from the core of my being because I was afraid of exposure and rejection.

Gradually I overcame my fear of girls enough to make a preoccupation out of seducing them and going as far sexually as I could. As this new outlet for my lust gained proficiency, my abuse of my brother slackened and stopped. I realise now the awful consequences for each of the victims of my lust. They were violated, their boundaries trespassed, their bodies used without care or respect. At the time I could only think of more ways to indulge in evil, each thought more perverse and against society's standards than the last. Masturbation became such a preoccupation that my grades suffered and my social relationships eventually dried up. My constant search for stimulating fantasies and experiences hurt other people, invaded their privacy and drove them away.

When I met my wife-to-be, I was on the rebound from a sexually obsessive relationship that had no solid basis. Although I knew my new love was a Christian, I had only had fleeting contact with 'Bible thumpers', as I called them. She was pretty, intelligent, caring and needed nurturing; her childhood had been unhappy, too.

I thought she would give up Christianity as soon as she learned the truth; she thought I would convert as soon as I heard the gospel. Neither of us received wise counsel against the relationship, much less the marriage, although we talked to several pastors before getting married. It was a hodgepodge of a ceremony. My bride read from 1 Corinthians 13 and other Scripture passages, while I said nothing religious in my speaking parts and quoted from secular and mystical sources. Significantly, I didn't vow to be faithful or to honour or cherish my wife. At the time, I was very much 'in love', but I hadn't the faintest idea about the commitment my bride was making to love me in the love of Christ.

Initially, my wife, in her eagerness to please her new husband, satisfied my lust. Even in the marriage bed I considered her just another object placed there for my pleasure, to make me feel adequate and loved. I didn't really look very hard for ways to enhance her pleasure, other than to order a copy of a Hindu treatise on sex that included hundreds of acrobatic activities that we weren't athletic enough to accomplish (much to my disappointment). I was still looking for the ultimate sexual high promised by the pornography but never delivered. Such notions as commitment, nurturing, caring, communication and fidelity were hard for me to understand.

After our first child was born, many bitter arguments ensued about the religious upbringing of our children. I insisted that they would have none. My wife tearfully shared her fear that they would be condemned to hell if they didn't know Jesus as their Lord. She wanted them to learn about Jesus while they were little. I was adamant that our children not be 'brainwashed' but somehow learn about religion from someone else when they were adults. Although I took a course on the life of Christ and earned an 'A', I still rejected the gospel. I was abusive, hostile and blasphemed the living God in my petulance and anger. Meanwhile, my life was in disorder, although I was the last to notice.

Finally, in a time of crisis, having seen many responses to my wife's prayers that I couldn't explain away, I decided to accept the gift of salvation freely offered by the Father through His Son, Jesus Christ. I committed my life to follow Him, having very little idea what that commitment meant. For a time, I was so grateful at having been saved from hell that my lust was put on the back burner. But that didn't last long. I had privately renounced my past sins, but was unwilling to undergo the self-examination and cleansing that are necessary for a child of God to truly express the joy associated with following God in loving obedience.

When preachers or commentators talked about God as a 'loving Father', that term seemed an oxymoron; I had not experienced such a father. I was expecting punishment, not praise. At the time, I didn't know what God had said about the matter: 'Therefore judge nothing before the appointed time; wait till the Lord comes. He will bring to light what is hidden in darkness and will expose the motives of men's hearts. At that time each will receive his praise from God' (1 Cor 4:5, NIV).

Shortly after I became a Christian, I engaged in my first act of adultery. I had already had adulterous thoughts, but an opportunity to put my lust into practice presented itself, and I jumped (not fell) into sin. Afterward I was so ashamed that I didn't attempt to continue the relationship. I felt remorse and tried to pray, but I didn't acknowledge to myself or to God my full responsibility in the matter. Three more times over the next several years I took advantage of opportunities to have sexual contact with other women, and my involvement with pornography continued on an episodic basis, adding fuel to the fantasy life that detracted from my relationship with my wife.

Some misguided person might offer the 'consolation' that perhaps my wife was unattractive physically or emotionally, and that somehow she drove me to these sins. I have two responses: First, my wife was (and is) very lovely, and during those times she was trying to be supportive; second, I am responsible for my actions regardless of the external circumstances. My focus on sex as the means for meeting my emotional needs led to decisions to demand or take that which was not properly mine.

As years passed, my wife began to be troubled by my increasing demands for unusual sex practices, those she considered kinky or perverted. At the same time, my occasional impotence or delay in climax became more frequent. We didn't talk about these things because my wife's occasional ventures into discussing sex were met with hostility, defensiveness or silence. I was so ashamed of the 'rest' of my sex life that I felt it could not be discussed with anyone, including my wife. If anyone knew, my life would be over because I was uniquely sinful and worthy of condemnation or death.

I definitely didn't go to God; He only accepted those who were completely obedient to Him, at least in the 'big things'. I knew I was going to heaven, but I believed that God was only keeping a bargain. He couldn't really love me with the accretion of sinful things I had done. I felt out of control, powerless to stop my behaviour. Even more serious brushes with the authorities didn't stop me from seeking the magical sexual 'high' that would make me feel loved.

At the same time I pursued those fantasies, I was rejecting any real friendship or intimacy with my wife, with friends or within Christ's church. In our local church I was an elder, I led home Bible studies, I even pursued evangelism and saw several people accept the salvation of Christ after I had shared the gospel with them. But inside, I knew no peace.

Some of the pornography I read was 'Family Reading', a euphemism for stories about incest. At first the theme seemed repulsive; then it was stimulating like other perverted subjects. I didn't apply it to my own family at first. Then, as my daughter reached fourteen, I began to notice her maturation in an unhealthy way. My language at home became more suggestive, my remarks less appropriate, the jokes I brought home from work more sexual in content. I was less careful about modesty in my dress. When I saw my daughter in swimwear or nightwear, it became more difficult to avert my eyes.

Finally, when telling my daughter good-night in her bedroom, I would find one pretext or another to 'accidentally' brush a hand against her breast, even while praying with her. This happened over a period of several months. I became afraid of what would happen next, but told myself I couldn't help it, that I really loved my daughter. My ambivalence interfered with my sex life with my wife, and I found myself increasingly impotent with her. Even masturbation failed to satisfy.

One evening I offered to tell my daughter good-night. 'No, thanks, Daddy, I'm too tired,' she said, as she went into her bedroom and firmly closed the door. There were no more good-nights after that. She didn't want me to hug her or even touch her, claiming that her muscles were tender from workouts. A gulf grew between us, but in my deception I didn't attribute her rejection of me to the abuse of our relationship, to violating her boundaries as a person, to transgressing God's law. I attributed her coldness to 'growing pains', failing to recognise that I had hurt and frightened her and had perverted our relationship.

Several months later, relationships in our family had deteriorated severely. No one was communicating effectively with anyone else, and we were all barely coping with day-to-day existence. After a thoroughly botched holiday, with no one talking all the way back home, things became even worse. My wife became severely depressed, entering a psychiatric unit for more than a week. While she was there we were all distraught, yet I did not confide in anyone what was going on in my secret life that corrupted everything in our family.

Although I did not abuse our daughter during that tumultuous period, I failed to take decisive action and she became more depressed than ever. A couple of weeks after my wife returned from the hospital, our daughter ran away. When we finally tracked her down a few days later in a nearby community, she was defiant and didn't want to come back home. One of her acquaintances told us she had narrowly been prevented from committing suicide. So our daughter went into the hospital for a month.

While she was in the hospital, not a hint of the story of her sexual abuse came out until the last week. In spite of repeated questioning by the mental health team and by my wife, she denied there was anything between us and so did I. It was as if we believed we could wish away the incidents, that nothing had really happened. But it had, and that monstrous sin festered beneath the surface, becoming more foul. There was little progress in our daughter's depression and anger, and daily my wife and I were becoming more distant from one another.

Finally I woke up at four o'clock one Thursday morning, sitting bolt upright in bed with a compelling urge to confess everything to my wife. Although my intent was to tell everything, my almost-as-great compulsion to protect and defend myself produced a protracted confession lasting four days. There were falsehoods, half-truths, whole truths, all tumbling together with tears and remorse. She heard about the adultery, the incest with my siblings, my seduction by the older man, the confrontations with the authorities. And she kept asking about our daughter while I kept denying there was anything amiss.

Finally, on the fourth evening, I told my wife I had abused our daughter. She sat there in stunned silence and horror. 'That explains a lot,' she finally said. 'I couldn't put things together in my mind, but now events make sense.' Just then our son walked in and you know what the rest of that evening was like. A couple of elders from our church came over that night, prayed with my family, encouraged them as much as they could and offered their help. One of them took the guns from our house. My wife contacted the Child Protection Agency the next day (an essential action, mandated by law, when abuse is discovered).

I moved to a less-expensive motel for a couple of weeks while my wife decided what to do. I couldn't call the house because my son was there. My days were spent in pain, grieving my losses, berating myself. I found a Bible and began reading verses about those who are in Christ and God's love for us. I cried a lot. I read Psalm 51, King David's confession of sin with Bathsheba, over and over. I prayed aloud to God; I screamed into my pillow and drenched it with tears. I wept over the remains of a wasted life, of broken relationships.

I began to realise slowly how my sins had produced consequences in the lives of others that couldn't be erased. I talked to our friends from church from my motel room, pouring out my anguish to them. I was amazed that they didn't hang up on me. They didn't approve of my behaviour, but they were still talking to me.

I couldn't attend the church my wife and daughter were attending, so I looked in the Yellow Pages for a church close to my motel. I was sure my shame was written all over my face, but I knew that I had to be with God's people, even if they threw me out on my face. The first service I attended was about sin and God's mercy. I sat there with tears blinding me, the lump in my throat preventing me from singing.

After the service I asked the man who had been sitting next to me to recommend a mature Christian I could talk to. Sensing the urgency in my voice, he introduced me to a man about my age who took me outside to talk. Sobbing, I told him the whole story, sparing nothing. 'I didn't want your church just to accept me as some kind of super saint, welcoming me with open arms,' I said. 'I've hurt a lot of people and my sin has hurt me as well.'

I'll never forget that man's response: 'Friend, this church is a place for healing. You are welcome here.' Unmerited grace flooded my heart and I wept uncontrollably at this generosity. I had never considered the church to have a ministry to people wounded by their sin. But I returned the next Sunday and took the risk of meeting some of the elders of the church and the pastor and sharing my story with them. I asked for prayer for my family and for me. The response didn't excuse my sin, but made it clear that they considered me a child of God worthy of respect. I was overwhelmed by gratitude.

My wife was grief-stricken, angry, fearful and depressed over the revelations of my infidelity. In spite of that, she took time to call me at the motel and check on me. She got me the essentials for living out of the house and smuggled them to me. She spent hours in secluded places with me, talking out her frustrations and encouraging me to deal with reality as I confronted my sins.

We had periods when emotions were so high we didn't talk to one another for days at a time, but God always brought us back to each other.

One of our friends from our old church recommended a Christian counsellor he had known for years: 'He's a gentle man, full of wisdom, and I've heard that everything he tells you he backs up with scriptural truths so you can check it out.' Although I was seeing a secular psychiatrist, we decided to go to this man for help. He listened to the whole sordid story and said, 'There are major problems here, but none that God can't handle.' He began to teach us to communicate the feelings in our hearts with one another without killing one another's spirits in the process. He taught us the basis for sin and our reaction to it, beginning with Adam and Eve in the Garden of Eden and working from there through the Bible. We began to see hope.

In addition to the counselling sessions, our counsellor recommended several books to read as we went along. One book he recommended was *Victory Over the Darkness* by Neil Anderson, a book about Christian maturity. For the first time, I began to understand that because I am in

Christ, certain things are true about me that are also true of Christ.

Because of my identity in Christ, I have power over the things in my life that I always assumed were beyond my control. In particular, I learned that my emotions and my actions are governed by who I believe myself to be. If I believe a lie about my essential nature, whether it is from the world, the flesh or the devil, then I will act according to that belief. Similarly, if I choose to believe what God has said about me, then I will govern my thoughts and my actions that proceed from those thoughts in accordance with God's will.

I experienced a dramatic sense of joy and freedom in realising the permanence and solidity of God's love for me that transcends any particulars of sin. It was a profound revelation to see from the Scriptures that I am not just 'a sinner saved by grace', but I am a saint who sins, one who is called out and sanctified by God. I learned from our counsellor how to appropriate the truth that I have an advocate before the Father who is constantly there to counter the charges made by Satan against God's elect. I began to experience periods of real joy for the first time, interspersed with periods of melancholy and deep, abiding sorrow before God for my sins against Him and against other people, particularly my daughter and my wife.

Times of self-hatred were finally terminated by my wife reminding me that, 'You need to remember that if God has forgiven your sins in Christ, you must now forgive yourself.' I have had to work toward forgiveness of those who hurt me in the past, not because those hurts are an excuse for sins old or new, but because the unforgiveness kept me bottled up. I have asked for and received forgiveness from those family members I hurt (with the exception of my children who are still struggling with it), and have been reconciled to them, knowing true intimacy for the first time in my life with my brother and sisters and mother. My father died an unbeliever a number of years ago, rejecting the gospel till the last. It has been hardest forgiving him for the rage and neglect, but God has called me to that as well.

I had been attending two different twelve-step groups for 'sexual addiction', and finally quit when I realised that they were elevating sexual sobriety on a pedestal as the end of their efforts. Although they acknowledged a 'Higher Authority', they weren't permitted to identify that Authority as Jesus Christ. And when they had a split vote on whether sex was permitted only in marriage or just in a 'committed relationship', whether homosexual or hetero-sexual, I realised I was in the wrong place and left the groups for good.

The only thing those groups did for me was help me to realise a context for my sexual dysfunction in society: There are plenty of people out there involved in sexual sin. But these groups could not offer the spiritual perspective that identified the life-changing power of Jesus Christ inside the heart of those who trust and obey Him. Because of that, I am hesitant to recommend their 'self-help' approach, par-ticularly if it detracts from relationships within the body of Christ. These groups often claim in meetings that the 'addicts' are the only ones who can understand one another, that they are the addict's true family. To a Christian, such an attitude misses the point of the body of Christ caring for its members who are hurting.

The second book I read that shed tremendous light and was a pivotal work in giving hope and direction to my struggle was Neil Anderson's *The Bondage Breaker*. This book deals extensively with spiritual warfare and the demonic side of habitual sin. I learned how we enable Satan and his unholy angels to establish footholds, then strong-holds in our spiritual lives as we fail to live in our identity with Christ and appropriate the aspects of His character that are already ours. In reminding me that Satan is a vanquished foe who has no power over me that I do not relinquish to him, the book gave hope for victory in the spiritual and the physical struggle over sin.

I began to read aloud the spiritual truths that Neil had included in both books that show our identity in Christ and the results of that identity. As I affirmed my identity and then struggled with the discrepancy between my attitudes, thought life and behaviour, in contrast to my nature in Christ, I was often overwhelmed with grief and self-condemnation. I renounced the strongholds that Satan had established, experiencing progressive freedom as each trouble area was identified. It was only after months of struggle that I have come to where God wants me: confident in Him, not in myself, and confident in His love for me that will not fade or fail.

My wife and I have worked for the last year toward re-establishing our relationship, based not on lust and exploitation but on the solid foundation of Jesus Christ. Gradually we have dealt with issues of sin and forgiveness, and we are friends again. We still have arguments, conflicts and hurt feelings to deal with, but our tools are better. We are building a track record of success in resolving our past and present conflicts.

I still struggle with my emotions, but I am able to feel the full range from profound sadness to great joy, and God is with me in all of them. Do I still sin? Surely, but I am a saint who occasionally sins, and I am able to confess to God, remembering 1 John 1:9: 'If we confess our sins, he is faithful and just and will forgive us our sins and purify us from all unrighteousness' (NIV). And very importantly, I have been freed from the sexual compulsion that grew out of believing Satan's lies about my true nature.

With the help of my therapist I have been learning to recognise and acknowledge emotions. With the help of the

Holy Spirit I have the power to will to do good rather than evil. I have not been magically freed from temptation: The more closely I draw toward God, the more the tempter presents opportunities for sin. Recognising that my thoughts will bear fruit if they are allowed to, I constantly am making choices for what is right. The bondage to sin that I allowed to happen through my sinful choices has been broken. In the midst of the evil around me, I am learning to flee temptation, resist the devil and be in the world but not of it. I stand on God's promise:

> No temptation has seized you except what is common to man. And God is faithful; he will not let you be tempted beyond what you can bear. But when you are tempted, he will also provide a way out so that you can stand up under it (1 Cor 10:13, NIV).

Still, I am confident that God's timing and His methods are perfect, that His plan of redemption has no flaws. I am grateful for His restoration and I look forward to the time when all wounds are healed, all tears are wiped away and reconciliation in Christ is perfected. Until then, I am learning how to function as a person who takes responsibility for his actions, and I am learning to love my wife the way God intended. Now I am able to pray, to study Scripture with gratitude, to praise God for His grace, to rest in His provision for my life. Thanks to understanding my identity in Christ, I am free! I can live the life God calls me to live!

Who are the hurting?

Every spring I teach a class called 'Church and Society', our basic class on ethics that tries to determine the church's role in society. In the second half of the semester we invite local experts to address specific moral issues. I enjoy the class because every spring it is a learning experience for me as well. As the guests come to give their presentations, I warn the students not to 'pick up everybody's burden' or they will be overwhelmed. However, the concerns must be heard because these speakers are striving to meet the needs of hurting people in our society, and that is also the ministry of the church.

The continuous concern I hear from Christians who work with the abused in parachurch or secular agencies is their frustration with the church. They say the church is living in denial and actually harbouring wife beaters, child abusers and alcoholics. That most often we fail to defend the victim and provide sanctuary for the abuser, under the disguise of not wanting scandal. Consequently, neither the abuser nor the abused get help. Their lives continue to go farther and farther off course as was the case with Charles.

Male and female sexuality

We are created as sexual beings: female vaginal lubrication and male erections take place in the first twenty-four hours after birth. Infants need to experience warmth and touch in order for parental bonding to take place, and trust is developed during the first few months of life. Abuse or neglect even during this time will have lasting detrimental effects, so it shouldn't be hard to see how severely a child can be affected if he is abused a little later in early childhood when there is even greater awareness. There is actually a sick organisation of paedophiles that promotes incest, proclaiming, 'Sex before eight or it's too late!' They seek to destroy normal sexual functioning even before it has a chance to develop.

All sexual anatomy is present at birth and becomes developed in early adolescence. Hormones start secreting three years before puberty. In the female, oestrogen and progesterone are very irregular until a year after puberty when a regular rhythmic monthly pattern is established. The wall of the vagina thins and vaginal lubrication decreases after menopause, as hormone secretion decreases.

In the male, testosterone increases at puberty, reaches a maximum at twenty, decreases at forty, and becomes almost zero at eighty. Normal aging causes a slower erection and less sexual functioning, but not a complete stopping of those functions. While a man is sleeping he will experience an erection every eighty to ninety minutes.

All this is a part of God's wonderful creation which we are to watch over as good stewards. But as already noted, this beautiful plan for procreation and expression of love can be grossly distorted.

Healing distorted sexual development

God intended sex to be for pleasure and procreation within the boundaries of marriage. But when sex becomes a 'god', it is ugly, boring and enslaving. Heaping condemnation on those who are enslaved is ill-advised. Increasing shame and guilt will prove counterproductive and will not produce good mental health, Christian character or self-control. Guilt does not inhibit sexual arousal, and may even contribute to it and keep us from using our sexuality wholesomely as God intends. Instead of condemnation, I would offer the following steps for those who have had a distorted sexual development.

1. *Face up to your present condition before God.* There are no secrets with God. He knows the thoughts and intentions of your heart (Heb 4:11–13), and you don't ever have to fear rejection by being honest with Him and confessing your sin and need. Confession is simply being truthful with God and living in continuous agreement with Him. The opposite of confession is not silence but rationalisation and self-justification, attempting to excuse or deny your problem. This

will never lead you to freedom. Your journey out of sexual bondage must include God in an honest and intimate way.

2. *Commit yourself to a biblical view of sex.* All sexual expressions were intended by God to be associated with love and trust which are necessary to insure good sexual functioning. Recent evidence indicates that trust may be one of the most important factors determining orgasmic capacity in women. To ensure trust means that we never have the right to violate another person's conscience. *If it is wrong for your spouse, it is wrong for you.*

Too many wives have tearfully asked me if they have to submit to their husband's every request. Usually their husbands are asking for some kinky expression hoping to satisfy their lust. Some actually appeal to Hebrews 13:4, saying the 'wedding bed is undefiled' and claiming that the Bible permits all expressions of sex in a marriage. No four words are taken out of context more than those. Finish the verse: 'for fornicators and adulterers God will judge.' The idea is to keep the wedding bed undefiled with no adultery or fornication. A wife can meet the sexual needs of her husband, but she will never be able to satisfy his lust.

A biblical view of sex is always personal. It is an intimate expression of two people who are in love with each other. People who are in bondage to sex or are bored with it have depersonalised it. They become obsessed with sexual thoughts in hope for more excitement, and because obsessional sex is always depersonalised, boredom increases and obsessive thoughts grow stronger. One man actually told me that his practice of masturbation is not sinful because in his fantasies the women have no heads! I told him that is precisely what is wrong with what he is doing. Fantasising another as a sex object, as opposed to seeing them as a person created in the image of God, is precisely the problem. And even the porno queen is some mother's daughter, not just a piece of meat.

A biblical view of sex is also associated with safety and security. Outside of God's plan, fear and danger can also cause sexual arousal. For instance, sneaking into a porno shop will cause sexual arousal long before an actual sexual stimulant is present. And voyeurism is very resistant to treatment because arousal is not just from the viewing — the act violates a forbidden cultural standard. The emotional peak is heightened by the presence of fear and danger.

One man said he was into exciting sex. He would rent a motel room and commit adultery in the swimming pool where the possibility of being caught heightened the climax. Such people must separate fear and danger from sexual arousal. A biblical view of sex includes the concepts of safety and security so that the maximum fulfilment comes from a complete surrender of oneself to another in trust and love. Some people buy the lie that the forbidden fruit is the sweetest, denying the crucial importance of the relationship between a man and woman in finding pleasure and fulfilment in sex.

I also advocate abstaining from any use of the sex organs other than that which was intended by the Creator. I was not built upside down, nor intended to walk on my hands. Parts of my body are created to dispose of unusable body fluids and substances. I do not believe that oral sex reflects the Creator's design for proper use of body parts. Even personal hygiene would suggest that this expression isn't what God intended.

Why are we continually looking for the ultimate sexual experience? Why aren't we looking for the ultimate personal experience with God and each other, and letting sex within marriage be an expression of that? Good sex will not make a good marriage, but a good marriage will have good sex.

3. *Seek forgiveness from all those you have sexually offended.* I encourage every man to go to his wife and ask

for forgiveness for any violation of trust. Our wives can sense when something is wrong; don't let them guess. They are actually a critical part of our living sexually free in Christ. Men are incredibly vulnerable sexually and need the caring support and discernment that a loving wife can provide. Both Doug, from our last chapter, and Charles finally confessed everything to their wives. Humbling? Yes, but that is the path to freedom.

Charles also had to seek forgiveness from his children. In some cases, it may take years before that comes. Sadly, some never come to the point of forgiving their abuser, and so the cycle of abuse continues. Abused children usually become abusive themselves, and their children will suffer the result of yet another parent in bondage. If the victim chooses not to forgive the abuser, he or she is living in the bondage of bitterness. Yet for the restored abuser to live in condemnation because he or she has not been forgiven by the victim is to deny the finished work of Christ. Christ died once for all for the sins of the world. We must believe, live and teach that in order to stop the cycle of abuse.

4. *Renew your mind.* Abnormal sex is a product of obsessive thoughts. These thoughts become self-perpetuating because of the physical and mental reinforcement that comes from each mental perception and repeated action. The mind can only reflect upon that which is seen, stored or vividly imagined, and we are responsible for what we think and for our own mental purity.

I remember when I first became a Christian and committed myself to clean up my mind. As you can imagine, the problem became worse, not better. If you are giving in to sexual thoughts, temptation doesn't seem that strong, but when you determine not to sin, temptation becomes stronger. I remember singing songs just to keep my mind focused. My life and experiences would be quite innocent compared to most people I have talked to, but it took years to renew my mind from the images I had programmed into it earlier.

Imagine your mind to be the coffee in a pot. The fluid is dark and smelly because of the old coffee grounds (pornographic material and sexual experiences) that have been put into it and left there. There is no way to rid the bitter taste and ugly colouring that now permeate it, no way to filter it out. You can, and must, get rid of the 'grounds'. All pornographic material must go!

Now imagine a bucket of crystal clear ice alongside the coffee pot. Each ice cube represents the Word of God. If we were to take at least one ice cube every day and put it into the coffee pot, the coffee would eventually be watered down to the point where you couldn't even smell or see the coffee that was originally in there. That would work, provided you also committed yourself not to put any more coffee grounds in the pot.

Paul writes in Colossians 3:15: 'And let the peace of Christ rule in your hearts, to which indeed you were called in one body; and be thankful.' How are we going to let Christ rule in our heart? The next verse says, 'Let the word of Christ richly dwell within you, with all wisdom teaching and admonishing one another with psalms and hymns and spiritual songs, singing with thankfulness in your hearts to God.'

Just like Jesus, we must stand against temptation with the truth of God's Word. When that tempting thought first hits, take it captive to the obedience of Christ (2 Cor 10:5). 'How can a young man keep his way pure? By keeping it according to Thy word. Thy word I have treasured in my heart, that I may not sin against Thee' (Ps 119:9,11)

Winning the battle for our minds is often two steps forward and one step back. Eventually, it is three steps forward and one back. Then it's five steps forward and one back, until there are so many positive steps forward that the 'one back' is a fading memory. Remember, you may despair in asking God to forgive you when you fail again and again, but He never despairs in forgiving.

5. *Seek legitimate relationships that meet your needs of love and acceptance.* People with sexual addictions tend to isolate themselves. We need each other; we were never designed to survive alone. Charles sought out Christian help and fellowship. Few do that, however, because of the shame. Consequently, they stay in bondage. When we are satisfied in our relationships, deep legitimate needs are met. Finding fulfilment in sexual expressions instead of relationships will lead to addiction.

6. *Learn to walk by the Spirit.* Galatians 5:16 says, 'Walk by the Spirit, and you will not carry out the desires of the flesh.' A legalistic walk with God will only bring condemnation, but a dependent relationship with Him, with His grace sustaining us, is our real hope. In my book *Walking Through the Light*, I seek to define what it means to have God's guidance and a life that is enabled by His Spirit.

Admittedly, sexual bondage is a difficult bondage to break, but every person can be freed from Satan's grasp in that area. The terrible cost of not fighting for that freedom is too high a price to pay. Your sexual and spiritual freedom are worth the fight.

8

A FAMILY:
Freed From
False Teachers

The most insecure people you will ever meet are controllers.
They are external, not internal, people; shallow, not deep.
Subconsciously, they labour under the false belief that their
self-worth is dependent upon controlling or manipulating
the world around them. Consider the Hitlers and Husseins
of the world. Their insecurities have gone to such extremes
that the lives of millions have been lost. Controllers of this
nature simply eliminate those who oppose them and sur-
round themselves with puppets who outwardly affirm them.

In a similar and sinister way, false prophets and teachers
have crept into the church. We have been clearly warned
about them in Scripture: 'For false Christs and false
prophets will arise and will show great signs and wonders,
so as to mislead, if possible, even the elect' (Mt 24:24). It
still surprises me to learn that the followers of cultish-type
leaders come from educated, middle-class and usually religious homes. Are we that susceptible to deception? Yes, we
are!

In 2 Peter, we find the entire second chapter devoted to
false prophets and teachers who will rise up, appearing to
be Christian. Notice the first two verses:

> But false prophets also arose among the people, just as there
> will also be false teachers among you, who will secretly
> introduce destructive heresies, even denying the Master who
> bought them, bringing swift destruction upon themselves.

And many will follow their sensuality, and because of them the way of truth will be maligned.

The sinister side of religious deception

When the way of truth is maligned, the result is bondage instead of freedom. Who will follow such deceivers? Usually, dependant people and those who are products of controlling, manipulative parents. Some are idealists disillusioned by a promiscuous society.

Abuse by religious deception is even more sinister than the physical or sexual abuse we have been discussing because this masquerade comes with high commitment, noble-sounding ideas and rigid controls. Thus it destroys decent people who are looking to be led by someone they can trust. Without realising it, they end up following a man, not God. Paul warns us in 2 Corinthians 11:13–15:

> For such men are false apostles, deceitful workers, disguising themselves as apostles of Christ. And no wonder, for even Satan disguises himself as an angel of light. Therefore it is not surprising if his servants also disguise themselves as servants of righteousness; whose end shall be according to their deeds.

Stifling legalism

In *Walking Through the Darkness*, I discuss the nature of false prophets and teachers, and false guidance. Nothing is more repugnant to God than those who would lead His children astray. False teachers have an independent spirit; they won't answer to anyone. They will demand absolute allegiance to themselves and charge you with not being submissive if they don't receive it. Instead of liberating people in Christ they exercise rigid controls, often under the disguise of discipleship. They insist that they are right, everyone else is wrong, and their pawns can do nothing unless it is approved by them. The fruit of their spirit is leader-control, resulting in a stifling legalism. The fruit of the Holy Spirit is self-control, resulting in freedom.

God is holy and we are to live holy lives, but legalism is not the means by which we will be able to do so. External controls cannot accomplish what only the indwelling Holy Spirit can accomplish. Legalists are driven, compulsive people who are trying to live up to some standard and never able to do so. They even require others to try and ironically reject them when they can't. They live under the curse of condemnation: 'For as many as are of the works of the Law are under a curse' (Gal 3:10).

Legalists try to establish their sufficiency in themselves, not Christ:

> Not that we are adequate in ourselves to consider anything as coming from ourselves, but our adequacy is from God, who also made us adequate as servants of a new covenant, not of the letter, but of the Spirit; for the letter [of the law] kills, but the Spirit gives life (2 Cor 3:5,6).
>
> Now the Lord is the Spirit; and where the Spirit of the Lord is, there is liberty (2 Cor 3:17).

A family, in and out of bondage

Our next story is of a family who, over a ten-year period of time, journeyed into and then out of bondage. When I met him, Joe was competent and successful in his profession, but his marriage was in jeopardy. His wife had gone away for a few days in order to contemplate separation from him. His eyes expressed his deep concern as he came to ask for counsel. We will hear first from this conscientious man who unwittingly led his family into the bondage of a cult leader disguised as a righteous mentor. Joe's great difficulty was to admit to the deception; once he had, he struggled with whom to trust next.

Then we will hear from his wife, who discerned that something was wrong but was charged with not being submissive. Finally we will hear from their two daughters who chaffed under this oppressive atmosphere. I will not comment after their testimonies because they say it all.

Joe's Story

*My mother did everything she could
to hold the family together.*

My parents divorced when I was very young. After that, I remember feeling more trauma at the death and separation from others that I loved. My mother did everything she could to hold the family together, but her own insecurity demonstrated itself in a need to control.

Mum and I were always very close, but looking back, I see that she pressured me in my decision-making, and moulded me into being a person who needed someone else to guide me. This has had a profoundly negative effect on my entire life. I still often go through a 'hell' of indecision in trying to choose a course of action. And once I do make a decision, I find myself evaluating it over and over again.

I did well in school and especially university, gaining second place in my major field upon graduation, and I was chosen for an all-star sports team composed of students from all the universities on the eastern seaboard of America.

Cynthia and I met at seventeen, when she came to our home as my sister's guest. She was pretty and had a sparkle in her eyes, and I was attracted to her. We fell in love, dated through the university years and married upon graduation. We attended church after we were married, but I didn't come to know the Lord in a personal way until about a year later; for Cynthia, it was several years later. We went to a very legalistic church which Cynthia hated, but I gave my life to it. As a result of my dedication, many people there told me I should go into the ministry.

We moved to another church where I also became extensively involved: leading worship, assisting the pastors, writing curriculum, leading in small groups. That's when I began to realise that my relationship with Cynthia was suffering. Finally I resigned from all 'ministry' activities to focus entirely on my home and family.

We became acquainted with a couple from another church who modelled a good family life and really helped us in our relationship and in raising our young children. It was through them that we were introduced to the discipleship movement that eventually shattered our family. We attended a service at their church to hear the leader of the movement who was from another state. I responded to his message and listened to his tape series over and over again. I became convinced that we should become involved in this movement.

Cynthia found it difficult. When she listened to the tapes, she was filled with fear. Our church leaders were also opposed to our becoming involved. So I submitted to Cynthia and to our leaders for a period of two years until, finally, there was agreement that we would join the movement.

I look back and see now that Cynthia never did feel good about that decision; in effect, I simply wore her down. But at the time I believed I was waiting on God to act on our behalf and that He had removed the barriers to our going.

We joined the new church and gradually my perspective of Cynthia began to change. In my new interpretation of authority and submission in the home, I began to view her resistance to me as rebellion against the Lord.

I was hungry toward God and excited by the vision of the movement and the answers I believed it had for the problems of the church and society today. I genuinely thought that the church needed order and discipline, and that God had brought about his work to accomplish that goal.

I moved into some major responsibilities in the movement, both legally and administratively. We sold our home in order to move closer to the church and gave the equity to the furtherance of the vision.

Looking back, I see that in that movement there was one man, the leader, who was abusing his position of authority and using, controlling and manipulating people. I was one who was responding to his leadership, but I did it in the firm belief that I was responding to the Lord.

The warning I missed all along was Cynthia's concern. She continued to hold back. I realise now that in her spirit she could feel things were wrong, but she couldn't explain them to me, and I probably wasn't ready to listen. I should have paid attention to the reservations she was feeling; they were a part of the God-given guidance which I ignored. Instead, I saw her resistance as self-protection and my responsibility as having to help her.

Finally we were asked to move to another state where I thought we would be able to be even more involved, but that never happened. I didn't know it then, but after we were there awhile, the leader was telling Cynthia things about me that were hurtful and divisive. At the same time, he was telling me that I couldn't lead my wife and was not fit to have responsibility in the church. I was set aside.

That all happened as I was questioning the legal affairs of the movement. I had seen a red flag, and when I spoke about my concerns to the leader he reacted in anger. He told me that I was touching things out of the sphere of my responsibility and had no right to interfere.

I spent the next five years agonising before God, trying to respond to what I was being told were my 'problems'.

Meanwhile, an even greater barrier grew between Cynthia and me. I felt that much of what God had called me to do was being blocked because she always resisted me, the leaders and God. This attitude was nurtured by the leader in ways that were so subtle I didn't realise what was going on.

Gradually I found it more and more difficult to respond to the leadership's teaching and challenges. Yet we were being taught to keep responding to God by submitting to their authority. It was a painful and confusing time for me, and I did not see the many warning signals that things were not right.

When Cynthia got the idea to spend time in a training school — a live-in discipleship experience for the whole family — I was elated. I saw this as a change in Cynthia and we agreed together to go.

The following year the movement's leader was exposed publicly, both for his handling of the finances of the ministry and for abusing many of the women spiritually and sexually. Together with others from the group, Cynthia and I pieced the jigsaw puzzle of the movement together and saw a picture of control and manipulation by one man that is almost too complex and incredible to believe.

Everyone believed that they were the only ones being victimised, and that the 'problem' in their own life was the reason they could not move on to new responsibilities. Much of the control of people was maintained by dividing husband and wife; Cynthia and I were a classic example of that. But when the leader was exposed, that powerful controlling influence over all of us was broken.

We left immediately and returned to our home state to start life over again. Great damage had been done to our family relationships, the most treasured part of my life. I had lost the ability to relate to my children, especially my older daughter who had been struggling for a long time in the same way that Cynthia had.

There was a lot of change needed. I had drunk deeply of a wrong spirit, brought it into our home and modelled something that was fundamentally flawed. I acknowledged these things to my family but did not realise that this was only the start of a major journey, not the end of our problems.

A book was recommended to me: *The Bondage Breaker* by Dr Neil Anderson. I found clarity and freshness in the freedom in Christ it portrayed. I purchased his first book, *Victory Over the Darkness*, which Neil had referred to as being important to our identity in Christ. I devoured both of the books, reading and rereading them, and marking them throughout. There was not one area of the Scriptures in these books that I had not studied in depth, yet Neil brought a fresh perspective to it all.

I recommended the books to Cynthia and began to seriously consider going to California, hoping to see Neil. Imagine my delight when I heard he was coming to our area within a few weeks to give a week-long seminar! Cynthia was not that interested and went away on a trip to evaluate our relationship, so I attended on my own. At the conference, I was referred to a Freedom in Christ staff couple in response to my request for counsel. When Cynthia returned, she agreed that we would go together to talk as long as it was with someone totally independent, someone who had not been influenced by my perspective of the situation or of her.

I met with the husband while Cynthia met with his wife, each leading us through the Steps to Freedom. During that session, I began to see myself in a new light. I knew of my identity in Christ; I could have discussed the issues from a scriptural perspective. Yet I began to see that I had built up a strong wall around many locked-up emotions which I had held since childhood. I was not in touch with my own feelings, but related to God and others on a mind level only.

The walls I had built around me were a self-defence, a security system under the cover of spirituality: great personal discipline, consistent study of God's Word, regular quiet times with God; but still a system where I controlled as much as possible in order to hold myself together. I had spiritual pride in my ability to respond 'correctly' to situations, to control or suppress my feelings and emotions, to do the right thing.

It was my own 'goodness' that was blocking a sense of personal poverty and need of God. What I didn't know was the humility of being in need of God in a personal way day by day. I knew the right thing to do, always had the 'right' answer and could always back it up scripturally, but I did it in my own power. This aggravated Cynthia; to her, I wasn't real.

I found it very hard to be wrong, especially in spiritual matters, and often would not listen to Cynthia. She was the one who was 'out to lunch' and needed help. I was encouraged to stop insisting on being right, to be free to be wrong, and to let Cynthia help me.

I finally realised that I had, in effect, destroyed Cynthia. I had given myself to God's work and, more specifically, to the vision and call of our discipleship leader, disregarding my own wife. What kind of person could do that? I had idolised a man, needing his approval because of my own insecurity. I had not understood the wonderful approval and acceptance of God even though I could teach all about it.

Coming to this realisation has been very difficult because I sincerely felt that everything I was doing was for God and had His approval.

It is still difficult for me to understand how, in my longing for God, I could have been so deceived by the enemy of our souls. The explanation, of course, is that Satan is a liar and a deceiver and very subtle in his ways. This ten-year experience has been a tremendous object lesson and it has left an indelible mark on my life and family.

Even after the Freedom in Christ seminar, I was still discovering more about the frightened person who had spent the past twenty years living for God while staying personally independent of Him — having spiritual knowledge, but living in emotional unreality.

Thank God I was able to face the truth about myself. The biggest barrier to the restoration of my family had been the need for me to realise my own sin. After asking forgiveness from the Lord and Cynthia, I spoke to the children, telling them something of what I was seeing about myself and how wrong I had been — that I was not a good reflection of what God is really like. We cannot eradicate the past, and we are far from perfect, but now we are on a new journey of grace together.

As Cynthia came into the lobby of the church, walking tentatively beside Joe, it was evident that here was a woman besieged by fear and disappointments. Her story follows…

Cynthia's Story

I used to cry myself to sleep at night.

There was conflict in my childhood home. While my parents bickered and fought in the living room, my sister and I held hands between our beds for comfort and cried ourselves to sleep.

I wanted peace so badly that when my dad became angry, I would stay out of his way and try to keep everything cool and calm.

My dad was a proud worker who felt that a good man does a hard day's work, and he drank as hard as he worked. Basically, he had a tremendous work ethic which he imparted to me. I always wanted to do well and did so, because to do anything less was to let myself down. And I did achieve my academic goals, though I was terribly insecure within myself and unsure of my future.

During my teen years my mum bought all of my clothes at the second-hand store, and they were always too big. I had to take them in with safety pins. When I complained, Mum said that boys only wanted one thing and that if they could see the shape of my body it would give them ideas.

I withdrew from the children at school out of embarrassment and just concentrated on my studies, especially English and imaginative writing. I enjoyed those courses because I could express myself through them. Once I wrote a paper on individuality out of the cry of my heart — a paper on being different but being accepted, being worthy in your own right even if you are different.

When I was in my final year of school, I went with a girl friend to visit a family in another city. I was stunned when my parents gave their permission because they were so incredibly protective of me. But then, my friend was the pastor's daughter. She had said that we would have a summer romance, though I was not sure what that meant.

There was another girl our age in the home where we stayed and she had a brother. I was afraid of boys, but Joe was kind, soft-spoken and a gentleman, just a few months older than I. Our friendship developed over the next few years and though I saw a tendency to control, I didn't recognise it as a problem that would pursue us.

Joe and I married, and for awhile I waited with excitement for him to come home at night. But I soon learned that he was a very insecure man.

His insecurity created serious relational problems when

we joined a legalistic church. He was a seeking Christian and he loved the legalism. He was looking for someone who would simply tell him what to do so that he would feel secure in doing it. I would cry every Sunday as we left the church because they were always pointing the finger at you and telling you what you were doing wrong.

I got to the point where I didn't go to church. I didn't want to be like those people: downcast, unhappy, with no joy. The pastor even said that if you were a Christian and taught in a public school, you were as the heathen. A nurse working on Sunday was also condemned.

One time, however, I heard a visiting missionary speak. He laughed a lot and sang songs. I had never seen such a joyful Christian before. Everything I had tried before, joining the church or Bible study groups, had turned out to be emptiness, but that missionary became my friend and we began to meet with him for Bible study. One night the light went on in me, and I saw a loving Saviour welcoming me and forgiving my sins. I received Him into my life and cried buckets of tears, saying, 'I understand! I understand!'

Then we joined another church, more legalistic than the first one. Joe was excited because the leader of a discipleship movement he was attracted to was a part of that church. He felt that this leader had the answers to the Christian life that he had been looking for. I felt just the opposite. I feared that we were getting involved in a cult; I had strong reservations about the teaching and methods of this group and about the leader himself. But Joe persisted and I followed.

Some of their teaching was that people should attend meetings, not only for long periods on Sundays but often throughout the week and again on Friday evenings. Children were supposed to be there at all times, so the young ones spent three to four nights in a row falling asleep on the floor. We were told that we needed 'religion' removed from our thinking, so meetings were held at other than traditional times on Sunday. We were taught that the church was now our family, and we were to choose any meeting called by the leader over any family activity.

It was a steady programme of indoctrination. If we didn't agree with anything the leader said or did, we had no right to come to him about it. Leaders were not accountable to their followers, their 'sheep'. They never had to apologise for any wrong done. However, sheep were supposed to be given what was called 'the right of appeal' if they felt they had been wronged by subordinate leaders. In reality, this never happened. Sheep were always wrong and were taught that they were attacking 'the throne of God' if they challenged or even questioned the leadership.

The leaders, or 'shepherds', taught that they were above the sheep. They were not to befriend the sheep, but simply to make their needs known so the sheep could serve them. I never felt that the shepherds were supportive — their job was to point out my faults and errors.

In the first few months of attending this church, I shared my concerns and questions with Joe. Unknown to me, he was relating all that I said to his shepherd. This was encouraged by the hierarchy, supposedly to help mature us. One day my husband calmly told me that I had a Jezebel spirit. Not knowing what that was, I asked him to explain. He said that I was a usurper, that his shepherd had come to that conclusion after hearing of my concerns. Joe was told that I was trying to run the home and was walking all over him.

For ten years, anything said or done in our home was judged by that perspective. Joe felt that he had no manhood if he couldn't lead his wife, and the church constantly reinforced that belief. He was told that he couldn't advance within the church until he had his house (me) in order.

When Joe and I had that first major conflict, I asked for a 'right of appeal'. We were given an appointment to see the leader. This shepherd told me that I wanted a 'puppy dog' for a husband, someone who would follow me around. He also told me that there are many levels of maturity in the Christian faith and that I was only in the kindergarten.

I left the interview feeling that it had been unfair and that I had not been heard. The leader had tried to weaken my resolve and crush my spirit. Actually, he only raised more questions and concerns about the whole situation.

Unfortunately, as I became more wary, Joe became more enamoured with the strong teaching and the leader himself, even writing long letters to the leader pledging himself as a bond servant to him. When I discovered this I was enraged — not only was my husband selling himself out to a man, but he was doing it at my expense.

My husband had always been loving, kind and thoughtful, but that changed. He became suspicious, distrusting and resentful, seeing me as the enemy, the one who thwarted his plans.

Knowing his longing to find God and to walk in His ways only made this whole process more difficult. At this point we were encouraged to sell everything and move some thousands of miles to be near the leader who had moved the headquarters of the church to another state. This was like a sentence to me, but since I had no other hope for our marriage I agreed. With much anxiety, we made plans to move. Our two children did not want to leave home, school or friends, especially our older daughter. However, I was holding on to a thread that maybe this could be the answer and we could work things out.

After the move, instead of finding help we were left alone with absolutely no personal contact for months. I found out later that the couple who were assigned as our shepherds had warned everyone with whom I became friendly, 'Be careful of Cynthia; she's trouble. You mustn't spend too much time with her.'

Joe was also ignored and even ostracised. Whereas he

had been quite heavily involved in the legal aspects of the church for some years and had held significant responsibility in this area, he was now told that he was not even to ask questions or in any way become familiar with the workings of the movement.

I struggled. He struggled. Unfortunately, we didn't pull together. Joe still maintained that the leadership had to be right and became extremely angry with me whenever I voiced my concerns. Quite frankly, I couldn't see much of Jesus in what was going on. I had long since decided that if what my husband had was Christianity, then I didn't want to have anything to do with it. But then, I had been told I was in kindergarten spiritually while my husband was viewed as being mature, so I kept those thoughts to myself.

After some time in the new state, I suggested to Joe that maybe we should go to the training school operated by the discipleship movement. That decision was born of desperation and a belief that I did need more discipline in my life.

The rules for family behaviour were very strict in the school, and our teenage daughter and Joe had many confrontations. The children were taught that their place was to listen, to obey and to have their will crossed so they would learn that life isn't fair. When Joe returned home from a trip, he would make a point of bringing a gift for only one of our children. It didn't matter if the same child was left out several times in a row — that only reinforced the lesson. This idea came directly from the leader himself.

Several months after graduating from the course, both Joe and I decided to return to our home at the end of the year. When we asked the leader for permission, he said that he didn't believe the Lord had finished with us yet and that he also had plans for us. But I didn't want his plans. Besides, the Lord had given me a Scripture personally, that 'He had plans for me. Plans for welfare and not calamity, to give me a future and a hope' (Jer 29:11). How I held on to that word.

As I studied Jeremiah the Lord gave me words about returning from exile. Joe, our children and I all felt we should return home and we were excited. For the first time in ten years, our family was in agreement.

Then a church meeting was called and the announcement was made that the leader had been asked to resign due to sexual impropriety with many women. The shock ran through the church, and then we absolutely knew what the Lord would have us do — go home!

Once home, the girls and I were euphoric, but Joe went into a deep depression that lasted for weeks. His belief system had been challenged. He was confused and angry and didn't know where to turn or from whom to seek counsel.

We were fighting again and we knew we needed help, someone we could talk to who was independent of the situation and who had a godly ministry. This was our cry.

Months went by, and Joe learned of Dr Neil Anderson's books, which he read with great interest. He purchased one, then another. Then he heard that Dr Anderson was coming to town to conduct a seminar on 'Resolving Personal and Spiritual Conflicts'.

Joe was determined to go and asked me to come with him, but I refused. I did read the books he'd recommended, but I wasn't about to deal with ten years of abuse and control in a room full of people. Instead, I took a trip alone to another city to try to sort through my confusion and perhaps decide to leave Joe. I returned near the end of the conference, and each night Joe would come from the seminar and share a little of what he was learning. But I wasn't too interested — I had lost respect for him in spiritual matters.

I did agree to meet with a couple from the Freedom in Christ staff near the end of the conference. I was scared. Too many times I had gone to talk to someone and hadn't been heard. When we walked into the church and met the smiling couple, I acknowledged their greeting but remained closed inside. I wasn't going to share a thing if I felt any suspicion of judgement or distrust toward me. I found none.

We had a brief prayer together and then the men moved to another room while the woman and I began to talk. She asked me to share my life and my hurts with her, and what transpired in the next couple of hours dramatically changed me.

I talked; how I talked. Realising there was a receptive, sensitive spirit in this woman, my guard came down and all that had been locked in for those many years came pouring out. I felt for the first time in ten years that someone could hear me without judgement — just an openness and unselfish giving of time to let me release the burden of those years. Finally she took me through the Steps to Freedom, renouncing any and all contact or involvement with the cult.

I was asked to list the name of all the people I needed to forgive. There were many. When I came to the former leader of the movement, I struggled — everything in me didn't want to forgive him for all he had done to devastate our lives. But I did. By an act of my will, I forgave him and a deep flood of emotion was released. Forgiving God for allowing all of this to happen was something I hadn't considered, but I realised that I did blame Him. Finally, I had to forgive myself for things I had and had not done through the years.

At the end I was tired and strangely humbled. I felt comforted by the fact that someone believed me, and cleansed because I had let go of the burden of unforgiveness. In talking about the leader of the movement afterward, I no longer experienced tightness in my chest and tension in my body; I knew I was free of him. My healing had begun!

My daughters agreed to accompany me, so I took them to the next conference that Neil was conducting. From the first evening, the girls relaxed and enjoyed the messages.

They had spent many weeks at church seminars before and had come to hate them, but this was different. This man was real; he was even funny, and what he had to say made sense. Later in the week, both girls went through the same freeing process that I had gone through the previous week.

The changes in our daughters' lives have been profound. Our oldest daughter has a softness restored and her heart is so open to the Lord. The younger one released burdens of pain and unforgiveness. We are all free.

Joe and I still have much to work through. Daily situations arise where we have to deal with old patterns of behaviour. But I no longer feel it's too big for me to handle. We know that it will take time to walk out of the old way of thinking, but we are on the road to wholeness. We have hope!

Joe and Cynthia's oldest teenager, Judy, is an illustration of the domino effect which can take place when parents repent and communication between themselves and the children becomes real and honest. Here is the account of Judy's search for truth and her struggle with her own anger and rebellion.

Judy's Story

*I wondered how adults could ever
do anything wrong.*

When I was little I thought Mum and Dad were happy, but when I got to about ten I began to feel a lot of underlying tension. But that didn't matter — I still thought my parents were perfect and wondered how adults could ever do anything wrong.

Mum would cry a lot, and she and my dad argued behind closed doors, sometimes for hours and hours. I would lie in bed at night and hear it and not know what to do. It was frightening. Then Dad would come up and tell us good-night, but he wouldn't say anything else.

I became a Christian when I was very young. When I was a teenager, we went to another state and it was awful. The people there, and especially the children my age, were so fickle. They were friendly on the outside, but it seemed their underlying motive was to hurt you and bring you down. I wasn't used to that and it took a while for me to toughen up. I would come home in tears because I couldn't handle the fact that people would gossip about me for no apparent reason.

I hated the church we went to and the pastor. When he walked into the room I felt like there was a dark presence there, as though the room was filled with evil. I would feel suffocated or claustrophic and want to get out. I didn't like being near him at all.

When I went to church I withdrew inside myself. I didn't sing or join in the service. I just couldn't respond and that got me into a lot of trouble. My parents would say, 'What's wrong with you? You're fine before church and you're fine after church. What happens?' And I didn't know what to tell them; I just didn't want to be there.

I must have been feeling all of the wrong that was there. I felt that the whole movement was fake. The leaders would stand up and yell to the point where it would hurt your ears, and what they said didn't make sense to me. It was all theology and a lot of words that weren't helpful.

We had to go to youth meetings; we didn't have a choice. If you didn't go you were frowned upon as a rebel and a backslider. The good thing about it was that I would get to see my friends and that was one of the only times we saw each other.

In the authority structure, the big word was *framework*. It was all rules, very legalistic. From the top down, everything was the law and it affected me a lot.

The leaders were supposed to know everything about everybody. That wasn't so true of us because we were at the bottom level, but the higher up you were, the more you would know about everyone else. That was the power structure. They wanted to know things so they could lord it over you. It was my dad's responsibility to tell them everything about us.

When I was fourteen and my parents were in the training school, there were really strict rules. My dad was in favour of all of them, so he followed them all the way. I was under pressure all the time and eventually I rebelled against it. I fought a lot with my dad, and we were constantly at each other's throats. It got to the point where, during the last year we were away from our home, I hated him with every ounce of me. Everything he stood for, I was against. I knew that I shouldn't be that way, but I didn't feel bad about it.

My mother would share some of the difficult things she was experiencing and I would talk to her about what I was feeling, mostly the pressure from my dad. Whatever I would say, he took as criticism; he always thought I was pulling him down, even if it was just a little comment.

I didn't trust my dad. One time I told him something and he went straight to my teacher and told her. Then my teacher came and talked to me. I couldn't believe it. I had told something that was very important to me and now it was being held against me.

Sometimes my mother would say, 'There's hope; there's hope. He's changing; he's changing.' But I would say, 'I can't see it.'

When we came back home, my spiritual life was almost non-existent. I wasn't purposely trying to turn my back on

the Lord, but I made a conscious decision not to get into anything like we had been in. I didn't want to be a hypocrite.

When my dad started talking about the Freedom in Christ conference, I didn't want to have anything to do with it. He kept pushing and pushing, but we had been to so many conferences. We had attended teaching sessions where there were meetings every night of the week, and we had religion shoved down our throats. We had to go to those and it was awful, so I thought, *Here we go again.*

Dad said that he wouldn't make us go, but that he would really like it if we did. I don't know why, but this time he didn't seem to be insisting like he used to, and we were at a point where we were getting along a little better. But my mum, sister and I declined, so Dad went and just kept telling us how good it was. I thought, *Great, there's going to be some big changes here,* but nothing visible happened. Then Mum and Dad went to the counselling session together.

The next day my mother and I went out alone. We talked together for hours. She explained what had gone on at her counselling session, and the two of us cried together.

Mum told me about the couple she had met with who were not judgemental. I thought I would give that a try. We went to the next conference they were at and I loved it. All the sessions were enjoyable and refreshing — no legalism. And the speaker was funny. He didn't talk at you, but would give examples from his own life and family. You felt like he was coming alongside and saying, 'Look, I'm a person too, and I also have problems.'

I decided to see the same counsellor Mum had, and when I did I gave up a whole lot of resentment by my own choice. It was something I had to do. Now I pray for those people from my past.

Over the years there have been those times when I have had big, dramatic encounters with the Lord. But it never lasted, except maybe for a week or two. They were emotional, physical experiences with shaking and everything. There were good things, but there was also a lot of hype. Then I would be back to what I was before. It was always external; I wanted more. I wanted something deep that was going to last, and that's what this was. Something happened in me, and I feel different, definitely softer toward the Lord. I talk to Him and I feel content and peaceful. I'm happy. I'm really happy!

Our family still has problems, but we have an answer. Recently we had a disagreement and Dad got angry and withdrew, but the next day he apologised. He said he was still working through some things, and I have a lot of respect for him for doing that. He said he was wrong and accepted responsibility for what happened. Now we can go on because things aren't being pushed under the rug.

―――――――

Joan, the youngest teen in this family, expresses her fear and finally her hope as the family reunites in Christ. These two girls are above average in intelligence, looks and personality. Their response to their parents' choices to forgive and restore are proof that one of the greatest gifts you can give your child is to love your spouse.

―――――――

Joan's Story

*Our parents were fighting more and
more, and I was really scared.*

Before we left our home there was a time when I felt that Mum wasn't a Christian. I hadn't seen her pray and she wasn't participating in everything Dad did.

I loved doing things with my dad and believed every-thing he said. But when my sister and I began to observe our parents fighting more and more, I became really scared. Sometimes I thought they might be breaking up.

I became depressed and really didn't know what to believe. I just went off by myself. I would actually hide from people. If I heard footsteps, I would hide around the corner so I wouldn't be seen. And I really got into books. If some-one wanted to talk to me, I would avoid that person by burying myself in the books and play-acting the stories in my mind. What was happening in my family frightened me, and this was my escape.

I thought everything was my fault, and I wondered why God wasn't talking to me. Why couldn't I be happy like everyone else seemed to be? My dad helped me accept Christ into my heart when I was four years old, but now I was having questions about Him and whether anything had really happened.

When we moved to the other state, I hated going to church, but thought that when I got older maybe I would understand. Sunday was supposed to be the best day, but it was the worst day of the week for me. It was so boring to sit for so long, not understanding, not being able to do any-thing. We weren't even allowed to yawn.

One time I was so tired that I did yawn. Dad took me outside and told me not to yawn again or he would spank me. I did it again and he took me out to the car, but didn't spank me when I told him it was because I was so tired. I was confused when he did that. Now I understand that he did it because he was told to. He was supposed to be in con-trol and if his children made any disturbance he was sup-posed to punish them for it. It was the father's role to discipline and be in charge of the family.

When we moved back to our home, I was in bad shape. I would hide from my parents. I was scared of talking to them. School was frightening. I didn't have friends, and when the children were unkind I didn't defend myself. I thought I was supposed to have grace and not get angry, that it was the Christian thing to just take it and take it and take it. I was blaming myself for everything that was wrong in my life.

Satan had a real hold on me with fear. When I learned how to rebuke him, things really changed. Now, whenever I hear thoughts that I know are not true, I say, 'Satan, I rebuke you. Get behind me,' and he goes.

Before I learned about my freedom in Christ, I was really depressed a lot of the time and avoided handling my problems. Now I am learning how to face them. I know the Lord is with me. I call on Him for help, and I talk to Him. He's my friend!

9

THE CHURCH:
Helping People
to Freedom

In December 1989, I participated in a 'Power Evangelism Symposium'. Only seminary professors who were teaching something related to spiritual warfare were invited. The papers that were read in this formal conference resulted in the book *Wrestling With Dark Angels*. All participants were biblically conservative, but they represented a broad theological perspective. My paper was the last to be presented.

Before I read my paper, I said, 'I don't see the battle as a power encounter, but rather a truth encounter. I believe that it is truth that sets us free. Secondly, I'm afraid that in the past we've adopted a method out of the Gospels instead of the Epistles.'

There is no instruction in the Epistles to cast out a demon, but there is much instruction for individuals to assume their own responsibility to get and stay free. Prior to the cross, God's people were not redeemed and Satan was not defeated, so it would take a specially endowed authority agent to cast out a demon, such as Christ or the apostles (Lk 9:1). After the cross, Satan is defeated, and every child of God has the authority to resist the devil since we are in Christ and seated with Him in the heavenlies. The responsibility has shifted from the outside agent to the individual. We have a very definitive passage in 2 Timothy 2:24–26:

> And the Lord's bondservant must not be quarrelsome, but
> be kind to all, able to teach, patient when wronged, with

gentleness correcting those who are in opposition, if perhaps God may grant them repentance leading to the knowledge of the truth, and they may come to their senses and escape from the snare of the devil, having been held captive by him to do his will.

Not power, but truth

The ministry God has given the church is not a power model, but is better seen as a kind, 'able-to-teach' model that is utterly dependent upon God to grant the repentance. We can't set anybody free, but we can facilitate the process if we are the Lord's bond servant, know the truth, and can relate it with compassion and patience.

After I presented my paper at the symposium, I was asked if the truth encounter method works. I assured the friend who asked that it does because truth always works and God is the deliverer. He came to set us free (Gal 5:1). I have seen hundreds find freedom in Christ in personal counselling and thousands in conferences.

Then I was asked if the deliverance lasts. It will always last longer if the counsellees assume their own responsibility and make the decisions, rather than my doing it for them. It is the counsellee who has the responsibility to forgive, renounce, confess, resist, etc. We, as pastor-counsellors, can't do that for them.

Then I was asked if it is transferable. Truth is always transferable, but if we are basing our method on giftedness or an office of the church, then it isn't. Most pastors don't care to get into a power encounter, and some counsellors would probably lose their licence or get sued if they did. I advocate a quiet, controlled means of helping to free people — one that is dependent upon God and not some special person. It's not 'Neil's method'. It is simply God working through the truth of His Word to release people. Thousands of pastors and lay men and women around the world are using the Steps to Freedom to do just that.

A transferable ministry

One pastor attended a doctor of ministry class that I taught, and within one year he and his associate had led more than a hundred people in their evangelical church through the Steps to Freedom. When I spoke in their church, I was overwhelmed with the spirit of worship and the 'aliveness' I sensed there. Many of those people came to me and expressed their gratitude to God. They shared how thankful they were to have pastors who could help them resolve their problems. The pastoral staff is now in the process of training others from their church to lead people to freedom in Christ.

In this chapter you will hear from John Simms, a godly Pentecostal pastor who recognised the need for deliverance but grew tired of the marathon power encounter sessions. He was also frustrated with his lack of 'tools' to help a couple in his church who were in great need of his help. Then you will hear from the couple themselves who were taken to a fellow pastor, one of my former students, who freely gave of himself to guide them through the process.

I share their stories with you in order to convey that what we are sharing is transferable. Pastors can and must get involved in helping people like the couple in this story. And I believe that what we are sharing isn't an evangelical or charismatic issue, nor is it a dispensational or covenant theological issue. It's not even a Protestant or Catholic issue. It's a Christian issue, centred in the truth of God's Word, part of the eternal purpose of God.

Pastor Simms's Story

I'm just a pastor who loves people.

Pat and her husband, George, started coming to our church through the invitation of Pat's brother and sister-in-law. From the very beginning I knew that Pat had problems: She found it hard to sit in church, was always squirming, and would often just get up and leave. There was never any eye contact, and she was extremely quiet and withdrawn into herself.

It took awhile for her to gain enough trust to begin to confide in me and ask for help. I told her I'm not a trained counsellor, just a pastor who loves people and is willing to listen and pray with them. I agreed to meet with her.

Pat came to our house and began to share the story of her life with my wife and me. I try to limit appointments to an hour, but she would often become so emotional that they would easily stretch to a couple of hours or more. I worked with her every week or two, desperately trying to help free her from life-long struggles with rejection, depression and pain.

Pat had blocked out a lot of her memory because of her hurt and unforgiveness. I tried to keep her focused on Jesus and the Word of God. I told her that she was like a runner with many hurdles in front of her. She would knock down some of the hurdles, jump over others, and some would seem just too big to jump over — but Jesus was at the end of the race. That started a long journey over a period of at least a year and a half, meeting at an average of every other week.

Pat was always in need and became dependent on me, so I had to be blunt and forthright with her and keep turning her back to dependency on Christ and her husband. She accepted it well, but she still would call me constantly, sometimes three or four or five times a week. It was very wearing to have someone that emotionally dependent on me. I prayed about this all the time, wanting to do the best I could as a pastor but having responsibility to other people in my congregation too. However, she was one of the more hurting people that I was aware of at that time. Satan had such a stronghold in her mind that it was easy for her to be deceived. She often felt that I was mad at her, and I was constantly having to convince her that I wasn't angry.

I worked mainly with Pat, but would occasionally take George aside to talk about her needs and his as well. At that time, though, I wasn't yet aware of all that had been going on in his life.

It was in the midst of this ongoing counselling that God led me into contact with Freedom in Christ Ministries, a ministry I had never heard of before.

That contact with Freedom in Christ was significant because about eight years ago, when I was an associate pastor in another church, the Holy Spirit impressed upon me that God would use me in a deliverance ministry. That very day, two demonised people came across my pathway seeking deliverance and help. I wasn't looking for demons under every bush and had not even read any books on the subject, so I wasn't programmed to give that kind of help.

The first year I got every basket case around. One lady manifested demonic activity in my office and God graciously delivered her, but there was such a distaste in my heart for the laborious, all-night marathon of the deliverance ministry. After about a year I was ready to give it all up and just preach the Scriptures. I didn't want anything to do with deliverance any more. It just didn't seem like there was enough power. I prayed, 'Lord, I can't imagine You labouring all night with people. You spoke and people were healed instantaneously, and that's what I long for, what I want to see.'

It was then that I attended a ministerial meeting where Dr Neil Anderson spoke in preparation for an upcoming 'Resolving Personal and Spiritual Conflicts' conference. As he shared, I was pricked in my heart. I saw that there was something more I needed to learn, that deliverance was much broader than I had thought, and it excited me. I went home and told my wife, 'This guy has really got something, and I'd like to know more about it.'

About the same time, God brought a very tormented young man into my life. There were terrible things that happened in Frank's life that he had never told anybody. He had more compulsive habits and behaviours than anyone I had ever known and was diagnosed as schizophrenic and manic-depressive.

I knew Frank needed deliverance, so I took him to a couple of pastor friends of mine and we had several long sessions with him, trying to cast out demons. There were some definite manifestations, but he didn't get free and my heart just yearned for him to be free.

By then his dad was ready to ship him anywhere in the world for a spiritual cure. He gave me the name of a man who might be able to help, and my wife spent five hours on the phone trying to track him down. When I came home that night, my wife said, 'You're never going to believe this. I didn't locate that man, but guess who I was put in touch with?' And then she told me that she had been directed to Dr Anderson's office, the very same person I had heard at the ministerial meeting.

My wife and I, Frank's parents and Pat all attended Neil's conference. Frank was hospitalised and unable to go. The first part of the week was wonderful teaching about our acceptance as God's children. But when we came to the final session when Neil took everyone through the Steps to Freedom, Pat got up and left the meeting. She hit a wall at the forgiveness issue. She just couldn't forgive, and became emotionally and physically upset. Dr Anderson said that some might not be able to resolve their conflicts in a group setting and would have to go through the steps another time.

I pursued this with Pat. I told her I'd heard about a pastor in a nearby town who had studied under Dr Anderson and who was helping people through the Steps to Freedom. I offered to contact him. She was fearful and torn, wanting to do it and then not wanting to. The voices she had been hearing had become 'friends' to her and she was afraid to expose her past and problems to a stranger, but since I had become her trusted friend she did let me make the appointment.

Pat's appointment lasted almost four hours. I didn't do much except be there for prayer support. A couple of times she almost got up and left, but the pastor coached her through the steps. When we walked out of the office she was smiling and happy. I was almost in unbelief. How could she get free so quickly when I had dealt with her all those months and there had been no resolution? But I knew God had used everything that had gone before to get Pat to this place.

My wife, however, was more sceptical. I guess she had sat in on too many of the long and tiring counselling sessions with Pat for her to believe a healing could come so instantaneously after our months of counselling effort had failed. That scepticism was short-lived. The women from our church went to a retreat and Pat went with them. After that weekend my wife came back and said, 'I can't believe Pat. She is an absolute miracle.' And that's really the best way to describe what happened in her life.

Pat began worshipping the Lord in our services and clapping her hands during the singing. She became free and she has remained free. As with anyone, there are times of little discouragements and defeat, but Satan doesn't have that stronghold on her mind; she has been loosed from that oppression.

Her husband George also found freedom over sexual spirits by going through the steps with that same pastor.

Frank's parents hoped this would be an answer to his problem as well. Unfortunately, Frank is not coherent enough just now to walk through all this and know what he is doing, but his parents were freed from some things in their own lives and we continue to pray for Frank.

God has brought a new understanding of deliverance to me. I see that it is a broader picture. We are so narrow-minded at times that we don't see that it's not just deliverance — it's the need to know who we are in Christ and what our authority and resources are to stand strong against the enemy. Included in that is the necessity of forgiveness. I think an unwillingness to forgive ourselves and others is the big issue that keeps so many in bondage.

We have seen a glimpse into the lives of Pat and George, and the results of a faithful pastor's efforts to help a very needy member of his church. Now let's look at Pat's story in depth.

Pat's Story

Our family never shared our feelings.

I remember things that happened at school during my childhood but not very many from my home life, except for some flashbacks that came during my counselling. Our family never shared our feelings and no one seemed to care about what was happening in each other's lives.

From the time I was four until I was six, my dad

molested me sexually. Finally I told my mum, 'I'm afraid of Daddy. He's hurting me.' I heard them arguing that night and after that my mum stopped talking to me. She was angry at me and cut my long hair into a boy's cut. I knew then not to tell my mum or dad my problems.

The neighbour boy raped me when I was eight. I was confused, depressed and angry a lot of the time, and afraid of rejection. I never had a lot of friends and didn't like life. In junior school, I cut my hands with glass, feeling that I was a horrible person and needed to be punished.

If I thought life had been hard while I was younger, it became worse in high school. I felt as though I was at the end of everything. I could never drink enough alcohol to stop the pain I was feeling and the voices I was hearing. But I tried. I drank before school, during school and on weekends, just to get through the days. When I finally got my own room at home, that became my refuge and I spent a lot of time there. It was a place to be away from my grandmother who lived with us and didn't like me.

When I was fifteen I took a handful of my mum's pain pills. Thinking about that and planning to do it was the most peaceful time of my non-Christian life. I waited until everyone was in bed and gulped them down, but I didn't take enough and just slept all the next day. My mum didn't say anything about it and sent me off to school the day after that. I cried in all my classes, and finally my teacher phoned my mum and asked her to pick me up. She took me to the doctor, and he directed us to a psychiatrist who put me on anti-depressants and began regular counselling with me.

One day when my dad picked me up after a counselling appointment, I had a strange feeling — as if he were another person. His eyes had an evil expression as they did when he used to abuse me. I think he was afraid that I would expose him to my doctor. I tried to overdose two more times after that.

While I was still in high school I got a job as a waitress at a Christian conference centre. I think I got it by lying on the application about my experience with God. One day I talked with another waitress about my problems and she introduced me to George. I'd heard he was a 'Jesus person'. I really didn't know what to think about someone who talked about Jesus all the time, but he was nice and kind of cute.

As I got to know him, I really appreciated how he listened to me and tried to help. Then one starlit December night we were standing in the parking lot after work, and he said, 'Pat, we can talk and talk and talk, but the only thing that is going to help you in your life is not going to be me. It's going to be the Lord.' That's when, at the age of seventeen, I invited Christ into my life.

My life changed then, as though a big pressure and heaviness was released from inside of me. I hungered to read my Bible and it didn't bother me that my mum thought it was just a phase I was going through.

I was grateful to George for leading me to Christ. We began dating and later he asked me to marry him. When we told my mother about our plans, her response to George was, 'Don't get her pregnant. I don't want another bastard in the family.' She had been pregnant before she married, and my sister had also been pregnant before marriage. Since sex was something we never discussed, it made me very angry and embarrassed that my mother would mention it that way in front of George.

When George started to put pressure on me sexually, the heaviness I had felt before I became a Christian came back. It was such a disappointment, since all the other men I'd known had also done that to me. But I felt that I really cared for George and I gave in to him, figuring, 'That's just the way men are.' A subtle change took place in my thinking at that time, the beginnings of a disillusionment with Christianity.

I was pregnant when we married, but a month later I lost my baby and spiralled down into depression. George began bringing marijuana home for us to smoke together, and I again contemplated suicide.

We were attending church sporadically and hearing glorious stories of others' victories. I agonised over why we were struggling so much. People said we should be different because we were new creatures in Christ, and that just made me feel more rejected, confused and hopeless.

I thought that having a baby would perhaps fill the void in my life. It seemed that no one needed me and that having a child who depended on me might make me feel better. When I found I was pregnant, I told George I wasn't going to use marijuana any more. He got angry and we fought over almost everything until our arguments became violent and he would often stomp out of the house.

I continued to be depressed most of the time, but I didn't realise my need for help until after my son was born. I would become angry with him to the point of rage. Two-and-a-half years later when my daughter was born, I began having nightmares of my son molesting or hurting her, and I found myself over-reacting to the simplest things he did wrong. This bothered me and I talked with friends and my pastor about it (not Pastor Simms), but they simply passed it off, saying, 'You're a good mum.'

I felt that the pastor rejected me because he expected a Christian to be able to live a perfect life. He was unkind and accusing and we did not feel welcome at that church. I also did not feel accepted by George's dad and stepmother, so we had conflict there as well.

Then George lost his job. It was at the time our associate pastor was moving to work at a church in another part of the state, and he suggested that we make a change and move with him, which we did.

A job opened up for George on a ranch that put us out in the middle of nowhere. We worked seven days a week and seldom went to church as a family. It was a difficult time, but George and I did get closer, having to depend on each other instead of everybody else.

We lived there for two-and-a-half years. All during that time I sensed hatred from my husband's boss. He kept asking, 'When are you leaving?' Finally, when we did leave, he didn't come to the farewell dinner the staff arranged for us.

We were offered a part-time job and given money to move back to our previous town. This angered the pastor who had invited us to move with him, so he dissociated himself from us as well.

I continued to live in torment, hearing voices, having terrible nightmares and drinking. I was anorexic, had struggles with suicide and was masochistic, cutting myself as I had in junior school.

After the move, George and I began attending the church my brother and his wife were attending, and I really loved Pastor Simms. He seemed to genuinely care about people. Yet, when I went to church it was torment for me. Suddenly I would feel an intense hatred for him. As I looked at him, flashes of terrible things happening to him would fill my mind. I dreaded it and looked for excuses not to go.

A friend told me about a care group for victims which I attended for a long time, but it was hard. The minute I entered the care group, the voices in my head and the horrible thoughts got worse. Nevertheless, I was able to let some of my anger go and not vent my rage against my son all the time. That helped me because I had felt so guilty, like I was destroying my son.

When I started counselling with Pastor Simms, I looked forward to every session. He was the first one who didn't just tell me that I was a new creature in Christ, that old things had passed away and I shouldn't be having any problems. Never did he make me feel like I was going crazy. I remember the first time I told him I was hearing voices in my head. He didn't laugh at me; he believed me.

Pastor Simms went through a lot trying to help me. I called him repeatedly, and when I struggled with suicide, he really supported me.

I was in a cycle of bulimia for two years, but I never told my husband about it. I don't know why, because he already knew of my struggle with drinking, voices and suicidal thoughts. But when I was hospitalised for a month because of my eating disorder, it was a major shock to him, and he felt betrayed.

Later, George told me that just before I was released from the hospital, he had slept with a girl from work. That sent me into shock. I didn't want to deal with that or anything: not the voices that tormented me every time I went to church...not the things that happened before, during or after the hospital...not my childhood...not anything. For two months, I withdrew to my house and closed up inside myself.

That's when Pastor Simms gave me the brochure about Dr Anderson's seminar. I wanted to go because I knew that somehow the Lord didn't want me to live like this for the rest of my life.

Listening to Neil was like hearing the story of my life. He talked about people hearing voices and thinking of suicide, and that was me. His teaching gave me incredible hope, until the last day when we were asked to go through the prayers of the Steps to Freedom. On that day I got terribly sick to my stomach, my head felt like it was going to explode, and I thought I was going to throw up.

I moved to the back of the auditorium and finally left. I just couldn't stand it. After awhile, I forced myself to return;

it was at the time when everyone was going through the for-giveness prayers. The voices inside me were screaming. I felt there was no one I was mad at, no one to forgive. Everyone was perfect; the only problem was me.

A couple of weeks later, I called Pastor Simms and told him that I couldn't make the list of people to forgive in a group setting. Besides, when I was sitting in the back of the church there had been no one crying around me. No one else seemed to be struggling with anything, while just think-ing about my problems brought me to tears. I didn't want to make a fool out of myself.

Pastor Simms said he had heard about another pastor who could take me through the prayers and that he would make an appointment and even go with me if I wanted. The day of the appointment, he met me there. I was feeling very nervous, but immediately felt safe as Pastor Simms and I sat down in Pastor Jones's office. I had never met this man before, yet as I looked into his face I sensed a peace and knew he was sincere and caring. He began by saying that if anything caused interference, such as the voices or feeling sick, I should let him know so that we could stop and pray, and it would go away.

I'd had daily, constant headaches since childhood, and they had increased in intensity during the last three years, ever since I went to the first care group. And now my head began to pound. When we came to the step on forgiveness, I got sick to my stomach as I had at the seminar. My hands were trembling. The voices were so loud they just about drove me crazy, and I remember asking, 'Don't you hear this?' At each one of these interferences, Pastor Jones prayed or led me to pray, 'In the name of Jesus, I command you, Satan, to leave my presence,' and the disturbance quieted. Going through those steps was the hardest thing I have ever done in my entire life, but with Pastor Jones's help, I did it.

At first, it didn't seem like anything had changed. But

then my mum came over and criticised my housekeeping as she had so often in the past. When that happened and it didn't bother me, I knew things were different! I was apprehensive starting back to church, but that was different, too. I enjoyed the worship and listening to Pastor Simms, and for the first time I could hear what he was saying because there were no voices. I don't think I've ever smiled so much! I'm so grateful for Pastor Simms's unconditional love that kept pulling me back to the church.

I have underlined all of the verses about who I am in Christ in my Bible. I still have lying thoughts condemning and accusing me, but I don't hold on to them like I used to. I recognise them sooner. Life still has its problems, but it is the difference between night and day, nothing like it was before. Actually, my whole outlook has been totally different from the day I walked out of Pastor Jones's office.

Pat's husband, George, was so encouraged and glad that she had finally been released from so much torment that he was eager to find help for himself as well.

George's Story

Nothing in my life had worked to free me.

I was excited when I looked over the books Pat brought home from the seminar. *This will work,* I thought. And how I desperately needed the help it promised, because nothing else in my life had worked to free me from Satan's sexual stronghold that was destroying me and my marriage.

I grew up with a dad who was a perfectionist, the kind of dad with whom you do your best and it still isn't good enough. I'd hit the ball over the fence in the back garden and he would say, 'Well, that was good, but let me show you a better way to swing the bat.'

My parents divorced when I was about five, and even though I was very young my mother began to depend on me. Then she married again, and my stepdad was an alcoholic and verbally abusive. As I grew up I worked for him and he, too, would tell me how much he needed me. I believe it was because of that I developed the attitude of needing to work for acceptance and approval, something I tried very hard to do.

The first time I saw pornography was when I was still with my real dad. He had some very vivid sexual-intercourse types of pornography. Also, my grandfather had a cabin with full centrefold pictures from *Playboy* on the walls. Both my dad and granddad had an attitude of disrespect and exploitation toward women.

My grandfather was also a 32nd degree Mason. He wore a Mason ring and was very politically influential in the city in which he lived. When he died, his funeral was a Mason funeral.

When I was thirteen, I began attending a small Catholic school. I wanted to be accepted, so I responded when one of the boys who seemed very popular showed an interest in me. He invited me over to his house when the only other person there was his older brother. We went into his bedroom and he wanted to have sex with me. I remember thinking, *I don't really want to do this, but I will if you will be my friend.* I had never had a desire for other boys before, but somehow there seemed to be a seed planted at that time that had a profound impact on my behaviour.

I never felt good about myself. I never felt accepted, so pornography was my way of feeling good. I never bought pornographic magazines myself because I could see all that I wanted from my dad's supply. I devoured my dad's

Playboy magazines and fantasised about the women pictured there, as well as those in the women's sections of catalogues.

I began masturbating when I was fourteen. I would pick out a girl in school and then I would go home at night and think about her and masturbate. I fantasised about the girls, but I didn't date any of them — I didn't talk with them and I didn't want a relationship. I just wanted sexual gratification. The whole focus was sexual.

I had intercourse for the first time when I was seventeen, and that wasn't even a date. I met the girl shopping where we were introduced by a mutual friend, and then we went to her house and had sex together.

When I was eighteen, I began to date. One date was the girl next door. The thing I remember about her is that I couldn't stand her laugh, but that didn't keep me from having sex with her. Again, it was all a sexual focus; I didn't even want to know her. That became a concern to me, because I felt I might never be able to really love a girl but would just keep finding things wrong that would break the relationship.

I would purposefully date only those girls I thought I could have a relationship with sexually, not looking for girls who had character or were respectable. Sex was all that I wanted.

When I was twenty, I became totally depressed and, for about a year, I didn't date any more. The Lord began to work in my life as a result of a human ecology class at university. I found out that our world is falling apart and that started a deep depression. To counteract that, I was smoking marijuana and drinking. I didn't know what my purpose was in life. I wanted to be loved, but I went with the wrong people. I wanted a future, but it frustrated me that there wasn't one.

During that time I was given a Gideon New Testament

by someone who was handing them out at the university. I began reading it and later, when I saw the movie *The Ten Commandments*, I began reading the Old Testament.

As I read the New Testament, it excited me that God could have a relationship with me. As I read the Old Testament, all I could think about was the rules I had broken. I thought, *How am I going to get out from under this? I'm so guilty.* So I got more depressed.

Another thing that made me feel helpless was my marijuana habit. I knew it was wrong. I wanted to quit but I couldn't. I remember telling God, 'Please do something. I want to quit. I want to be right before You, but I just keep hurting You and sinning against You.'

One day I took my bicycle, lunch and Gideon New Testament and said, 'I'm going to go out and have lunch with God.' I read the parable of the sower and, as I did, I understood the meaning. When I read the interpretation in the following verses and saw that my understanding was correct, it dawned on me that God was actually talking to me through the Bible. But I couldn't understand why God would when I had broken all His laws.

I knew that I needed to break my unhealthy relationships, so I moved back to the state where my mother lived. That summer I met a lesbian who invited me to her home with some other guys. They invited me to a bar where I began drinking and ended up French-kissing a man. A powerful, lustful feeling came over me, far more powerful than anything I had ever felt being with a girl, and it scared me to death. It was an inflamed, aggressive desire that came out of nowhere, and I realised that I was opening myself up to homosexuality. That scared me so much that I quit.

Around that time I read a weird book by Roy Masters who talked about Jesus in a twisted way. I got it at a bookstore where they were having a seminar on New Age. I started to meditate in my closet. I would put my hand in front of my head and bring it toward me and it was supposed to feel like my hand went right into my head. I was searching, and because this teaching had a 'Jesus' flavour to it, I was open to it.

I probably would have gone further into New Age had someone not left a copy of *The Late Great Planet Earth* with my sister. I read the whole book and, when I finished, I went outside and asked Jesus to be my Saviour. However, I wasn't sure that He really was.

A friend said, 'You have to meet my grandmother. She can help you.' When I did, I thought, *I've never met anyone so on fire for the Lord.* She had a deep personal relationship with Jesus. After talking with her one evening, I realised that I needed to take a definite stand and surrender my life to Christ. I went with her to church the next morning and when the invitation was given, she asked me if I wanted her to go forward with me. I told her, 'You don't need to. I'm on my way,' and that's when I gained my assurance of salvation.

From that day, I really wanted to obey the Lord. For a solid year I didn't masturbate and had no sexual problems of any kind. Then I moved back to the state where my dad lived and went to work at the Christian conference centre where I met Pat.

I loved the Lord and just wanted to serve Him, but one day I was listening to a national Christian radio programme and the speaker said something that gave the enemy a loophole. He talked about masturbation and didn't really treat it as a sin. He spoke of it lightly and said it was only a problem if it occurred over a long period of time. When I heard that, I went home that very night and said, 'Well, if You understand, Lord, then I guess I can do that.' The bondage was back, and once I started, it continued for years, even long into my married life.

A lot of girls worked at the conference centre, but Pat

stood out from them. I liked her quiet personality and I wanted to help her with her problems. She was also attractive and after a while we dated. Then I realised I loved her and wanted to marry her.

That marriage could have been so great, but I messed it up by coaxing her into having sexual intercourse with me before marriage. I'm responsible for that. She said later that she thought, *Why does he want to do this? We're going to get married.* But she didn't express herself and I wasn't sensitive to her feelings. I know the Lord has forgiven me, but this had its effect. The marriage night was a disappointment for her and for me.

With my sexual addictions and Pat's harassment with voices, nightmares, anger and depression, you can imagine what our marriage was like: Everything was out of control.

While doing some extra work for my dad, I found explicit pornography in his desk and would look at that and masturbate. Then I found that he had video-tapes. I had never seen a pornographic video before, and it was so powerful I couldn't believe it. It was ten times more powerful than a magazine. My sexual desire was building and building and got to the place where every time I looked at a girl it would be with lust.

At the same time Pat was trying to get free from her past through counselling with Pastor Simms, there was a girl at work to whom I became sexually attracted. It was like 'The grass is greener on the other side'. I was tempted on and off for about six months — a little cat and mouse thing, very subtle. The devil had set it all up, but I took the bait and had an affair with this girl. And the saddest part is that it happened at a time when Pat was in the hospital trying to get help. Afterward, I cried all night long, consumed with guilt like a huge rock on my heart. I was afraid I would lose my marriage. God had given Pat and me so much, and I took the chance of throwing it all away.

I was so totally bound. I had developed a strong desire for oral sex. One time, just before Pat went to the conference, I looked at myself in the bathroom mirror before taking a shower and felt like someone was grabbing me for sex. Another time I awoke at night feeling a woman on top of me with her mouth on me. It was a physical thing, beyond a dream. I know that there was something more than me involved, but there was no other person in the room.

After Pat went to the conference and I read the books she brought home, I wanted to go to see Pastor Jones, the one who led her through the Steps to Freedom. I was ready; I knew I needed that.

The appointment was arranged and I went. Afterward, I had an immediate confidence that I was free: The sexual desires were gone, but now my concern was whether I could stay free or if the bondage would return again.

I have to be honest in saying that even after I saw Pastor Jones and went through the Steps to Freedom, I did fall back into masturbation a few times. But I am learning how to resist now, and I know that when I fall it is an act of my will, a behaviour pattern, not an uncontrollable compulsion. I know that I am loved, forgiven and accepted by God, and I want my mind to be renewed and transformed by Him.

I used to think the battle with Satan was already over and that we couldn't have that kind of problem. I thought we had a new nature and it was just the flesh we were struggling with, not a spiritual issue. Now I know that just as there are angels around, so there are spirits around, and that they can suggest things to you but you don't have to choose to do them.

Pat was the one who reminded me of this by saying, 'You have a choice.' When she said that, it all came back to me. Jesus said, 'You shall know the truth and the truth shall make you free' (Jn 8:32). He is the truth and He has set me free. As I depend on Him, obey Him and choose His truth, He's keeping me free.

———————

A ministry for the church

Pastor Jones (a former student) got involved in helping to free people from spiritual bondage when he sat through a counselling session that he asked me to lead. He has since taken further training and has set up a group called S.W.A.T. (Spiritual Warfare Against Trauma!) Not only has he personally helped many find freedom in Christ, but he has seen several from his congregation receive training to help others as well. I always encourage pastors not to attempt this ministry alone as they will quickly get swamped and, eventually, forsake other important ministries of the church.

If your church is going to take this vital ministry seriously, then start with a small group of the most spiritually mature people whom you can prayerfully select. These people must themselves be free in Christ and living a balanced life. They must be committed to the authority of Scripture and the study of God's Word.

Patience is a prerequisite since no session can be done in the short time that is normally allotted for Christian counselling. If you start to lead a person through the Steps to Freedom, finish them in that session. If you don't work through all of the steps to a resolution, that person will leave and have the worst week of his life. The only exception is when you are dealing with severely traumatised people, which we shall look at in the next chapter.

The spiritual side of addiction

George's statement, 'There was something more than me involved,' brings up further issues on sexual addiction. I have already said that there is a spiritual side to addictive behaviours, but what he was experiencing is referred to as *incubi* and *succubi* (Latin terms for male and female sexual spirits). Most people will never divulge having had that kind of experience because it is so perverted. If I know that there has been incest or major sexual addiction, I ask coun- sellees if they have ever felt like a presence was coming at them for the purpose of sex. Oftentimes the image they see will be a man with a goat bottom or a woman with a snake bottom or any variety of grotesque images. Sometimes they wake up compulsively masturbating.

One man felt something fondling his genitals at night and at first thought it was his wife. Rather than stand against it, he participated with it. The experience grew until he could feel the weight of a female body upon him. Then he started to feel the presence in his car as he drove to work. Finally, he started to think, *What am I doing? Am I going crazy?* Since he participated with it, it grew in intensity and wouldn't go away.

When he saw me, he was going to bed at night with a Bible between his legs and pictures of Jesus on his body in an effort to stop that attack. No, it didn't work! He was not freed from that until he renounced his involvement with the sexual spirit, renounced using his body as an instrument of unrighteousness, and then asked God to forgive him. This sexual bondage can be really sick and evil. I have had peo- ple tell me that they feel a compulsion to tie something around their neck while they masturbate, and some people have thus died of auto-erotic asphyxiation.

The addictive nature of perversion

George's brief encounter with homosexual behaviour vividly depicts the diabolical nature of perverted sex. The rush that he felt when kissing the man, like the rush from mind-altering drugs, was not from his natural self nor from

God. Wilfully going against God's standards opens the door for Satan's sirens, and feeling that high is intoxicating and enslaving. Never indulge in perverted sex in the first place, but if you have already done so, renounce it immediately and determine to flee from immorality. Paul summarises this in Romans 13:12–14:

> The night is almost gone, and the day is at hand. Let us therefore lay aside the deeds of darkness and put on the armour of light. Let us behave properly as in the day, not in carousing and drunkenness, not in sexual promiscuity and sensuality, not in strife and jealousy. But put on the Lord Jesus Christ, and make no provision for the flesh in regard to its lusts.

10
Ritual Abuse and MPD

While conducting a conference in another state, I was asked to visit a young woman hospitalised in a psychiatric unit. She had read my books and wanted to see me. Her doctor permitted it, but a nurse had to be present and the session had to be taped. Marie had been ritually abused as a young child. I knew I wasn't going to be able to resolve much in the hour I was allotted, so I just tried to offer her some hope. To accomplish anything significant, the initial session with ritual abuse victims may take several hours.

I asked for her co-operation by sharing with me any mental opposition that she might experience during our time together. As mentioned before, the mind is the control centre. As long as Marie actively maintained control of her mind and brought to light the lying thoughts that were trying to distract her, we wouldn't lose control. It was a struggle, but Marie was able to maintain her focus for the hour. During that time I affirmed who she was as a child of God and the authority she had in Christ. I tried to help her understand the battle going on for her mind. As I started to leave, a different voice spoke out, 'Who are you, why don't you like me?'

What was that? A demon? An alter-personality? Your theological education and biblical world view will greatly influence your response. Since secular psychology doesn't accept the reality of the spiritual world, there is only one possible diagnosis: multiple personality disorder (MPD). In contrast, some deliverance ministries see only demons in such situations. Which is correct? How can you know? Are there other possible explanations?

Before you are too quick to answer, let me share another story. After a church speaking engagement, several people swamped me with questions. One inquirer was an attractive lady in her early thirties. She was describing her childhood abuse when her eyes started to glaze over. I could see that she was being mentally distracted and I didn't want her to be embarrassed. So I asked her if she would wait until the others left and then I made an appointment to see her the following week.

Elaine was an extremely intelligent lady with an established career. However, in her inner-personal life she was barely hanging on, even though she was seeing a secular counsellor and attending a twelve-step recovery group. While sharing her story, she suddenly proclaimed that one of her multiples didn't want to leave. I asked if she had been diagnosed as having a multiple personality disorder (MPD). She said she had; her counsellor had informed her that she had twelve alternate personalities.

I asked permission to address only her. After we walked through the Steps to Freedom, there was no trace of the multiples. In her case, I believe the voices were clearly demonic. In other extreme cases, I believe there is a combination of a spiritual stronghold and a fragmented mind caused by severe trauma.

A fragmented mind

What is a fragmented mind? It is a divided mind, the result of choosing to mentally detach from immediate, surrounding circumstances. Everybody chooses to do this in a limited sense. I remember times when my children were young when I would choose to disassociate from my surroundings. They would be arguing rambunctiously in the other room, and I would tune them out. I was caught up in what I was doing (maybe studying or watching my favourite sports on television), and I consciously (or subconsciously) chose not to deal with them because I didn't want to deal with something unpleasant, or I just didn't want to be distracted from what I was doing. Mentally, I was 'out in my garden' as my wife would say. 'Earth to Neil' was her way of getting me to tune in to what was going on around me.

No, I'm not weird. We all do that on a regular basis. People who live by the railway lines or airports learn to ignore the noise. A friend can be in the house when a train goes by and say, 'How can you stand this?' And the home-owner replies, 'Stand what? Oh, the train! It bothered me for about three weeks and now I don't even notice it.' We choose to think about that which is true, lovely, pure, etc. (Phil 4:8). We can choose not to deal with something that is unpleasant, to disassociate, and to think upon something else. But this can be unhealthy if we are detaching from reality as a means of coping. It can also become a pattern of denial.

Multiply the unpleasantness of children fighting and passing trains by one thousand, and you will get a sense of what it is like for those who suffer from a dissociative disorder. It is a defence mechanism caused by severe trauma whereby the person dissociates in order to survive. Unfortunately, the atrocities they have been subjected to are recorded in their memory bank. Physically, their eyes continue to see, their ears continue to hear, and their bodies continue to feel, but the mind chooses to ignore all those haunting horrors and creates an imaginary, 'safe' world in which to live.

Only one birth certificate

How are we going to resolve this dilemma? First, I don't prefer the term 'MPD'. It gives the impression that there are many people present in one body. There is only one birth certificate and there will be only one death certificate for these people...only one name will be written in the Lamb's Book of Life...and only one person will stand before God some day and give account for the choices made in this life.

Those who attempt to surface the various personalities and integrate them recognise that there is usually one dominant self, and they usually identify that part as the host personality. The MPD picture as seen by most mental health experts looks like this:

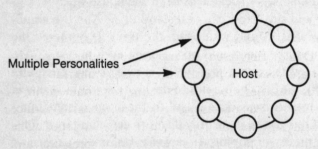

Multiple Personalities

Host

I don't believe this is the right perception. I prefer to think that there is only one person who has a fragmented mind. The picture would then look like this:

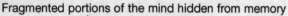
Fragmented portions of the mind hidden from memory

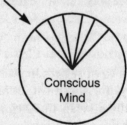

Conscious Mind

What to do with the old self

The psychological integration of personalities goes beyond the scope of this book, but I do want to set forth the necessity of establishing these dear people in Christ and resolving their spiritual bondage first. In many cases, the victims themselves cannot tell if a voice in their minds is an alter personality or a demon. As I was taking one young lady through the Steps to Freedom, she suddenly confessed on the step dealing with rebellion, 'I always thought that part of me was a personality.' She renounced the evil spirit and her participation with it, and commanded it to leave. The change in her countenance was remarkable to both of us. Many godless counsellors are trying to integrate demons into people's personalities, and many well-meaning pastors are trying to cast out personalities. Both extremes must be avoided.

Host personalities don't always like to admit that they are MPD and often resent the intrusion of other personalities that are less developed and sometimes embarrassing to them. Personalities are developed due to certain environmental factors. Each personality will involuntarily surface to perform the function for which it was developed. One personality may take over at work under pressure, and another personality may come out for social functions. Every MPD is different. In most cases fragmented personalities have not developed or learned to handle life in a Christ-centred way. In severe cases the fragmented personality may even be loyal to the cult that caused the fragmentation. Numerous cases have arisen where a committed Christian has split off at night and actually participated with satanists.

I usually explain to host personalities that their mind is like a house. They are the most dominant room in the house. As I help them clean up their room and establish them in Christ, they may be aware that there are other rooms in the house. The other rooms haven't been cleaned up, nor are they aware that they have been established in Christ. They must be acknowledged, won over, and set free from their past. Eventually they must all agree to come together in Christ. The following verses offer hope and provide direction for treatment.

Now those who belong to Christ Jesus have *crucified the flesh* with its passions and desires (Gal 5:24).

For you were formerly darkness, but *now you are light* in the Lord; walk as children of light (Eph 5:8).

Brethren, I do not regard myself as having laid hold of it yet; but one thing I do: *forgetting what lies behind* and reaching forward to what lies ahead, I press on toward the goal for the prize of the upward call of God in Christ Jesus (Phil 3:13,14).

Do not lie to one another, since you *laid aside the old self* with its evil practices, and have put on the new self who is being renewed to a true knowledge according to the image of the One who created him (Col 3:9,10).

When I was a child, I used to speak as a child, think as a child, reason as a child; when I became a man, *I did away* with childish things (1 Cor 13:11).

Whole in Christ

Nowhere in Scripture are we told to resurrect the old self or heal the flesh. We are made whole in Christ. 'And we proclaim Him, admonishing every man and teaching every man with all wisdom, that we may present every man *complete in Christ*' Col 1:28). We can't fix our pasts, but we can be free from them.

I tell all fragmented children of God that in the deepest part of their beings they are already whole. They are whole because they are complete in Christ (Col 2:10). All we need to do in our pastoral counselling process is resolve the issues that caused them to fragment when they were young. When those issues are resolved, they can be fully integrated. I pray, asking the Lord to put them back together again and make them complete in Him. Each individual personality must decide to become a part of the whole person and complete in Christ. We can't make them whole, but Jesus can. He came to bind up the brokenhearted and restore the soul.

God redeemed us and established our identity in Christ and then waits until we have an adequate support structure before He peels off layers of the onion to show us more and more of ourselves (see chapter two). I'm often asked, 'What if I have blocked out periods in my life that I can't remember?' Then keep pursuing God and be a good steward of what God has entrusted to you. At the right time He 'will both bring to light the things hidden in the darkness and disclose the motives of men's hearts; and then each man's praise will come to him...' (1 Cor 4:5). The only reason it is necessary to surface the past is to recall the experiences so that they can be resolved. If there isn't anything hidden in the darkness, then don't worry about it. If there is, it will be revealed at the right time.

Deal with the person

When past atrocities start to surface in a person, how can we tell if we are talking to a demon or a fragment of the mind? Sometimes it is difficult even if you have a lot of experience and spiritual discernment. Even the most experienced and mature people can be deceived. I certainly have been. In one sense, I don't try to differentiate; I always seek resolution by dealing only with the person. I never want the person to mentally lose control. Dialoguing with demons is always wrong, because that process totally bypasses the person and will surely lead to deception, since the demons all speak from their lying nature. People who believe what a demon tells them run the risk of being deceived.

At the time of the abuse, people may mentally disassociate as a defence mechanism in order to survive. When I counsel them, I don't want them to fall back into that old defensive pattern for survival. Christ is their defence now, and I do everything within my power to help them maintain control of their mind. If you encourage clients to repeatedly split off into fragmented personalities and explore their dissociative states without ever resolving anything or winning them over to Christ, you strengthen the existence of a defence mechanism instead of establishing Christ as their only necessary defence. Legitimate Christian counsellors don't want to reinforce the existence of any other defence mechanism. Why this one? Let's expose it and find a better way to cope in Christ. If you use secular counselling techniques on multiples that don't even work for a whole person, the multiples will disassociate even more. We must learn to resolve issues in Christ so that they can get on with their lives.

Just like the person who is hearing voices, people with disassociative disorders will be reluctant to share what is really happening in their minds. They will function like adults in society, but take on different traits at home. They could behave like a parent in the living room and then behave like a child behind closed doors in the bedroom.

One counsellor that I respect, who also understands the demonic, asks troubled clients, 'Do you ever feel as though you aren't whole?' If they acknowledge that as the case, he asks permission to talk to the other part of them. The *only* reason it is ever necessary to do this is to get at the memory of what happened to cause the person to disassociate in the first place. I prefer asking the Holy Spirit to reveal the things 'hidden in darkness'.

If you do probe around in a person's altered states, I strongly recommend that you pray together first, and have the person pray, asking the Holy Spirit to guard their heart and mind and to protect them from any deception. In asking permission to address a fragment, make sure that the person remains actively involved. After you have found out what happened to cause the disassociation, resolve the issues by having the person forgive the offenders and renounce any cult or occultic experiences.

In every case, I strongly recommend that you go through the Steps to Freedom with the host personality first, before you start probing into his or her mind. The process of going through the steps will resolve the issues for the host personality and hopefully eliminate any demonic strongholds. I have had people switch personalities as they go through the steps. I usually just continue on if they are co-operative. Often there is a need for one personality to forgive another. One Christian group takes every personality through the steps. I don't believe that is necessary, but each part must resolve his or her own issues. I will probe only after going through the steps when I (or they) sense that there hasn't been complete resolution.

When the issues are resolved, I've never had to return to those same experiences with them again. The causes for fragmentation and demonic strongholds are simultaneously resolved. The person will continue to recall the experiences, but the past no longer has a hold on him. His mind begins to look like this:

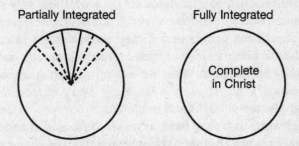

Partially Integrated   Fully Integrated

Complete in Christ

Old things have passed away

Many counsellors who try to integrate personalities from the past into the host personality without resolving the issues have bizarre experiences with their clients. Some of them will take on the various personalities in destructive ways — some will wander into the night and then call home or get picked up by the police, unable to explain how they got there. This kind of behaviour only happens when they disassociate. So why are we helping them to disassociate? Should we be encouraging victims to lose mental control by getting in touch with fragments of their minds without resolution? No person would want to leave a counselling session not knowing what happened. No one wants to disassociate. James 1:8 says that a double-minded man is 'unstable in all his ways'. It is that instability that we are trying to avoid by helping them to not lose mental control.

Whether the problem is a fragmented mind or a spiritual stronghold, I ask for one major co-operation from them. They must share with me what is going on inside. I explain that their minds are the control centre, and if they don't lose control there, then we won't lose control in the session. There are two reasons why they may not share. First, they won't reveal what is going on in their minds if they suspect that you won't believe them. They may also be embarrassed by the foul nature of their thoughts. I tell them that it doesn't make any difference if those thoughts are coming from within or from a loudspeaker on a wall, the only way they can be controlled by them is if they believe them. Sometimes I tell people that if they could see a demon, it would look like a little gnat with a great big mouth. Satan is a bully and a bluff. What we are up against is a major deception.

Some have a thought and immediately believe it or do it, not knowing that they have a 'no' button. It's as though they have no will. Rather than believing the thought or acting upon it, I ask them to share what they are thinking with me. It is very intense working with severe cases because it is so easy to lose them. Sometimes I make them get up and walk around just to prove to themselves that they have control and can exercise it. Sometimes it may be necessary to back off by slowing the process down.

The second reason they may not share with you what is going on inside is because they are being intimidated. Usually it is a threat that they will be thrashed when they get home, or a threat of harm to others if they get free. Parents are often threatened that the evil spirits will attack their children. I sensed that one person wasn't sharing everything with me, so I asked her, 'Are you being threatened that if you divulge what is going on you will be punished when you get home?' She acknowledged that she was. I said, 'This has nothing to do with your house or when you get home, only your freedom now. If you resolve it here, it will also be resolved at home, because the problem isn't in your home, it's in your mind.' She said immediately, 'I wish you could prove that to me.'

Getting it out in the open is what maintains control. God does everything in the light because He is the light of the world. The power of Satan is in the lie. When you expose the lie the power is broken. The power of the Christian is in the truth, so we are to speak the truth in love because we are members of one another.

A present popular psychological concept is the 'inner child of the past'. I have heard inner child of the past proponents say, 'There are two people I am counselling, an adult and a little child within him.' I disagree. Biblically, what is the inner-child of our pasts? Is it a part of our new identity in Christ, or is it a part of our old nature? Scripture assures us that we are not primarily products of our pasts but that we are new creations in Christ. 'Therefore if any man is in Christ, he is a new creature; the *old things passed away;* behold, new things have come' (2 Cor 5:17).

Don't misunderstand me; I have seen people curl into foetal positions as they recall childhood experiences. I have seen spontaneous age regression in personality when horrible atrocities are recalled. I know that many have stopped developing emotionally because of traumatic experiences, but there is only one person sitting in front of me, not two. For his or her sake, I don't want that person to disassociate as they recall a painful memory. I want them to learn a new way to deal with the past, a way based on truth.

'In reference to your former manner of life, you lay aside the old self, which is being corrupted in accordance with the lusts of deceit, and that you be renewed in the spirit of your mind, and put on the new self, which in the likeness of God has been created in righteousness and holiness of the truth' (Eph 4:22–24). We must acknowledge the emotional pain of our pasts and seek the healing that comes through forgiveness and establishing our new identity in Christ. We can't fix our pasts, but we can be free from them. In order to be free, we need to have a biblical means to get at repressed memories.

Getting at things passed away

I'll say it again because it is so very important. We need to first establish a person's present identity in Christ before we attempt to expose the past. That is the order of Scripture for a very important reason. When we examine the past from our present position in Christ, we are assured that we already have victory in Him. We are already whole in the inner man and complete in Christ.

Suppose the most skilled secular counsellor in the world was able to perfectly reconstruct a person's past, so that he or she is able to explain with precision what you are doing today and why you feel the way you do. So? Now what? The alcoholic would say, 'You're right, that is precisely why I drink. Care to have a drink with me?' Reconstructing the past has value, but by itself it offers no resolution. There must be knowledge of who we are in Christ in order to adequately deal with past problems. We don't want to put a bandage on a symptom, we want to heal the disease which is separation from God.

Legitimate counsellors know that they need to hear a person's story in order to resolve his or her conflict. Most counsellor training programmes focus on counselling techniques such as trust, warmth, congruence, accurate empathy, concreteness, immediacy, transparency, etc. These are essential if the person has total recall and just needs a trusting relationship in which to open up. But when memories are blocked, only God can reveal the things hidden in the darkness and disclose the motives of our hearts (1 Cor 4:1–5).

God brings things to light

'It is He who reveals the profound and hidden things; He knows what is in the darkness, and the light dwells with Him' (Dan 2:22). Satan does everything in the dark; like a thief in the night, he fears exposure. However, when a child has been subjected to satanic ritual abuse, even if it has been in his or her own home, be assured that God will bring it to light. 'If they have called the head of the house Beelzebul, how much more the members of his household! Therefore do not fear them, for there is nothing covered that will not be revealed, and hidden that will not be known' (Mt 10:25,26).

> And this is the judgement, that the light is come into the world, and men loved the darkness rather than the light, for their deeds were evil. For everyone who does evil hates the light, and does not come to the light, lest his deeds should be exposed. But he who *practices the truth* comes to the light, that his deeds may be manifested as having been wrought in God (Jn 3:19–21).

Most often, what God reveals will not be admitted to by the perpetrators. Most abusers will never admit their sin;

satanists won't because they are under penalty of death should they ever reveal their deeds. Their deeds are evil and they hate the light, and rarely will they come to it.

I don't ask a person to try to remember what happened; I have him ask his Heavenly Father to reveal truth to him. 'If you abide in My word, then you are truly disciples of Mine; and you shall know the truth, and the truth shall make you free' (Jn 8:31,32). Facing the truth can be a frightening thing for many. Some would rather not face it, but freedom can come only as the truth is known — the total truth, the truth of God's word and the truth about ourselves. David cries out in Psalm 51:6, 'Behold, Thou dost desire truth in the innermost being.'

God's Spirit at work

Making this truth known in the inner man is the great work of the Holy Spirit. Jesus said, 'I will ask the Father, and He will give you another Helper, that He may be with you forever; that is the Spirit of truth' (Jn 14:16,17). 'But when He, the Spirit of truth, comes, He will guide you into all truth' (Jn 16:13). We don't have any power to reveal truth in the inner man, nor is there a learnable technique that can accomplish this task. Our part is to work with God as told in 2 Timothy 2:24-26:

> And the Lord's bondservant must not be quarrelsome, but be kind to all, able to teach, patient when wronged, with gentleness correcting those who are in opposition, if perhaps God may grant them repentance leading to the knowledge of the truth, and they may come to their senses and escape from the snare of the devil, having been held captive by him to do his will.

This passage is not a power model for deliverance, but a kind, patient, 'able to teach' model that requires the pastor/counsellor to be dependent upon God. Only God can grant repentance, leading to truth, which sets the captive free. Part of our role is to be patient; it takes time to process major atrocities. Satanic ritual abuse (SRA) victims require many sessions, and even then I am careful not to move too fast. If you move too fast, the person will lose control.

I haven't had a person lose control in a long time, but if I did, I would stop the counselling process. Recently, and momentarily, I had a demon manifest and say, 'Who the (blank) do you think you are?' 'I'm a child of God,' I said, 'You shut up!' Immediately the lady was back. We can't be intimidated by these liars. I frequently have people say during a session that they have to get out of there. I say, 'Okay, I'm not going to do anything to violate your mind.' Every person who has left my office has been back within five minutes. Remember, it is the person's own responsibility to think.

Prayer journaling

Memory retrieval as enabled by the Holy Spirit may be divided into four categories. The first is prayer journaling. I sometimes encourage people to personally ask God to reveal the truth to them at home, between appointments, and then to keep a journal of what the Holy Spirit brings to their minds. Some have a trusted prayer partner they ask to assist them. When we meet again, I help them process what they have remembered. It's not uncommon for them to bring two or three pages of sordid detail.

If they are trying to do this on their own, I ask them to pray for God's protection. I suggest that they record exactly what the Holy Spirit reveals, not questioning, only recording every minute detail. Many will wonder if they are making it all up. One lady visited the home she was raised in to see if the details about her neighbourhood were what she thought the Holy Spirit enabled her to recall. To her surprise, the neighbourhood was exactly what the Holy Spirit revealed, even though she hadn't seen the place for twenty-five years. My memory of early childhood is vague at best, so how can these people remember early childhood experiences with such clarity? They are not remembering it: God is revealing it to them.

Praying through stalemates

A second retrieval method is to have people in your presence, asking God to reveal what it is that is keeping them in bondage. Usually I will do this if our time together has come to a stalemate, or after I have gone through the Steps to Freedom and there has not been a complete resolution. We have processed all we could, but something has not yet surfaced.

One lady was working through forgiveness and stopped at her third-year teacher. All she could remember was leaving the class and feeling bonded in some way to her. She forgave her for that, but we both knew that wasn't the real issue. I encouraged her to pray, asking the Lord to reveal what really happened in her third year at school. She did, and saw herself in a ladies room with the teacher, who was sexually abusing her.

How do we know that wasn't a mind game or satanic deception? One way is to see if there is any external confirmation. In this case, classmates shared years later that her teacher treated her badly. Also, she was sent home bleeding from her uterus with the explanation that she fell, though she never did remember falling. The bonding was spiritual, due to the sexual abuse, not the psychological bonding that can take place because of a close teacher/student relationship.

Never put suggested thoughts into another person's mind, even if you suspect abuse, because the mind is very vulnerable to suggestions. The vague memory of an honest hug by a parent can be easily distorted into inappropriate fondling or worse. As a pastor/counsellor, I pray for wisdom and guidance for myself, but I always have the person ask the Lord to reveal what it is that is keeping them in bondage. I would be suspicious of any details that come from a dream. Nightmares usually indicate some spiritual assault but are usually eliminated after a person has found her freedom in Christ. One lady accused her parents of sexual abuse because she had a dream, and a friend confirmed it through 'words of knowledge'. That is far too subjective to make accusations. There will almost always be some external confirmation of what they recall.

Satan attacks the minds of hurting people and does seek to discredit spiritual leaders by putting thoughts into the minds of their children or associates. I know of several cases where parents have been falsely accused by their children. Satan is crafty. If he can induce phony memories of ritual abuse and the accused are cleared of all charges, many will think that all the legitimate cases are phony as well.

What if people pray and nothing surfaces? Then I encourage them to continue their pursuit of God. Possibly the timing isn't right. Maybe there is nothing there and we need to explore another reason for their difficulties. You can only process that which you know. I don't think we ought to search for things in the past, but wait until God reveals the things hidden in the darkness.

Prayer for light on areas of bondage

The third way is to ask the Lord to reveal specific areas of bondage. Usually this is done as I walk people through the Steps to Freedom. In the first step, they pray and ask God to reveal all cult, occult, and non-Christian experiences they have had. After they pray, I ask them to check those involvements on a list of non-Christian experiences included in that step. But that list is not exhaustive; there are thousands of counterfeits, and sometimes people will add to the list. If I sense that they are brushing over that step, I will ask them to pray again that God will remind them of all the involvements they have had in this area. Chapter two of this book recounts the story of the woman who had completely forgotten that she had actively pursued the occult as a child. It was only after she had forgiven others that the Holy Spirit revealed her childhood pursuits.

When going through the forgiveness step, a person is asking God to reveal the names of people he or she needs to forgive. In most cases, some names will surface that they had consciously buried, and when they go through the process of forgiving, God will often bring back memories that have consciously (or subconsciously) been buried in the past.

If there has been sexual abuse, I have the person ask the Lord to reveal every sexual offence so they can renounce each one, saying, 'I renounce that (specific violation) of my body.' When they have finished, I lead them in a general declaration based on Romans 6:1,2,13 and 12:1,2: 'I renounce the use of my body as an instrument of unrighteousness, and I present my body to God as an instrument of righteousness, a living sacrifice holy and acceptable unto God.' If they are married, I will have them add, 'I commit my body to my spouse only.'

These people don't just remember an experience, they relive it. To wallow in the past is to keep them in bondage and strengthen the hold, so we should never reinforce what has happened by dwelling on it. When God grants repentance leading to the truth, we must participate with His leading, helping the person come to full repentance. Repentance literally means a 'change of mind'. The idea is, 'I used to believe that; now I believe this.' But the concept is much broader than mental acquiescence. Complete repentance means, 'I used to walk one way, now I have totally turned around and I am walking according to the Way, the Truth, and the Life. I renounce the lie and all the satanic experiences that I have had, and I announce the truth and all the reality of salvation that is mine as a new creation in Christ.'

Renouncing the kingdom of darkness

The fourth method of dealing with the past is to lead a person through several renunciations. I use this method early in the counselling process whenever a person has periods of his life blocked out. It is a generic means of checking out his past as well as resolving certain issues that accompany satanic ritual abuse (SRA). You have nothing to lose if there is no SRA.

In SRA, satanists do everything in direct opposition to Christianity. Satanism is the antithesis of Christianity. Satan is the anti-Christ. So I have clients renounce any possible involvement in the following way:

Kingdom of Darkness	Kingdom of Light
I renounce ever signing my name over to Satan or having my name signed over to Satan.	I announce that my name is now written in the Lamb's Book of Life.
I renounce any ceremony where I may have been wed to Satan.	I announce that I am the Bride of Christ.
I renounce any and all covenants that I made with Satan.	I announce that I am a partaker of the New Covenant with Christ.
I renounce all satanic assignments for my life, including duties, marriage, and children.	I announce and commit myself to know and do only the will of God and accept only His guidance.
I renounce all spirit guides assigned to me.	I announce and accept only the leading of the Holy Spirit.
I renounce ever giving of my blood in the service of Satan.	I trust only in the shed blood of my Lord Jesus Christ.
I renounce ever eating of flesh or drinking of blood for satanic worship.	By faith, I eat only the flesh and drink only the blood of Jesus in Holy Communion.
I renounce any and all guardians and satanist parents who were assigned to me.	I announce that God is my Father and the Holy Spirit is my Guardian by which I am sealed.
I renounce any baptism and all sacrifices that were made on my behalf by which Satan may claim ownership of me.	I announce that only the sacrifice of Christ has any hold on me. I belong to Him. I have been purchased by the blood of the Lamb.

For SRA victims, the above renunciations are an expansion of the confession made by the early church, 'I renounce you, Satan, and all your works and all your ways.' However, even the above renunciations are generic since all SRA victims have been subjected, in one form or another, to the above rituals and more. Again, as the Holy Spirit reveals the specific things hidden in darkness, they must be specifically renounced.

The way Satan counterfeits

Satanists refer to the book or scroll where they have people sign their names as the 'goat's book of life', and often the signing is done in blood. A colleague at our seminary brought in a fifteen-year-old who had participated in satanism for ten years. It was difficult, but she gave her heart to the Lord. Without looking up, she said, 'It's burning up, it's burning up.' 'What's burning up?' I asked. 'The book I wrote my name in!' Apparently, God gave her a visual aid to help her accept the fact that her name is now written in the Lamb's Book of Life.

Satanists also perform wedding rituals where the child or adult is wed to Satan, and afterward the wedding is consummated in horrible sexual violations. Eating flesh and drinking blood are also a regular part of their rituals as a counterfeit of John 6:53, 'Truly, truly, I say to you, unless you eat the flesh of the Son of Man and drink His blood, you have no life in yourselves.' John equates eating and drinking with believing (Jn 6:40,47,48), but they take it literally. One person I counselled couldn't eat meat because it solicited the recall of eating raw flesh. He renounced it in light of 1 Timothy 4, where we are told that it is those who are deceived (v 1), who 'forbid marriage and advocate abstaining from foods, which God has created to be gratefully shared in by those who believe and know the truth.

For everything created by God is good, and nothing is to be rejected, if it is received with gratitude' (vv 3,4).

Ritualistic cutting for the purpose of shedding blood is common in many pagan religions where people ritualistically cut themselves as a counterfeit of Christ shedding His blood for us. The idea is, we will become our own god and shed our own blood for ourselves. All blood pacts need to be renounced, even 'innocent' ones that were made with 'blood brothers' and 'blood sisters'.

Satanic sacrifice

Sacrificing is an attempt to establish ownership. We were redeemed 'with precious blood, as of a lamb unblemished and spotless, the blood of Christ' (1 Pet 1:19).

In satanic ritual abuse, children are often forced to do the sacrificial killing themselves for two reasons. First, it conditions them for future participation in the ritual. Often drugs are the means whereby they are forced into this compliance with horrible sexual abuse and sacrificial rituals. Or, they may comply because of threats of harm to others, as was the case with one girl who was told that her brother would be harmed if she didn't participate. And why do satanists perform these killings on innocent victims like babies, foetuses, and animals? They say, 'Your God sacrificed His only Son, who was perfectly innocent.' For them, the greater the sacrifice, the greater the power. And satanists are into power.

Second, children are forced to kill because it forces them into secrecy — a person is not about to tell the outside world that she killed an innocent child or animal. Her memories may be blocked out, but when she does recall the atrocities years later, she still can't share them because she assumes responsibility for having done it. She must take into account drugs or other ways she was forced into compliance. These people fear for their lives, both then and now,

because they know that sacrificing a life means nothing to
a satanist. If they refuse to do the killing during ritual, then
they will be killed, or at least they fear that possibility. Fear
is what keeps them from disclosing the things done in
darkness, and the present guilt and grief they feel is overwhelming.

Symptoms of ritual abuse

Two major symptoms of SRA are sexual dysfunction and
zero affect (no emotion). Most satanic rituals are ripping,
banging, violent sexual orgies, not sex as normal humans
would experience it. The ultimate high is sexual orgasm at
the time of the kill. This is the stuff extremely hard-core
pornography is made of, using animals, objects, and sado-
masochistic acts. In fact, hard-core pornography and
satanism are often linked together.

Those who have been abused in this way need to
renounce this sexual use of their body and forgive the sexual abusers. One victim could clearly recall twenty-two sexual abusers. Could we honestly expect her to forgive those
multiple offences? Remember, for her to forgive them is not
excusing what the abusers did; it is freeing her from the
past.

The zero affect is the result of programming. The victims
are conditioned to believe that if they cry, someone or
something will be killed, or great physical harm will come
upon them. One lady recalled her pregnancy being aborted
for the purpose of sacrifice. When she screamed in horror,
they told her that if she cried another baby would die. As a
result, she had not been able to cry for years. I told her to
renounce that experience and renounce the lie that her crying would result in the death of anything or anyone. As
soon as she did, she sobbed for several minutes.

A pastor's wife drove several miles to attend a conference. She had just started recalling SRA and was puzzled by

her own inability to cry. She had no specific memories of events, only vague, shadowy images. I said, 'You may not understand this, but I want you to renounce the lie that your crying would result in the death of anyone.' As soon as she did, a tear started to trickle down her cheek.

Every specific assignment needs to be renounced. Like curses, assignments are made during rituals. For instance, I was working through the step of forgiveness with one victim. When she came to her mother, she couldn't forgive her. Not because she didn't want to, but because she couldn't connect emotionally with one particular experience. She had already forgiven her father who took her to the rituals, which was a painful and emotional process that took a great deal of time. She could clearly recall one experience where her father raped her and she cried out to her mother to rescue her but she didn't. It was like she was telling a story but couldn't connect emotionally to the experience. (Usually when they describe the experience, there is a great deal of emotion expressed because they don't just recall it, they relive it.)

We weren't able to resolve that so we went on to the other names on her list (which I never prefer to do), and she came to the name of a woman she recalled from the SRA who, she said, 'was assigned to be my mother.'

'That's it,' I exclaimed. 'Renounce that assignment.' She said, 'I renounce the assignment of that woman being my mother and announce that I have only one mother who is (name).' As soon as she did that, she cried hysterically, 'My mother abandoned me.' She spent the next ten minutes reliving the horror of her mother rescuing her brother from her father, but not her.

Another person recalled a family being assigned to be her satanic parents and their son to be her husband. This was a prominent family in the church she was raised in. She, too, didn't have any emotional freedom to cry or feel deeply.

She was impregnated by the son, and her baby was aborted and sacrificed. When she cried hysterically, a baby was put in her arms. That baby would also die if she cried, they said. When she renounced that lie, she was freed to feel emotion and cry. She also renounced the assignment of the son to be her husband. When she left my office, she said, 'Now I can get married, now I can have children.' Until those assignments are recalled and renounced, they keep people in bondage.

One lady recalled an assignment given to her when she was in her fourth year at school. A young boy in the group was to be her husband and they were to bear a child. Any other man would reject her and any other offspring would be killed.

This lady eventually married another man, but was paranoid about being rejected by him and was fearful of having children. When I encouraged her to renounce that assignment, she became terrified. She told me she just couldn't do it, and I assured her that she not only could, she must. I learned later that her mind was being pummelled with lies and visions of babies dying. I said, 'This has nothing to do with any future babies, this has only to do with your present freedom.' I told her that God would protect any future offspring. She renounced the assignment, broke the satanic stronghold, and collapsed in tears. She is now free to have babies, understanding why she wasn't before.

As the Holy Spirit brings back memories, I have the person renounce the lies and assignments, proclaim the truth, and accept only God's will for their life. (Knowing God's will and understanding His leading is the subject of my book *Walking in the Light*.) This needs to be done specifically and verbally as memories are recalled.

It's only the Lord who freed captives

As we seek to help others, we find that every case is different and in each circumstance, we need to wait patiently upon the Lord and rely upon His leading, because He is the only One capable of setting captives free. Our role is to cooperate with God in helping His children find their identity and freedom in Christ.

You have heard from several dear people in Part 1 of this book who were desperately crying out to God for freedom. I pray that their stories will help you understand what is happening to many people in your church. Perhaps it is happening to you. It is my prayer that we have given you some hope and direction to find the freedom that Jesus purchased for you on the cross. God loves you. He wants you free *in* Christ!

Here is one final testimony, but this one you will recognise from Psalm 18:16–19 (NIV):

> He reached down from on high and took hold of me; he drew me out of deep waters. He rescued me from my powerful enemy, from my foes, who were too strong for me. They confronted me in the day of my disaster, but the LORD was my support. He brought me out into a spacious place; he rescued me because he delighted in me.

Praise His Name!

Part 2

A WAY OF ESCAPE

Acknowledgements to Part 2

The time it took to write this book was but a fraction of time I have spent with hurting people. Most have been victims of sexual abuse, and many have been carried away by their own lusts, enticed by a world spiralling out of control into a cesspool of sexual madness. Some had become abusers, while others degenerated into deviant sexual behaviours. They all bore the shame of a defiled temple and cowered under the accusation of the evil one.

If you saw only their behaviour, you would never let your son or daughter marry one of them or let your children be around them. Ironically, they *are* your sons and daughters, other family members, friends, and co-workers. If you heard their story you would weep with them. Perhaps you are weeping now, because you know this book is for you. I want to acknowledge all of you who had the courage to face the truth and find the way of escape. Your willingness to share with me may have been motivated by desperation, but your story has helped shape my life and has driven me to search the Scriptures for the only hope for sexual freedom.

I also want to thank Dr Robert Saucy for his wonderfully guided theological mind and helpful suggestions. I thank Dr Charles Mylander for his feedback and his thoughtful comments in the Foreword. I appreciate your friendship and support of our ministry more than words can express.

I am especially grateful to Russ Rummer, a dear colleague in ministry, for his extensive contributions to this book. Some of the illustrations and insights have come from his many hours of counselling people who struggle in sexual bondage. Russ, you are a highly valued and much appreciated member of the Freedom In Christ staff.

Again I am indebted to the editorial contribution of Ed Stewart. Ed, your gift of writing is a gift to the Church. Special thanks to Barb Sherrill and Eileen Mason, who were a delight to work with, as was the entire crew at Harvest House. I am also grateful for my faithful staff at Freedom In Christ Ministries, who filled in for me during my absence and stood behind this project in prayer.

The actual credit goes to the Lord, who is the way of escape. He first delivered me from my own struggles and enabled me to stand.

Finally, I want to thank my wife, Joanne Anderson. You prayed for me, read my unedited first attempts, and generally put up with me. You are my helpmate, best friend, and confidante. I love you and dedicate this book to you, and I commit myself to be faithful to you until Christ calls me home.

Neil T. Anderson

11
There Is
a Way Out

Jon's problems with lust and sexual bondage literally began
in a bin. That's where he came into contact with pornography for the first time as a boy. Curiously pawing through a
rubbish bin on the military base where his father was sta-
tioned, Jon discovered more rubbish than he had bargained
for. Somehow he knew he should bury the dirty magazines
and leave them there. But the lewd, tantalising pictures captivated him. As Jon poured over the pages in secret wonder,
the images burned into his mind. The hook was set.

Abruptly awakened to a sinister but exciting new world,
young Jon began looking for other sources of stimulation.
He soon discovered his father's stash of *Playboy* magazines
and secretly returned to that hiding place often to fuel his
unhealthy desires.

As he entered puberty, Jon became more adept at finding illicit material. He became entranced with sexual fantasy and frequent masturbation. With every experience, the
grip of pornography on his mind strengthened. Jon's covert
forays into the darker side of life also led him into experiments with alcohol, drugs, and sexual activity. Ironically, he
retained the external image of a nice Christian boy. During
high school he was active in Youth for Christ and involved
in church, even though his parents did not attend.

When Jon turned 18, he enrolled in a Christian university.
But his secret vices accelerated rapidly. His use of alcohol
and drugs turned frightfully self-abusive. His uncontrolled

desire to satisfy his sexual cravings escalated into the hard-core realm of pornographic movies. His focus at university turned from his studies to wild parties and sexual escapades. To his embarrassment, Jon ended up failing his exams at university.

Hoping to find direction for his life by following his father into a military career, Jon joined the Navy. But things only got worse. Temptations to substance abuse and pornography seemed even more abundant. A random test-ing programme uncovered Jon's drug problem, and he was repeatedly passed over for promotion.

Lying in the base hospital after a job-related injury, Jon came to the end of himself. He cried out to the Saviour he had only pretended to serve during his youth and turned his miserable life over to Christ. The change was miraculous and instantaneous. His dependence on alcohol, drugs, and tobacco seemed to vanish. His desire for pornography and illicit sexual encounters was suddenly gone. Such peace at last!

But Jon's relief was short-lived. Three weeks later he chanced to find an enticing magazine in a men's room on the base. Yielding to the temptation, he began a new cycle of sin, guilt, and frustration. He was overwhelmed by shame at letting God down and plunging himself back into the mire of immorality. He knew of no one he could talk to who would understand his plight. He felt terribly alone.

After an honourable discharge from the Navy, Jon met and married Angela, a beautiful Christian woman who knew nothing of his sexual addiction. Hoping to appease the God he had disappointed, Jon returned to university, prepared for the ministry, and entered Christian service. Yet he remained in secret slavery to pornography and substance abuse. The inner conflict tortured him and his relationship with Angela with severe stress. He desperately yearned for something to break the destructive stranglehold he seemed powerless to escape.

Jon hoped the birth of their first child and a lucrative new job in sales was the answer. But business trips far from home only opened a new chapter for his sexual addiction. Pornographic movies were plentiful on the hotel cable channels, and printed material, cleverly hidden by previous guests, could be found in dozens of places in each room. Instead of finding release in his new position, Jon was further encouraged in the downward spiral of his bondage.

When Angela discovered the depth of Jon's problem and confronted him with it, he broke down and confessed everything. Angela forgave him and promised to stand with him through his recovery. Jon felt relieved at last to be free of the secrecy and to walk in the light of the truth.

But sadly, Jon didn't remain in the light for long. Soon he was back to his old destructive habits. Only this time Angela dropped a bomb. She would no longer tolerate the lies and selfish behaviour that were ruining their family. After six years of marriage, she wanted a divorce — and she was determined to get it.

Jon suddenly realised that his dreams for a family and a lifetime of happiness were gone. His success in marriage, business, and Christian ministry had been torpedoed by a dark appetite he felt helpless to control. In despair, he flogged himself repeatedly with the thought, *If I had only left that rubbish in the bin...*

An all-too-common trap

Jon's sad experience as a Christian enslaved to lust and sinful habits is, unfortunately, neither an anomaly nor an isolated incident in our culture. I have talked to literally hundreds of individuals like Jon. Some of them come to me perplexed that their minds are constantly peppered by unholy thoughts related to sex. Others confess their failure

to completely overcome sinful habits in this area which have
stunted their daily victory and spiritual growth. Still others
vent their secret agony at being slaves to uncontrollable lust
and sexual immorality.

You may say, 'You must be talking about unbelievers,
especially when you mention people being slaves to sexual
sin.'

No, I'm not talking about unbelievers. The vast majority
of the people I counsel are evangelical Christians attending
churches like yours and mine. Many of them are in positions of service: teachers, choir members, committee members. Some are in positions of lay leadership: deacons,
elders, board members. A surprising number of the people
I deal with are even in full-time Christian ministry or in
preparation for it: pastors, missionaries, officers in parachurch organisations, students at Bible college and seminary. It's very obvious to us that Christians at every level of
growth and influence are vulnerable to temptation, bad
habits, and bondage related to sex.

Sexual bondages are nearly as prevalent inside the
church as they are outside. I surveyed the graduates of one
of America's better theological seminaries on the topic of
sexual temptation. Sixty per cent said they were feeling
guilty about their sexual life. Nearly half of that sixty per
cent stated that they would sign up for an elective class for
credit — if confidentiality could be ensured — which
promised to help them find sexual freedom.

Several years ago a well-known Bible teacher presented
a series of messages on sex in our seminary chapel. He
urged students to get their sexual act together before they
began their ministries. 'We don't need another pastor falling
into sexual immorality and bringing more embarrassment
to the name of our Lord Jesus Christ,' he exhorted.
Recently this man lost his ministry due to sexual immorality.

Two Christian leaders who taught in our Doctor of

Ministry programme lost their ministries for the same reason. Many other Christian leaders have fallen. Some of them are friends of mine for whom I care deeply. And I am keenly aware that, apart from the grace of God, I also could end up like them. Don't be fooled: Christian people are not impervious to stumbling into sexual sin. And those who think they are beyond the range of the fiery dart of sexual immorality tend to be the ones most vulnerable to be pierced by it.

You may also be thinking, 'You're surely talking about men here, not women. Unhealthy preoccupation and involvement with sex is a man thing.'

No, I'm not only talking about men. Clearly, the masculine gender seems to be the primary target of Satan's assault on biblical morality, as evidenced by the tidal wave of pornography catering to men which floods the print and electronic media. But my experience has revealed that many women are also captivated by the lure of lustful fantasies and carnal activities.

Count the number of television soap operas in syndication — daytime dramas that cater to the fantasies of women. Consider some of the sleazy topics being discussed on the daytime talk shows. Notice the amount of shelf space in secular bookstores given to romance novels — those books with a bare-chested hunk and a swooning heroine entwined on the cover. Think about the increasing number of tabloids crowding the supermarket stands offering to tell all the juicy details about the immoral liaisons of Hollywood's hot stars.

Judging by the billions of dollars invested, there is clearly a huge market niche of women devouring this material. At every turn the biblical values of virginity, marital faithfulness, and even heterosexuality are being subtly or blatantly mocked. And sadly, many Christian women have been unwittingly sucked into this dark whirlpool of temptation to immorality — if only in their thoughts.

Like the frog in the kettle

When Jon first became involved with pornography, you could have asked him, 'Do you intend to come under the control of this stuff?' He probably would have answered, 'Of course not. I just want to look at it and think about it and enjoy it for a while. I won't let it control me.' But when his life hit bottom many years later, he was forced to admit that what began as a titillating fascination had subtly enveloped him in its paralysing tentacles. Jon had lost control and come into bondage to sex.

That's the ultimate destination of even the most 'innocent' or insignificant sexual temptation which remains unchecked: loss of control, leading to sexual bondage. None of the men and women I have counselled ever intended their sexual fantasies to control them. But, like the proverbial frog in the kettle of water, they were unaware that their secret fascination with pornography or sexual fantasy was slowly cooking them into submission. Early in the process both the frog and the sexually tempted Christian are able to jump out of the hot water. But after continually compromising with and acclimatising to their potentially deadly environments, both become weak and unable to escape the trap.

I call that trap sexual *bondage*, even though much of society today labels it sexual *addiction*. What's the difference? Virtually none. Both describe the condition of being under the control of sexual lust. However, I prefer the term 'bondage' because it relates to the biblical concept of being a slave to sin, which is at the root of the problem. The apostle Paul referred to himself as a bond-servant of Jesus Christ, and that's what all Christians are called to be. Whenever we allow anything or anyone to have a greater hold over our lives than Christ, we become a slave to it. We have elevated the power and authority of that person or thing over the power and authority of Christ in our lives, and that's sin.

I want to show in this book that, as bond-servants of Christ, we can and should have victory over sexual immorality and bondage to sex because Christ has defeated Satan and sin. Since we can do all things through Christ who strengthens us (Phil 4:13), we can find freedom in Christ from sexual bondage. The recovery movement believes that the answer to sexual *addiction* is therapy and behaviour modification. I contend that the answer to sexual *bondage* is repentance and faith. When we renounce what we have done as sin and choose to believe the truth, we will be set free.

The issue of losing control to sexual desires was clearly illustrated to me when the 'free sex' movement was gaining momentum in America. I was asked to visit a Marriage and Family class in a local secular college and present the Christian perspective on the topic, which I'm sure few students really understood. The class was made up primarily of women with a few men also present.

One young man was clearly disinterested in my presentation. He pulled his desk away from the group and read the newspaper while I talked. Apparently he was listening, however, because he frequently interjected a vulgar noise in protest of my beliefs.

When I opened the floor for questions, one young woman asked, 'What do Christians believe about masturbation?'

Before I could answer, the young man announced proudly so everyone could hear, 'Well, I masturbate every day!'

There was an awkward silence as the other students

anticipated my response to his challenge. 'Congratulations!' I said at last. 'But can you *stop* masturbating?'

The young man was silent for the rest of the discussion. When class was dismissed, he waited for the other students to leave. As he strolled by me, he taunted, 'So why would I want to stop?'

'I didn't ask if you *wanted* to stop,' I replied. 'I asked if you *can* stop, because if you *can't*, what you think is freedom is really bondage.'

That's the issue: freedom versus bondage. If you are involved in sexually impure thoughts or deeds — activities that are clearly in opposition to God's Word, stop. If you *can't* stop doing what you know you shouldn't do, then you, like Jon, are in bondage to those thought patterns and activities and need to find your freedom in Christ. This book was written to help you succeed where all your self-determination, will-power, and counselling appointments have fallen short.

Levels of involvement

What is included in the broad category of sexual bondage? We can find some helpful answers in the work of those who study sexual addiction. Dr Patrick Carnes, arguably the leading secular expert in the field of sexual addiction, has studied persons caught in the trap of compulsive sexual activity. In his book, *Contrary to Love*, he describes three descending developmental phases of sexual addiction.[1] An individual can be in bondage at one level without necessarily descending to the next. Each successive phase is characterised by increased relationship-avoidant behaviours.

Phase one: normative activity

The first level consists of behaviours that are generally considered normative in secular society, meaning that they are fairly common and accepted — though reluctantly by some — in our culture. These behaviours often employ exploitation and victimisation — short of criminal violence — as a basis for greater sexual excitement. They include:

Sexual fantasy and masturbation. Our secular society generally views fantasy, whether or not it is accompanied by physical self-stimulation to orgasm, as an accepted and sometimes healthy diversion from the stresses of real life. Sexual fantasy is judged by many to be a harmless release of sexual energy because, technically speaking, a mental act won't violate anyone or constitute unfaithfulness to a spouse.

Thus, a man may see nothing wrong with fantasising about having sex with a female colleague, a friend's wife, an erotic dancer in a nude bar, a seductive image on the video screen, etc. A woman may project herself into a romance novel and vicariously submit to the love-making of the handsome, flawless hero. Fantasising is often accompanied by masturbation as the individual seeks the physical climax his or her fantasy partner cannot provide. But every fantasy becomes another link in a chain encircling the soul. Eventually such a person has difficulty interacting with others without being dominated by impure thoughts and desires.

Pornography. Anything which is intended to arouse sexual desire falls under the heading of pornography. Though some pornographic materials are still considered illegal, our society is inundated with expressions of pornography which, though perhaps offensive to some, are acceptable to many. Magazines offering 'entertainment for men,' such as *Playboy* and *Penthouse*, abound. Novels line the shelves of our bookstores and libraries which describe in graphic detail every possible perversion of God's design for sex.

Sexually explicit films rated R, NR-17, and X have migrated from the adult bookstore into our local cinemas as films for 'mature audiences'. Cable television channels can be accessed which broadcast one sex act after another — homosexual as well as heterosexual — under the banner of 'adult entertainment'. And network television doesn't seem to be far behind.

Add to this list the sexually explicit lyrics in some popular music, live sex shows in many city centres, phone-in sex lines, and now even computer sex. The seemingly unquenchable demand in our culture for sexual stimulation is matched by a seemingly endless and varied supply. And most of it is legal and easily accessible.

Satan, the god of this world, has orchestrated the subtle erosion of moral standards in the Western world. He has numbed the senses of this generation to sexually explicit material so we no longer react to it. A Christian who dabbles in pornography is like a soldier marching blindfolded through a minefield. Sooner or later poor judgement and careless experimentation will explode in his or her face.

Illicit affairs and/or prostitution. Premarital and extramarital sex seems to be widely accepted today (except perhaps by the individuals who are cheated on). Conversely, abstinence and marital fidelity are often viewed as outdated and prudish.

The media is doing a high-powered sell job on the issue. Movies and television sitcoms make light of adolescents losing their virginity and singles hopping from bed partner to bed partner. Characters who can't or won't 'score' are often pictured as oddballs. Daytime dramas in America glamourise the violation of marriage vows and justify adultery in the name of 'true love'. Frequenting houses of prostitution or sexual massage parlours or bath houses to pay for sex is often treated comically. Furthermore, homosexual relationships are being pictured as a viable alternative lifestyle. The relentless theme is that consenting adults are free to follow their sexual urges apart from a commitment of marriage.

Christians who allow themselves to be influenced by the world's declining standards with regard to sexual activity are morally drifting downstream toward dangerous waters and an eventual waterfall. Every compromise leads to another, and a plunge into sexual bondage awaits them.

Phase two: indecent activity

The second phase of sexual addiction finds the individual taking liberties which are considered indecent if not criminal by much of society. Persons involved in these types of activities often seek to intensify their sexual pleasure by performing for an audience — usually an *unwilling* audience. These people may already be in bondage to one or more activities in phase one. But like a drug addict seeking a higher high, they seek greater risk in order to secure a greater sexual thrill.

Behaviours in this category include exhibitionism (also known as indecent exposure, displaying genitals in public, flashing, or streaking), voyeurism (sexual arousal through viewing sexual objects or activity, 'peeping toms'), transvestism (cross-dressing), bestiality (sex with animals), obscene letters or phone calls, fetishism (sexual arousal from objects such as clothing), necrophilia (sex with corpses), and a variety of indecent public acts.

Phase three: extreme activity

Persons at this level violate their victims with painful and criminal acts. The nature of these acts is generally considered so vile that the perpetrators are often viewed as subhuman and incorrigible. This is the level where we find sociopathic sex criminals such as serial murderers Ted

Bundy and Jeffrey Dahmer. Behaviours at this level include child molestation, incest, rape, and sadomasochism (giving and receiving pain to heighten sexual pleasure).

According to Dr Carnes, not everyone progresses automatically from one phase to the next. Rather, the phases are a means of categorising sexual addiction according to the degree of personal risk involved. He notes, however, that a person's sexual behaviour seldom remains frozen at one level but includes a wide range of expressions drawn from other tiers. Thus someone who victimises others with indecent exposure may also be in bondage to pornography and involved in an illicit relationship.

It may seem unthinkable to you that someone who is 'innocently' hooked on *Playboy* or peep shows could descend to the depths of a serial sex criminal and murderer. But don't underestimate the power of the kingdom of darkness when a doorway is willingly and persistently opened to it. The only safe recourse is to slam that door shut and return to the light of moral purity as presented in God's Word.

You can be free!

You may have picked up this book because you have a problem with nagging sexual temptations or defeating bad habits in this area. For example, perhaps you have trouble staying away from sexy reading material. You once rationalised that *Playboy* magazine, the lingerie catalogues your wife receives in the post, or novels with explicit sex scenes were harmless entertainment as long as you didn't act out the temptations and fantasies that filled your mind. But now you're aware that you have flown far past the browsing stage. You know where to get the materials you want without being recognised. You throw away your stash from time to time, but in a few days or weeks you're back for more. You're hooked on the stuff, and you find yourself craving even more risque pictures and stories.

Maybe your biggest problem is with obscene movies and videos. You tell yourself that you watch them for the story while trying to ignore the steamy sex scenes. After all, a lot of Christians attend movies featuring sex, violence, and nudity without consequences — or so it seems. But not so with you. You can't get enough of the erotic scenes which are steadily lining the walls of your mind with posters that feed your sexual fantasies.

Perhaps you have jokingly told your friends that you are a soap opera and romance novel addict. But deep inside you know it's no joke. You plan your day around the soap operas, and the Bible on your bedside cabinet has been buried under a stack of trashy books for months. You don't want to be dependent on that stuff for a sexual and emotional buzz, but you can't seem to help it.

Or maybe you are secretly trapped in another unscriptural sexual behaviour: an extramarital sexual relationship; an insistent fascination and attraction to homosexuality; or tendencies toward exhibitionism or sadomasochism. You know that what you're doing is wrong. You wish you could retrace every misstep that got you into this mess in the first place. And you realise that every act drives you deeper into the darkness of your bondage.

But try as you might, you can't stop — and you don't know what to do about it. You long to be free, but you're afraid that you are headed down the same dark, dead-end street that caused Jon and Angela, at the beginning of this chapter, so much pain and heartache.

If you really want to be free from your sexual bondages, I have good news for you. You can be free! Jon, who is an acquaintance of my colleague in ministry, Russ Rummer, is living proof. You will be interested to hear the rest of his story.

When Angela told Jon to leave their home, it drove him to the breaking point. He went to the mountains with some friends to pick up the pieces. One of Jon's friends gave him my book, *The Bondage Breaker*, and he devoured it. He learned about the origin of the sexual strongholds which had ruled his life for so many years. Then in one three-hour session with God, Jon followed the Steps to Freedom found in *The Bondage Breaker* and in the Appendix of this book. He renounced the strongholds in his life and dealt with a number of issues which had contributed to his bondage. Jon later told Russ, 'It was the most freeing time I have ever spent with God.'

Then Jon became involved in a small group of others who had been set free from various bondages. Jon states, 'God began a process of rebuilding me from the ground up. It appeared that He wanted me to learn something clearly. I had to be real about the pain I had caused my wife and how broken I felt about being kicked out of our marriage.'

For the next couple of months God put Jon through a kind of spiritual army training camp. Through the support and prayers of his friends, his group, and Russ Rummer, God began to renew Jon's relationship with Angela. During this time she also went through the Steps to Freedom and began attending the support group with Jon. After three months of separation, Jon and Angela were reunited. Today Jon is free from his sexual bondages, and his marriage is growing stronger.

Jon concludes, 'My job still takes me on the road a lot, but things are different. Angela and I support each other during this time. When I check into my hotel room, I get down on my knees and pray for strength. Then I expose all the hiding places in the room and get rid of any pornography I find, and I use a block-out code on the television to keep the trashy movies out of my room. When I feel particularly tempted, I call Angela and have her pray with me.'

Jon admits that he isn't perfect; he has slipped a few times. But he no longer cycles through the guilt, anger, and remorse that used to dominate his thinking. When the temptations come, he now knows what to do about them. His greatest relief is that he doesn't have to hide any more. Jon is free!

The following pages were written to help you find your freedom from whatever sexual bondages are robbing you of your victory in Christ and hindering your maturity in Christ. (Or if you're reading so you can assist others find their freedom in Christ, chapters 18 – 21 of this book will be a great help to you as well.) There are no magic formulas to follow. Rather, the information in this book will reacquaint you with the truth of God's Word regarding sexual temptation, sexual bondage, Satan's destructive role in the struggle, your identity in Christ, and God's provision for your freedom. Also, the Steps to Freedom in Christ will guide you in renouncing behaviours which have kept you bound and in appropriating the freedom which is your inheritance in Christ.

It is important that you understand not only the freedom Christ has provided for you but how you got into bondage in the first place. Chapters 12 – 17 of this book identifies the pathways to sexual bondage, traces these pathways back to Adam and Eve in the Garden of Eden, exposes Satan's insidious lies about sex, outlines God's design for sex and marriage, and explores the negative consequences from ignoring that design.

In the appendix the Steps to Freedom in Christ centres on the way of escape from sexual temptation and bondage which Jesus Christ has provided for us. You will learn what you need to *believe* and what you need to *do* to secure your freedom in Christ. You will discover how to win the battle for your mind over sexual temptation. And you will be encouraged to begin your recovery in Christ and walk free of the sinful strongholds blocking your joy and growth in Christ.

Chapters 18 – 21 will also be helpful for those who have been sexually exploited by others through rape, incest, molestation, etc. Most of the people who come to Freedom in Christ Ministries for help can trace their problems to some kind of sexual abuse. I want to show how the gospel will put an end to victimisation and stop the cycle of abuse. I believe that Christ is the only answer, and that the truth can set both the victim and the perpetrator free.

As I worked on this book, it has been my prayer that you will find the sexual freedom that Jesus Christ purchased for you on the cross. No matter how you got into the shackles of sexual sin that now hobble you, there is freedom for you if you will throw yourself upon the mercy of God. Freedom comes through 'Christ in you, the hope of glory' (Col 1:27). Jesus Christ is the bondage breaker. He is the way of escape.

NOTE

1. Patrick Carnes, Ph.D., *Contrary to Love* (Minneapolis: CompCare Publishers, 1989), adapted from pp. 79–85.

12
The Lure of a
Sex-Crazed World

Elaine, a Christian woman, divorced her adulterous husband ten years ago. As a single mother with one child, she had done her best to provide for herself and be a good parent. But she struggled with loneliness and craved meaningful social interaction which her church wasn't providing.

I first met Elaine at a meeting of Parents without Partners. As a seminary professor, I had been asked to speak to the group on the topic of parenting. My presentation was sandwiched between happy hour and the dance! Elaine had a cigarette in one hand and an alcoholic drink in the other. As I watched her, it was obvious that she neither smoked nor drank, for the cigarette burned to ashes in the ash tray and the ice cubes melted in her untouched drink. She just wanted to fit into the group.

The next time I saw Elaine was in my office a few months later. She was in tears. Her overwhelming need for companionship and acceptance and the pressure of the worldly crowd had led her to compromise her moral convictions. A one-night stand with her boss had left her pregnant. 'Why did God do this to me?' she sobbed.

I wanted to say, 'Lady, God didn't shove you into that bed.' But instead I felt compassion for her and frustrated that some of our churches are unable to meet needs of people like Elaine, turning them out into a world that glitters with temptations which lure people into immorality.

Is it any wonder that sexual bondage is a major problem

in the Western world, considering the moral nosedive we are in? We couldn't be more hospitable to the influences of the world, the flesh, and the devil in the area of sexual immorality if we posted a sign at every border inviting, 'Come on in and take over — we're open to anything.'

For example, the evening news recently captured the anguished outcry of a woman in an upper-middle-class area in America. Thrusting a pamphlet toward the camera, she proclaimed, 'This kind of literature cannot come into our schools!' We would understand her concern if the pamphlet promoted sexual licence, homosexuality, or abortion. But the material was a clear, well-documented argument in favour of sexual abstinence before marriage. Although it was published by *Focus on the Family*, the pamphlet contained no reference to God and no mention of Scripture. But she was still against the promotion of abstinence among today's youth by a Christian organisation. I couldn't help but wonder what she was teaching her children. Most people only a generation ago were incensed at the idea of promoting premarital sex, condoning homosexuality, and offering free condoms in our schools.

Sexual promiscuity is rampant today, and many consider unrealistic the expectation that our young people will abstain from sex until marriage. But have we given up on our children too easily? Interviewing several honour students from mainland China, a news woman in America, Connie Chung, asked if Chinese youth engaged in sex before marriage. 'That would be wrong!' they responded.

'Do you mean to tell me that none of you have had premarital sex?' Chung pressed. The students shook their heads and again expressed their conviction that sex before marriage is wrong. What is deemed an unrealistic expectation in a 'Christian' nation is a socially accepted norm in a country where Christianity is officially suppressed! In each case the youth are living up to the expectations of their respective societies. We simply expect too little from our children. In reality, we can't impose a morality on them that we refuse to impose on ourselves.

Is America a Christian nation? Hardly! More pornographic filth is produced in America than in any other nation of the world. For example, the majority of all child pornography comes out of the Los Angeles area, where Freedom In Christ Ministries is headquartered.

Within the dark realm of pornography, nothing has greater potential to undo the West than uncensored cable or satellite television coming into our homes. There was a time when a person had to attend a public adult cinema to view hardcore pornography. This 'inconvenience' kept many people from getting involved, fearing that their reputations would be lost if they were seen going into these sleaze parlours.

But with the proliferation of VCR's and the cable and satellite networks, any home can become a sleaze parlour with the customers veiled in virtual anonymity — only the television company knows who has signed up for the porn channels. Furthermore, almost every hotel provides in-room 'adult entertainment' via satellite or cable, with the viewing guests cloaked in privacy.

Even national television networks are influenced by loose morals. My colleague, Russ Rummer, recently shared with me his evaluation of an evening of television programming.

> A few nights ago while I was exercising my male prerogative with the remote control, I flipped between two popular television sitcoms. In a span of three to four minutes I was shocked by two separate, overtly sexual segments.
>
> One involved the lead female character being asked to spend the night with a man she had just met — and she agreed. It was as casual and matter-of-fact as if they had decided to have lunch together. But the next

scene really struck me. The character's sister was seated on the couch telling a friend about her sister's impending sexual escapade. She said she hoped her sister didn't hurt the man, because she hadn't had sex in a long time. The line got a big laugh from the studio audience.

The other programme dramatised various expressions of the young male character's raging hormones. In one scene he was giving kissing lessons to a girl his age. When I flipped back a few minutes later, he walked through the door and sat down on the couch next to his dog. He commented that he bet his supposedly sexually inactive dog wished he could be like him — an accomplished sex athlete. A voice dubbed in for the dog said, 'No, I don't. I've already had sex.' And that line got a huge laugh.

The vast majority of all references to sex on television or in movies pertain to sex outside of marriage. Seldom are the negative consequences of immoral behaviour shown. James Bond never contracts a sexually transmitted disease, and we rarely see the damaging emotional effects of one-night stands on future relationships.

Living in a world of sexual myths

A major reason for the West's preoccupation with sex in general and sexual immorality in particular is the myths about sex which dominate our society. Although these myths are contrary to the teaching of Scripture, many Christians are swept up in them because the expression of them pervades the media, as exemplified by Russ's night of television viewing just mentioned. Perhaps your struggle with sexual temptation and sin is the result of being deceived into believing one or more of the following myths as truth.

Sexual fulfilment is the ultimate panacea for personal happiness. This myth permeates our society's music, movies, television sitcoms, dramas, soap operas, and advertising. The message pounds at us like a frenzied drumbeat: Life will be perfect if all your sexual drives, needs, and wants are met. Don't let anything stand in the way of getting what you want, not the 'old-fashioned' values of abstinence and marital fidelity, and especially not archaic biblical morality.

The mythical happy ending always seems to include the hero coaxing the girl into bed — or vice versa. Sexual conquest is the game, and we apparently have the right to get our share no matter who we use or how we use them to do it. And Madison Avenue suggests that this new car, that brand of toothpaste, this exotic fragrance, or that line of clothes will help us get what we want just like they do in the movies.

It must be horrible to have someone 'love' you for his or her own personal sexual gratification. It must be heartbreaking to wake up and realise that all he or she wanted was your body. How many people are being used this way in the name of love? All that is developed is lust, and all that is fed is the ego. No meaningful relationship is established, nor is any legitimate need being met. How degrading! It seems to be the great ambition of man to be happy as animals instead of being blessed as children of God.

The world's concept of happiness is having what we want. God's concept of happiness is wanting what we have (1 Thess 5:18; 1 Tim 6:6–8), which includes the sexual area of our lives. What we have are God's guidelines for moral purity in the Bible, His blessings as we live within those guidelines, and freedom in Christ if we get entangled in sexual bondage. If you really want to be happy, ignore the myth that sexual licence is the key. Learn to be thankful for what you have, not greedy for what you don't have.

Sex is the way to catch and keep the person you love, especially for women. According to this myth, everybody wants sex. If you aren't a willing and satisfying sex partner, you may lose the person you want and look like a prude in the process. So even if you don't feel like it or have qualms of conscience against it, you had better perform or you will lose out.

Enlightening research related to this myth was conducted by sociologist Wendy Luttrell of Duke University and health educator Peter Anderson of the University of New Orleans and presented to the Society for the Scientific Study of Sex.[1] Anderson's survey of 489 students showed that about one in five women and one in three men 'drink more than normal to make it easier to have sex'. Luttrell reported on thirteen student-designed surveys of 3,003 Duke University students over seven years. Although findings vary from year to year, there are key patterns:

- About 40 per cent of the students, both male and female, use drugs to affect their sexual behaviour and say it changes their willingness to make love.

- Between 20 per cent and 40 per cent of the women say they have been physically or verbally coerced into sex; 3 per cent of the men report that they have been coerced.

- More than 50 per cent of the women have pretended to enjoy sex when they didn't, versus fewer than 10 per cent of the men.

- Between 30 per cent and 85 per cent of the women — depending on the survey — say they have changed their minds during the sex act, deciding they didn't want to participate; 5 per cent to 20 per cent of the men report it has happened to them.

Diane Sawyer reported on 'Prime Time Live' that 33 per

cent of American girls have had sexual intercourse by the age of fifteen and 70 per cent by their final year of school. She interviewed several sexually active teenage girls, some as young as fourteen, who claimed to have had as many as ten different partners. At the end of the segment, Sawyer reported, 'Every single one of these sexually active girls confided with us that they wish they'd said no.'[2]

Does a woman or man have to perform sexually to be accepted and loved? No, that's a demeaning myth leading to sexual bondage.

Whatever two consenting adults do behind closed doors doesn't hurt anyone else. That's a lie. Those consenting adults are someone's son, daughter, brother, sister, mother, or father. Think of the shame and hurt these people may suffer as a result of their loved one's consensual but immoral behaviour. Also, the private liaison may result in a pregnancy leading to an abortion or an unwanted and abused child. That's serious hurt. And a sexually transmitted disease will surely affect the friends and family members of the persons infected.

Furthermore, God was in the bedroom with those two consenting adults. Secret sin on earth is open scandal in heaven. What we choose to do or not to do before God affects all humanity and eventually impacts eternity.

Activities that should be forbidden to children are all right for 'adults only'. This myth asserts that a child's mind will be polluted from seeing nudity in magazines or watching sex scenes on a cable channel, but an adult's won't. That's another lie. When did God establish a different standard of morality for children than for adults? He didn't. If something is morally wrong for your child, then it is morally wrong for you. You will never be so mature that pornography will not be harmful to you.

You cannot legislate morality. Nonsense! Of course we can legislate morality. That's what our elected lawmakers do all the time. If they couldn't legislate morality, we wouldn't have any laws against murder, rape, theft, etc. Every bill passed by the legislature is based on someone's concept of morality. What the secularists in America are saying is that Christians have no business imposing *biblical* morality on a secular society. They insist that the separation of church and state guarantees that government and due process of law are free from the intrusion of the church and its moral standards.

But that's not what the First Amendment is about. It guarantees that the government cannot interfere with the establishment and free exercise of religion. The First Amendment says nothing about the separation of church and state, nor does it forbid the influence of biblical morality upon our laws. Indeed, when the American Constitution was framed it was anchored to the bedrock of the Word of God. But our nation has slipped off its foundation to the shifting sands of popular opinion regarding righteousness and morality.

America and the Western world are paying a high price for accepting these myths about sex as truth and ignoring the moral decline these lies encourage. The epidemic of AIDS and other sexually transmitted diseases, a generation of babies sacrificed to convenience abortions, the breakdown of the nuclear family through adultery, abandonment, and divorce, and the rise of sexual abuse and sex crimes are glaring examples.

'But what about the Christian community?' you may ask. 'We're not being overrun by the AIDS epidemic. We're not flocking to the abortion clinics. We listen to Dr James Dobson on the radio and value the family. Is the declining moral climate really affecting us?'

Most definitely, though perhaps not as obviously. It may

appear that our values as Christian people have restrained us from following the world into immorality at the same breakneck pace. But our experience at Freedom In Christ Ministries has convinced us that believers are no less affected by the relentless, manifold temptations to sexual sin which permeate our culture. It's just that most Christians who get sucked into this trap, like Jon in the previous chapter, keep it a secret from their brothers and sisters in Christ in order to maintain an appearance of holiness.

So instead of openly engaging in an extramarital affair or homosexual relationship, they secretly toy with pornography, sexual fantasies, voyeurism, or whatever while trying to serve Christ. And they come to us by the defeated hundreds complaining of a lack of spiritual fervour, a nonexistent devotional life with Christ, marriages on the brink of collapse, and substance abuse addictions. And without exception, everyone we have counselled who was in bondage in some other way was also in sexual bondage at some level. Happily, when these people take responsibility for their bondages and take the Steps to Freedom in Christ, they are set free.

How do so many Christians get pulled into this quagmire? I see three major pathways to sexual bondage which are graded and paved by our culture's preoccupation with self and sex. In the next chapter I will describe these three pathways to help you identify how you found the dark detour into sexual bondage.

NOTES

1. Reported by Marilyn Elias in *USA Today* (November 8, 1993).

2. 'Christian Society Today', a publication of the American Family Association, Tupelo, MS (January 1994), p 3.

13
Pathways
to Sexual Bondage

No one purposely sets out to become trapped in sexual bondage. First, a person is tempted to fulfil legitimate sexual needs in the world, the flesh, or the devil instead of in Christ. Each temptation brings him to the threshold of a decision. If he hesitates at the threshold instead of immediately taking the thought 'captive to the obedience of Christ' (2 Cor 10:5, NASB), he increases his chances of yielding to that temptation.

Next, if he continues to yield to sexual temptation, he will form a habit. And if he exercises that habit long enough, a stronghold will be established in his mind. Once a stronghold of thought and response is entrenched in the mind, it is extremely difficult to act contrary to that pattern. Sexual bondage is a stronghold in the mind which causes the individual to act contrary to the will of God, even when he or she knows and desires otherwise.

In order to be set free from the sexual bondage which grips you, you must understand how you became involved in the first place. You must identify the pathway which drew you into sexual bondage so you can renounce those impure thoughts and behaviours. And you must identify any persons who may have aided or encouraged you in this wrong direction so you may forgive them.

In the process of teaching and counselling on this topic, I have discovered three broad pathways which lead to sexual bondage. The first pathway is *sexual promiscuity* — participating in activities that encourage lust and illicit sex: pornography, fantasy, voyeurism, sexual experimentation, etc. The second pathway is *sexual disorientation* — fascination with or exposure to homosexual influences. The third pathway is *sexual abuse* — hurtful experiences and negative influences from the past which predispose an individual to impurity. In this chapter we will examine these three pathways and identify how they lead the careless or unwitting victim into bondage.

It must be noted that few people find these pathways alone. The people in our past and present — parents, grandparents, siblings, other relatives, family friends, peers, colleagues — exert tremendous influence in our lives. Sometimes these individuals give us an intentional or unintentional push in the wrong direction. For example, a boy is introduced to pornography by his father, who carelessly leaves smutty magazines and videos where the boy can find them. A bachelor neighbour befriends an unpopular teenage boy and influences him into homosexuality. A little girl is molested by her uncle for years and grows up to be a sexually promiscuous teenager, or she shuts down sexually and cannot seem to enjoy a legitimate sexual relationship with her husband.

You may have been forced onto the pathway to sexual bondage when you were too young to understand or object. You may have been encouraged into immoral behaviour by someone you trusted before you knew the act was immoral. 'I'm hooked, and it's not my fault,' you contend.

It may be true that you are not fully responsible for the sin you got into. But you *are* responsible for choosing to remain there. As you explore the reasons behind your bondage, be encouraged that Jesus Christ has provided a way of escape. However, you can't blame anyone but yourself if you aren't free; you must take the exit God has provided. The last four chapters and the Steps to Freedom in Christ will help you do so.

Playing with fire

Andy came into sexual bondage by following the pathway of sexual promiscuity. He grew up in a church-going family in America. As a young boy he learned about pornography from his older brothers, who hid the magazines from their parents but not from him. All through his years at a Christian school, Andy's secret fascination with pornography intensified. The books and magazines he collected were increasingly more graphic and lewd. He restrained from physical sex because it was clearly a sin, but sexual fantasies consumed his waking thoughts.

By the time Andy entered a Christian university, printed pornography no longer satisfied his ravenous appetite for sexual excitement. He began sneaking off to adult cinemas and nude bars. He rented and viewed X-rated videos. He searched out live sex shows in the sleaziest parts of town. Yet he would not participate in sex, either in the dark dives he visited or with the available classmates at the university. Instead, he continued to be a model student and married a beautiful girl, Trish.

Moving to another part of the country to begin his career, Andy's sexual bondage held him like a vice. He quickly located and frequently patronised the porno attractions in the city without Trish's knowledge. His job permitted him time to rent videos and take them home while his wife was at work. As a twenty-five-year-old, Andy lamented, 'I'm a Christian, and I have never been unfaithful to Trish. But I have done almost everything a man can do without having illicit sex, and I have poured thousands of dollars into my disgusting "habit". I'm a sexual addict, and I don't know how to get free.'

Andy's pathway to bondage was sexual promiscuity. Although he did not have intercourse with anyone other than Trish for fear of disgracing his family or contracting AIDS, he admits that he has consistently violated Christ's instruction in Matthew 5:27,28: 'You have heard that it was said, "Do not commit adultery." But I tell you that anyone who looks at a woman lustfully has already committed adultery with her in his heart.' Andy has been sexually promiscuous with countless numbers of women in every way except physically. And it all began with the dirty magazines which captivated him as a child.

Sexual promiscuity is a major pathway to sexual bondage. I have heard variations of Andy's story from scores of men: pornographic magazines and movies leading to sexual fantasies, uncontrolled masturbation, and voyeurism leading to experimentation, adultery, prostitution, or worse. I hear similar accounts from women about being sucked into fantasy and unfaithfulness through their involvement with romance novels and dramas. People who play with fire by dabbling in impure sexual thoughts and activities invite a fire storm of sexual bondage.

Desperate for freedom from his bondage, Andy finally admitted his problem to Trish. The couple attended sexual addiction therapy sessions together for two years with little success. Recently, the women's Bible study group Trish belonged to at their church studied *Victory over the Darkness* and *The Bondage Breaker*, and she was filled with hope. At her encouragement, Andy read the two books and met with two men from the church who walked him through the Steps to Freedom in Christ. Andy is finally on the path to freedom from the pornography and mental promiscuity which had bound him.

The lie of the 'alternate lifestyle'

Thomas unintentionally discovered another pathway to sexual bondage: homosexuality. He was raised by a domineering mother and a detached father he could never seem to please. Possessing a brilliant mind, Thomas found his acceptance in academics, graduating from university with a teaching degree. He also found great happiness with Claudia, whom he married, and their shared faith in Christ. Together they moved to a large city where Thomas began his career as associate professor of history at a small private university.

Thomas's life was full and satisfying. Claudia's love and acceptance warmed him. His teaching position provided many opportunities for stimulating academic growth. He taught an adult Sunday school class at the church they attended. They were blessed by the birth of a daughter and, fourteen months later, a son.

But the responsibility of parenthood brought unexpected pressures and conflict to Thomas's marriage, activating old memories of his mother's dominance and his father's displeasure. The stress at home drove him deeper into his academic pursuits. He spent increasing amounts of time away from Claudia doing research for articles submitted to various professional publications. His relationship with God began to wane as he buried himself in his work.

That's when Thomas got involved with Aaron, a history department colleague whom he had once attempted to lead to Christ. As their friendship deepened, Aaron admitted to Thomas his years of inner turmoil over his sexual orientation. Thomas determined to guide his friend out of his delusion to the truth of God's Word.

Thomas accompanied Aaron into the seedy world of the gay bar scene, rationalising his behaviour as research for helping his friend. But instead of pulling his friend out,

Thomas was pulled in. The homosexual lifestyle was seductively fascinating to him. He was awakened to memories of boyhood experiences which had caused him to doubt his own sexual identity. Thomas remembered his father being more accepting of a younger brother, who was involved in athletics and deemed more masculine than the academically inclined Thomas. He recalled his father shaming him for crying over the loss of his pet guinea pig, saying, 'Only little girls cry about such a thing.'

In time, Thomas yielded to his first sexual encounter with a man. He felt compelled to seek 'freedom to be himself'. He found himself justifying his quest for personal sexual pleasure to compensate for the love he missed out on as a child. He felt wonderfully loved and validated by the homosexual community, which seemed far more accepting than the people in his church. So he became more deeply involved in homosexual affairs, but he kept his exploits a secret, leading a double life.

Yet a conflict raged within Thomas. On one hand, he believed — though his belief was based on deception — that God had created him to be a homosexual. What else would explain his inner turmoil over his father's disapproval and his conflicts with Claudia? What else could account for the satisfaction and acceptance he experienced among other homosexual men? On the other hand, he could not escape his understanding of God's Word on the subject of sexual purity. He felt convicted about being unfaithful to Claudia. He feared the consequences reaped by those who seek fulfilment in fleshly behaviours — and homosexuality was at the top of the list. Thomas was terribly confused about his relationship with God and how to balance his desire to be a Christian with his awareness of being a homosexual.

No longer willing to continue the charade at home, Thomas left Claudia and moved in with a homosexual friend. He began attending a gay church but was repulsed by the attempt to blend Christianity and the homosexual lifestyle. Gay pride and gay rights were emphasised and worshipped more than God. Sex play in the pews during services was condoned. Thomas felt caught between two opposing forces. Continuing to believe that he was created to be homosexual clashed with everything he knew about God and faith. But he didn't know how to extract himself from the punishing dilemma.

Thomas was in bondage to the lie that homosexuality is a viable alternative to God's design for human sexuality. Like so many people involved in homosexuality, he became trapped after repeated steps down a pathway of fascination with homosexuality, prompted by hurtful childhood experiences and clouded logic leading to poor choices as an adult.

'But it wasn't his fault,' some may argue. 'Thomas came from a dysfunctional family. His father and mother provided a skewed picture of male and female roles. His poor self-identity and subsequent behaviour is the product of his environment.'

As mentioned earlier, other people may be partially or substantially responsible for setting us on the pathway to sexual bondage. And Satan takes advantage of these failures to establish strongholds of control in the lives of misused or abused children and youth. These people and experiences must be dealt with in the process of finding our freedom in Christ from Satan's bondage. However, the focus at this point should not be on who is to blame but on finding the way of escape. On that count the individual in bondage is fully responsible to take those important steps.

The violation of the innocent

A third pathway to sexual bondage is the experience of being the victim of another person's illicit sexual exploits. Some of these people were molested as children by trusted adults. Some were the victims of incest by a parent or sibling. Some were date-raped as teens or violently raped as adults. Some were the victims of ritual sex abuse by members of a cult. The common thread among these victims is that they were sexually violated against their will. And the traumatic acts perpetrated by others on many of these innocent victims opened the door to their own sexual bondage.

Not all victims of sexual abuse end up in sexual bondage. But a surprising number of the people we counsel at Freedom In Christ Ministries admit that they have been sexually abused in some way.

As with many victims, Melissa's memories of sexual abuse were blocked by the trauma she experienced. At one point, had you asked her if she had been abused as a child, she would have said no. But her poor self-image and strange behaviour as a child signalled a deep, hidden problem. Melissa told her story to my colleague Russ:

> I felt so inadequate and unacceptable as a child. I avoided getting close to anyone, especially boys, fearing they would find out how terrible I was. Everyone seemed to react to me in a sexual way. As a girl of six or seven, men whispered to me what they wanted to do to me when I got older. As I grew up, women seemed threatened by me, as if I intended to steal their husbands. This behaviour only reinforced my belief that there was something wrong with me, and everyone saw it. I had become a Christian as a young child, but I was convinced that God had picked me out to be sexually tormented and abused.
>
> About the time I turned nine or ten, I began to experiment with masturbation. I also became quite self-destructive. I cut the insides of my legs and put alcohol on the wounds to make them hurt more. I cut pieces of skin off my knuckles just to feel the pain I knew I deserved. As a young teen I was shy and afraid of boys.

I didn't have many friends. When I dated, I either froze up after a little bit of necking or blanked out, unable to remember what I did or how I got home. I became bulimic at about fourteen.

I rededicated my life to Christ at the age of fifteen. But as I left school and entered university I continued to binge and purge once or twice a day. I also strayed into a few sexual involvements, and most of those boys were also Christians. I wanted to be loved and accepted, so I gave them my body. But when I did, they just used me and discarded me. With or without sex, the boys rejected me. I felt dirty and trapped.

When Melissa married Dan in her early twenties, their physical intimacy opened a floodgate of memories and nightmares about her clouded past. She dreamed about her grandfather raping her while her new husband watched with enjoyment. Gradually the repressed memories of her horrifying past came into focus.

Melissa remembered being molested by her grandfather when she was two. She was forced to accept and perform oral sex and other atrocities with him as a young child. At the time she was cutting herself, she also awakened often in the middle of the night with severe abdominal pains. An insightful doctor told Melissa's mother that she was being sexually abused. The mother blamed Melissa's stepfather, brother, and uncle — everyone but her grandfather, the man who was doing it.

Melissa felt betrayed by the doctor for revealing her 'secret'. She had never considered telling anyone how Grandpa 'loved' her, even though she felt it was wrong. She was confused. She loved her grandfather, but she also prayed that God would kill him to make the abuse stop. And when he *did* die before Melissa became a teenager, she felt responsible and mourned him. But the inner wounds he had inflicted continued to torment her for years.

Sexual abuse is a broad pathway to all kinds of bondage, including sexual bondage. Studies show that nearly half of all female children in America will experience some form of sexual abuse before they reach their fourteenth birthday.[1] Furthermore, the perpetrators of 85 to 94 per cent of sexual violations are either relatives, family friends, neighbours, or acquaintances of the victim, not strangers.[2]

Traumatic betrayal at such an impressionable age prompts distorted thinking in many victims of sexual abuse. Instead of blaming the perpetrator, who may be a relative she desperately wants to trust and love, a girl blames God for not protecting her. Others feel emotionally cut off from God, saying, 'I know God loves me, but my heart is numb to my relationship with Him, because He all but violated me Himself by letting it happen.'

The victim may also mistakenly blame herself for allowing such a thing to happen. As with Melissa, the thinking of abuse victims may centre on self-blame and poor self-image leading to self-loathing and self-destructive behaviour for 'allowing' the abuse to occur. Victims of rape often become their own victimisers as a result of intense feelings of shock, denial, fear, guilt, depression, and disorientation. These feelings may lead to disorganisation, suicide attempts, phobic avoidance of the opposite sex, and nightmarish dreams.[3]

Many young victims of sexual abuse, like Melissa, unconsciously protect themselves by blocking out the memories of these sad events. The intensity of the trauma overloads their young minds and pushes those memories into a dark corner. This defence against the pain works well for children, but as they grow older it hampers their hold on reality. Many begin acting out their excessive need for love and protection and find those needs satisfied by sex. This is why many who are caught in the web of sexual bondage cannot explain how they ended up there.

Melissa's pain didn't end with the realisation of her

grandfather's abuse. Unfortunately, her Christian husband Dan was in bondage to pornography and alcohol, and he sometimes subjected her to sexual acts against her will. But when Melissa pressed for a divorce after three years of marriage, Dan found help with a counsellor who led him through the Steps to Freedom in Christ. Melissa did the same, confessing the hurt, anger, and confusion that attended her history of sexual abuse. Their lives and marriage were so radically changed that it's hard to believe they are the same persons.

Melissa now understands how much God loves her and realises that her grandfather's sins can no longer touch her. She is free to enjoy life with the man who loves and accepts her completely. Her complete restoration from the bondage caused by sexual abuse is still in process as she walks in the truth of her freedom from the traumas of her childhood and adult years. The same victory is available to all of God's children who desire release from bondage.

Perhaps while reading this chapter you have recognised a pathway which has led you into the sexually impure thought patterns and behaviours which now seem to control you. And you have possibly identified thoughts, events, and persons which have ushered you down this path to bondage. As important as these discoveries may be, you yet need to get to the core of your sexual bondage. This issue is the subject of Chapter 14.

NOTES

1. Maxine Hancock and Karen Burton-Mains, *Child Sexual Abuse: A Hope for Healing* (Wheaton, IL: Harold Shaw Publishers, 1987), p 12.

2. Herant A. Katchadourian, M.D. and Donald T. Lunde, M.D., *Fundamentals of Human Sexuality*, 3rd ed. (New York: Holt, Rinehart, and Winston Publishers, 1980), p 379.

3. Barbara Chester, *Sexual Assault and Abuse* (San Francisco: Harper and Row Publishers, 1987), pp. 23–24.

14
The Pimp
in Your Mind

There is more behind sexual bondage than the sinking moral standards of our culture and the specific events or persons who were instrumental in ushering you down that path. The following story illustrates the point.

Before he met Christ, Rick's life was an endless quest for intimacy. As a child, he was sexually abused by his grandmother. After his father committed suicide, his mother became increasingly involved in religious activities, devoting her life to ministry. So as a young man Rick embarked on a desperate search to fill the hole which the sins of others had left in him. Even after his marriage to Emily, his university sweetheart, he kept trying to cover his bitterness and hurt with other sexual encounters, work, and the approval of others, but without success. Emily lost patience and left him.

One day while listening to a tape by Dr Charles Stanley, Rick fell to his knees and asked Jesus to save him from himself and from the sin that never delivered what it promised. He and Emily were reconciled and eventually had four children. They seemed to be the model Christian family.

But deep inside, Rick was still taunted by the lie that sex, food, work, and other people could meet his needs more fully than Christ. He began listening to that lie and fell back into his old patterns of immorality. He became sexually involved with numerous partners, including a married woman, while continuing to play the role of the Christian husband and father. He lived a double life in constant turmoil.

Devastated at the breakup of an affair, Rick confessed everything to his family and entered a twelve-step programme for his addictions. Emily was crushed and told him not to return home. Then she divorced him.

Rick made an attempt at renewing his faith in Christ. He prayed and committed himself not to get involved in illicit sex for the ninety days of his treatment. But he failed, deceived into thinking that the right woman would meet his deep and seemingly unquenchable need for love. He became involved with another married woman while continuing to have daily devotions, seek God's guidance for his life, and witness to his colleagues at work.

For years Rick rode a spiritual and emotional roller-coaster. Conviction would drive him to break off his relationships and return to the Lord. Then depression or problems would hit, and he would find himself seeking the same familiar ways of escape: illicit sex, food, success. He felt powerless to control his behaviour. Rick recalls:

> The 'pimp' in my mind repeatedly promised me fulfilment if I would only prostitute myself one more time. But he never fulfilled his promise. Life for me was like pushing a car. When things were going all right, it required only a little effort. But every time I tried to push the car over the mountain of my sexual bondage, the car rolled back over me, leaving me desperate, hurt, and without hope again. I couldn't stop this cycle no matter how much I sought God. My sexual addiction ruled everything in my life. I hated it, I knew it was destroying me from the inside out — but I kept heeding the pimp in my mind again and again.

Rick's mother invited him to attend my conference on resolving personal and spiritual conflicts. He consented to go, but during the first evening of the conference he was harassed by sexual fantasies prompted by Satan, the pimp in his mind. However, one statement did penetrate and give him hope: 'If the Son sets you free, you will be free indeed' (Jn 8:36). Rick says, 'I knew I wasn't free. I was powerless to stop the fruitless search for fulfilment and satisfaction in sex, food, and work.'

Rick's mother set up an appointment for Rick and me to meet privately during the conference. He continues his story:

> I knew while driving to the meeting that something was going to happen. My heart felt like it was going to explode. There was a war raging within me. The old pimp who had controlled my life for years didn't want me to go. But I was determined to experience the freedom Neil had talked about.
>
> I expected Neil to slap me on the side of the head and shout out an exorcistic prayer. Then I would surely fall to the floor and flap around uncontrollably until the effects of his prayer set me free. But it didn't happen that way. Neil listened quietly as I shared my story, then he said in a calm voice, 'Rick, I believe you can be free in Christ.'
>
> As Neil led me through the Steps to Freedom in Christ, I could hear the pimp's insistent lies in my mind. The inner battle was intense, but I was ready for the shackles to be broken. So I repented of my sin, renounced all the lies I had believed, renounced every sexual use of my body as an instrument of unrighteousness, and forgave all those who had offended me. As I did, peace began to roll in and drown out thirty-seven years worth of lies. I heard holy silence. The pimp was gone and, praise God, I was free.

Rick's freedom was tested right away. The next day during the conference he was bombarded by immoral thoughts. But he stood firm in the power of the blood of Christ to resist them. That night he was strongly tempted to pursue another destructive relationship. But the moment he called on Christ's all-powerful, cleansing blood, the holy silence returned.

Since that conference, Rick has experienced a genuine and growing relationship with his heavenly Father. He has stopped watching television and attending movies, which had played a large part in feeding his immorality. He now has an unquenchable desire to study the Bible and pray. And he has remained sexually pure. 'It's a miracle!' Rick says. 'I have been set free from that lying pimp in my mind.'

I believe that every child of God in sexual bondage can experience the freedom Rick has experienced. Jesus broke the power of sin on the cross by defeating the god of this world — Satan, the lying pimp Rick talked about. To appropriate and retain your freedom, you must understand the continuing work of the evil one. He is the lying deceiver at the core of sexual bondage.

Enemy in the Garden

God's plan for the sexual life and health of His human creation has been clear since the beginning.

> The Lord God said, 'It is not good for the man to be alone. I will make a helper suitable for him.' ...So the Lord God caused the man to fall into a deep sleep; and while he was sleeping, he took one of the man's ribs and closed up the place with flesh. Then the Lord God made a woman from the rib he had taken out of the man, and he brought her to the man.
>
> The man said, 'This is now bone of my bones and flesh of my flesh; she shall be called "woman", for she was taken out of man.' For this reason a man will leave his father and

mother and be united to his wife, and they shall become one flesh.

The man and his wife were both naked, and they felt no shame (Gen 2:18,21–25).

God created Adam in His own image, breathed life into him, and Adam became spiritually and physically alive. Something was missing, however. It wasn't good for Adam to be alone; he needed a suitable helper. None of the animals God had created could adequately fulfil Adam's need. So God created Eve from Adam's rib. The couple was naked and unashamed. There was nothing obscene about their naked bodies. Their sexual relationship was not separated from their intimate relationship with God. There was no sin and nothing to hide, so Adam and Eve had no reason to cover up.

The purpose and responsibility of this first couple was to 'be fruitful and increase in number; fill the earth and subdue it' (Gen 1:28). They were afforded a tremendous amount of freedom as long as they remained in a dependent relationship with God. They had a perfect life and could have lived forever in the presence of God. All their needs were provided for.

But Satan and evil were also present in the universe. The Lord had commanded Adam and Eve not to eat from the tree of the knowledge of good and evil or they would die (Gen 2:17). But Satan questioned and twisted God's command and tempted the couple through the same three channels of temptation that exist today: 'the lust of the flesh and the lust of the eyes and the boastful pride of life' (1 Jn 2:16 NASB). Deceived by the craftiness of Satan, Adam and Eve defied God, ate of the forbidden fruit, and thus declared their independence from God.

At that moment, Adam and Eve died spiritually, meaning that their intimate relationship with God was severed. In time they also died physically, which is also a consequence of sin (Rom 5:12). But in the intervening years, their perfect life in the garden was ruined by their sin. No longer innocent and without shame, 'the eyes of both of them were opened, and they realised they were naked; so they sewed fig leaves together and made coverings for themselves…and they hid from the Lord God among the trees of the garden' (Gen 3:7,8).

The fall affected Adam and Eve's daily life in many ways. First, it darkened their mind. In trying to hide from God, they revealed that they had suddenly lost a true understanding of God. Can you imagine trying to hide from God, who is present everywhere? They were no longer thinking straight. They were darkened in their understanding because they were separated from the life of God (Eph 4:18).

Second, the fall affected their emotions. The first emotions expressed by Adam and Eve after the fall — fear and guilt — had never been part of their existence before. When God came looking for the pair, Adam said to Him, 'I was afraid [fear] because I was naked [guilt]; so I hid' (3:10).

The fear of being exposed has driven many people from the light that reveals their sin. Without God's unconditional love and acceptance, they are forced to run from the light or discredit its source. Unable to live up to God's eternal standards of morality, they now face the prospect of living in guilt and shame or, like Adam, blaming someone else (Gen 2:12).

Third, the fall also affected Adam and Eve's will. Before they sinned, they could only make one wrong choice: to eat from the tree of the knowledge of good and evil, which was forbidden to them. Every other choice they could make in the garden was a good choice. However, because Adam and Eve made that one bad choice, they were confronted every day with many good *and* bad choices — just as we are today. We can choose to yield or not yield to a variety of temptations presented to us by the world, the flesh, and the devil. It is the pattern of consistent wrong choices in the area of sexual sin that leads individuals into sexual bondage.

Because of sin, we are totally helpless and hopeless to escape sexual bondage without God. In truth, no person living independently of God can live a moral life or withstand the conviction of His perfect light. 'Everyone who does evil hates the light, and will not come into the light for fear that his deeds will be exposed. But whoever lives by the truth comes into the light, so that it may be seen plainly that what he has done has been done through God' (Jn 3:20,21).

The first step in recovery for anyone in sexual bondage is to come out of the darkness of hiding and face the truth in the light. Many people have told me that they want to get out of sexual bondage because they are tired of living a lie. And bondage to sex is one of the easiest to lie about. For example, the effects of food addiction (either overeating or anorexia and bulimia) show up quickly in the physical appearance of the victim. Drug or alcohol addiction is noticeable within a couple of years. But there are no obvious clues to sexual bondage, unless it surfaces in the form of a sexually transmitted disease. It can remain a private nightmare for a lifetime unless it is brought into the light and dealt with.

A rebel takes control

At the root of the world's dilemma with sin and bondage is Satan. When Adam and Eve sinned, Satan usurped their role as rulers over the earth and became the rebel holder of authority. When Jesus was tempted, Satan offered Him the kingdoms of the world if He would bow down and worship him (Lk 4:6). Jesus didn't dispute Satan's claim to earthly authority and even referred to him as 'the prince of this world' (Jn 12:31; 14:30; 16:11). Paul called Satan 'the prince of the power of the air' (Eph 2:2 NASB). As a result of Adam and Eve's fall, 'the whole world is under the control of the evil one' (1 Jn 5:19).

The good news is that God's plan of redemption was under way immediately after Satan wrested authority from Adam and Eve. The Lord cursed the serpent and foretold the downfall of Satan (Gen 3:14,15), which was accomplished by Christ on the cross. Ultimate authority in heaven and earth now belongs to Him. Satan's days of authority on earth are numbered.

Because we are related to Adam and Eve, all of us were born spiritually dead and were subject to the authority of the prince of this world. But when we received Christ, we were transferred from Satan's kingdom to God's kingdom (Col 1:13; Phil 3:20). Satan is still the ruler of this world, but he is no longer *our* ruler; Jesus Christ is.

However, as long as we live in Satan's world, he will try to deceive us into believing that we belong to him. Even as members of Christ's kingdom we are still vulnerable to Satan's accusations, temptations, and deceptions. If we give in to his tactics, Satan can influence our thinking and behaviour. And if we remain under his influence long enough and fail to resist him, Satan can control us in those areas.

That's what happened to Rick, whose story opened this chapter. Before he became a Christian, he formed bad habits in the area of illicit sex. He had travelled the pathways of sexual abuse and sexual promiscuity into sexual bondage. After Rick gave his life to Christ, the pimp in his mind had him convinced that illicit sex was still the answer to his search for love and fulfilment. Only after Rick understood his identity in Christ and exercised his authority in Christ was he able to silence the pimp's lies and break free of his sexual bondage.

The seeds of sexual bondage

So why is this ongoing cosmic battle between God's kingdom and Satan's kingdom, between righteousness and sin, so often waged in the arena of sex and sexual behaviour? It dawned on me after years of helping people find their freedom in Christ that a person's sexual practices are a primary way by which seeds are sown in these two kingdoms. Most of the people who come to Freedom In Christ Ministries struggling against sin and Satan have some kind of sexual problem. In fact, every person who shared his or her story in Part One of this book had either been sexually abused, sexually disoriented, or sexually promiscuous.

People who respect and obey God's directives in Scripture regarding sexual purity are sowing seeds in the kingdom of God that will reap a harvest of peace and righteousness. People who ignore God's call to sexual purity are sowing seeds in Satan's kingdom and will reap a harvest of pain and heartache. And the fruit of seeds sown in these two kingdoms greatly impacts our relationships. For example, the seed of pornography was sown in Jon (Chapter 11) and Andy (Chapter 13) by other impure men who were careless with their pornographic magazines, resulting in these boys becoming addicted to pornography. Melissa's grandfather (Chapter 13) sowed seeds of immorality in Satan's kingdom by sexually abusing his granddaughter. The fruit of his sin was Melissa's own sexual bondage.

Satan's primary weapon for ruining relationships is sexual impurity. More Christian marriages and ministries are destroyed because of sexual misconduct than for any other reason. People who are in secret sexual bondage have no joy in marriage or ministry. Conversely, an individual who pursues a life of moral purity is nurturing a crop in the kingdom of God. The result is a positive impact for righteousness on his or her marriage, children, friends, and colleagues.

The strong link between Satan's kingdom of darkness and sexual bondage was illustrated to me during one of my conferences. David was referred to us by the pastoral staff of the host church. He was a successful businessman who appeared to have everything going for him. However, David's wife had just left him because of his pornography addiction. So one of our staff met with him to take him through the Steps to Freedom in Christ.

As we go through these steps with people, we routinely invite them to renounce any previous involvement in satanic or occult activities, even if they don't remember any. As David renounced making any covenants with Satan, he was shaken to the core when the Lord revealed to him a nightmarish experience from his past. He recalled a frightening encounter with a spiritual being who offered David all the sex and girls he wanted if he would just tell this being he loved Satan. At first David refused, not sure if he was awake or dreaming. Then he gave in and proclaimed his love for Satan. Sowing that seed in Satan's kingdom resulted in the sexual bondage that was ruining David's life and marriage.

After David renounced that experience and completed the Steps to Freedom in Christ, he was free from his bondage to pornography. His life and his marriage are being restored.

Darkness breeds impurity

Wherever you find the kingdom of darkness entrenched, you find sexual immorality and perversion flourishing. Several former participants have told me that satanic worship is a degrading and dehumanising sex orgy. Satanists practice selective breeding to propagate their super race. Inferior offspring are used for sacrifice.

The god of this world has not changed in his debauchery over the centuries. Pagans honoured Molech, a detestable

Semitic deity, by the fiery sacrifice of children, a practice God strictly prohibited (Lev 18:21; 20:1–5). God's people were also warned against worshipping the Babylonian goat idol or satyr (Is 13:21; Rev 18:2). A satyr is a demon that takes on the form of a shaggy goat. It was especially brutal and lustful in its nature.

There were many other pagan gods in biblical times whose worship involved sexual perversity. Chemosh, the national deity of the Moabites, required the sacrifice of children, and Diana of Ephesus had an explicitly sexual nature. Devotion to any*one* or any*thing* less than the God and Father of our Lord Jesus Christ is idolatry, and idolatry always leads into some perversion of moral purity.

Satan is still in the business of pimping his perversions of God's design for sex and marriage. To find your freedom in Christ, you need not only to understand how the seeds of impurity are sown in the kingdom of darkness, you need to understand God's view of sex. This is the topic of the next chapter.

15
The False
and the Genuine

It has been said that the way to learn how to recognise
counterfeit money is not to study counterfeit money. You
study the real thing — genuine currency — so thoroughly
that you will quickly spot a fake bank note if you look at it
closely. This must also be our approach when contrasting
Satan's perversion of sex with God's perfect plan. We
should know *something* about the pimp's dark plan and evil
methods. But it's the truth that sets us free, not a knowledge
of error (Jn 8:32). It is vital that we understand God's
design for sex and marriage in order to walk out of the
darkness and sow seeds of righteousness in God's kingdom.

God created us as sexual beings — male and female.
Gender is determined at conception, and the entire sexual
anatomy is present at birth. Even the molecular structure of
a skin sample, when studied under a microscope, will reveal
an infant's sexual identity. God is not anti-sex; He created
sex! David proclaimed, 'You created my inmost being; you
knit me together in my mother's womb. I praise you because
I am fearfully and wonderfully made; your works are wonderful' (Ps 139:13,14).

Viewing sex as evil is not an appropriate response to
what God created and pronounced good. 'Everything God
created is good, and nothing is to be rejected if it is received
with thanksgiving, because it is consecrated by the word of
God and prayer' (1 Tim 4:4,5). On the other hand, Satan is
evil, and sin distorts what God created. Denying our sexu-

ality and fearing open discussion about our sexual development is playing into the devil's hand. A Christian view of sexuality and sexual development, and helpful guidelines for presenting a healthy, biblical view of sex to your children, is found in Appendix B of this book.

A plan for the ages

God's ideal plan for marriage was outlined in the Garden of Eden before Adam and Eve sinned: 'A man will leave his father and mother and be united to his wife, and they will become one flesh' (Gen 2:24). Monogamous, heterosexual marriage under God was the divine intention; one man and one woman forming an inseparable union and living in dependence on God.

Adam and Eve were also commanded by God to procreate and fill the earth with their offspring. Had they never sinned, perhaps the world today would be populated with a race of sinless people living in perfect harmony. But Adam and Eve's sin in the garden marred God's beautiful plan. Lest we be too hard on them, however, had any of us been in the Garden instead of them, we probably would have done the same thing. Adam and Eve enjoyed ideal conditions and perfect light and still sinned. We could have done no better.

God did not abandon His plan for man, woman, and their sexual relationship despite the fall of Adam and Eve. Rather, He selected the procreative process of human marriage as the vehicle for redeeming fallen humanity. God covenanted with Abraham, 'In your seed all the nations of the earth shall be blessed, because you have obeyed My voice' (Gen 22:18). The 'seed' or descendant God was talking about was Christ (Gal 3:16), who would bless the whole world by providing salvation through His death and resurrection.

There was another facet to God's plan for marriage after the fall. From Adam and Eve to the present, the covenant relationship of marriage between husband and wife has been a God-ordained picture of the covenant relationship between God and His people. The church is called the bride of Christ (Rev 19:7), and He desires to receive to Himself a bride who is holy and blameless, 'without stain or wrinkle or any other blemish' (Eph 5:26,27). The purity and faithfulness of a Christian marriage is to be an object lesson of the purity and faithfulness God desires in our relationship with Him.

The Bible prohibits sexual immorality for two interrelated reasons. First, unfaithfulness or sexual sin violates God's plan for the sanctity of human marriage. When you become sexually involved with someone other than your spouse, whether physically or mentally through lust and fantasy, you shatter God's design. You bond with that person, thus blemishing the 'one man and one woman' picture and breaking the covenant with your spouse (1 Cor 6:16,17). We were created to become one flesh with only one other person. When you commit sexual sin, you become one flesh with every physical or mental partner, resulting in sexual bondage. That's why Paul calls sexual sin a sin against our own body.

Second, when you commit sexual immorality you deface the picture of God's covenant relationship with His people which your marriage was designed to portray. Think about it: A loving, pure, committed relationship between a husband and wife is God's illustration to the world of the loving, pure, committed relationship He desires with His body, the church. Every act of sexual immorality among His people tarnishes that illustration.

The plan in the Old Testament

Not many generations passed before the descendants of Abraham found themselves in bondage to Egypt. God raised up Moses to deliver His people and provide for them a law to govern their relationships in the Promised Land, including their sexual relationships. And six of the Ten Commandments listed in Exodus 20 dealt with marital fidelity.

You shall have no other gods before me (v 3). Illicit sex violates this commandment because it elevates sexual pleasure above our relationship with God. God is a jealous God. He won't tolerate a rival, including the god of our impure appetites.

Honour your father and your mother (v 12). Sin of any kind, including sexual sin, brings shame and dishonour to our parents.

You shall not commit adultery (v 14). God ordained sex to be confined to marriage. Adultery — sex outside of marriage — is a sin against your marriage partner and God (Gen 39:9).

You shall not steal (v 15). The adulterer robs his spouse of the intimacy of their relationship and steals from his illicit partner sexual pleasure that doesn't belong to him.

You shall not give false testimony (v 16). Marriage is a covenant made before God and human witnesses. Sexual sin breaks the marriage vow. In effect, the unfaithful partner lies about being faithful to his or her spouse. The adulterer often continues lying to cover up his or her sin.

You shall not covet (v 17). To covet is to desire something that doesn't belong to you. All sexual sin begins with a desire for someone or some experience that is not rightfully yours.

Though most are delivered in the negative, the commandments of God are not restrictive but protective. God's intention was to prevent a fallen humanity from sowing even more seeds of destruction through sexual immorality and thus enlarging the realm of the kingdom of darkness.

God's law also specified heterosexuality and condemned homosexuality. His people were to maintain a clear distinction between a man and a woman in appearance: 'A woman shall not wear men's clothing, nor a man wear women's clothing, for the Lord your God detests anyone who does this' (Deut 22:5).

Homosexual marriages and sexual relations were also clearly forbidden: 'Do not lie with a man as one lies with a woman; that is detestable' (Lev 18:22); 'If a man lies with a man as one lies with a woman, both of them have done what is detestable. They must be put to death; their blood will be on their own heads' (Lev 20:13). God commanded Adam and Eve and their descendants to multiply and fill the earth. The only way they could obey that command was to pro-create through the means of sexual intercourse as men and women. Men can't have children by men, and women can't have children by women. The alternative lifestyle of homo-sexuality is in direct conflict with God's plan of populating the earth, and He detests it.

God also instructed His people regarding the spiritual purity of their marriages: 'You shall not intermarry with [pagan nations]; you shall not give your daughters to their sons, nor shall you take their daughters for your sons. For they will turn your sons away from following Me to serve other gods; then the anger of the Lord will be kindled against you, and He will quickly destroy you' (Deut 7:3,4 NASB).

Ironically, the most glaring example of disobedience to this command is found in the man reputed to be the wisest who ever lived. King Solomon had 700 wives and 300 con-cubines, including some from the nations with whom God expressly prohibited intermarriage (1 Kings 11:1,2). Solomon was the sad fulfilment of God's prediction: 'His wives turned his heart away after other gods; and his heart was not wholly devoted to the Lord his God' (1 Kings 11:4, NASB). We cannot have God-honouring marriages if we seek spouses from outside the circle of God's people.

As I travelled and studied in Israel, I saw a memorial of what happens to the kingdom of God when the king violates God's commandments. Outside the walled city of Jerusalem is a place called 'the hill of shame', which is almost completely barren. It was on this hill that King Solomon allowed his foreign wives to build temples to other gods. Israel divided into two nations after the death of Solomon and never returned to the prominence it once enjoyed. The barren hill is a sad reminder of the fruit of disobedience.

The Old Testament also assures us that God designed sex within the confines of marriage for pleasure as well as procreation. The Song of Solomon portrays the joys of physical love in courtship and marriage. Furthermore, the law directed that the first year of marriage should be reserved for marital adjustment and enjoyment: 'When a man takes a new wife, he shall not go out with the army, nor be charged with any duty; he shall be free at home one year and shall give happiness to his wife whom he has taken' (Deut 24:5 NASB).

A destructive counterplan

As God's plan of propagation and redemption unfolded in the Old Testament, Satan was there attempting to ruin it.

On one front, he tried to prevent the descendants of Adam and Abraham from producing the Redeemer, Jesus Christ. Satan was behind Pharaoh's order to kill all the male babies when Israel was in bondage to Egypt. But God preserved Moses and raised him up eighty years later to set His people free (Ex 1,2).

When Christ was born, Herod also tried to annihilate

Israel's male babies. But the Lord told Joseph about the plot in a dream, and he took Mary and the infant Jesus to Egypt (Mt 2:7–23). As we watch the heartless slaughter of millions of unborn children today, we must wonder what great deliverance God has in store for His church and ask, 'What is Satan trying to hinder this time?'

Unable to prevent the birth of the Messiah, Satan prompted Judas, one of the Lord's own, to betray Him. That devious plan played right into God's hand. The grave could not hold Jesus, and His resurrection sealed Satan's fate forever.

On another front, Satan went to work to frustrate God's plan for monogamous, heterosexual, God-dependent marriages. Throughout the Old Testament we see the evil one encouraging God's people to ignore His design and sow seeds of destruction through their immorality. Genesis 6:2,4 reports, 'The sons of God saw that the daughters of men were beautiful, and they married any of them they chose.... The sons of God went to the daughters of men and had children by them.'

The 'sons of God' were apparently fallen angels. Mark 12:25 states that angels do not procreate after their kind, but on this unique occasion in Genesis 6 it appears that they cohabited with human women to produce human offspring.

How did God respond to this gross perversion of His design? 'The Lord saw that the wickedness of man was great on the earth, and that every intent of the thoughts of his heart was only evil continually' (Gen 6:5). God put an end to that wicked generation by bringing the flood, sparing only Noah and his family. If that evil seed-line had continued, who knows what the human race would look like today.

I have counselled many people who have encountered sexual spirits. The Latin terms for male and female sexual spirits are *incubi* and *succubi*. Every period of history records some reference to them. Mythology is replete with stories and images. They have caught the fancy of many artists and sculptors. Incubi and succubi are demon spirits who visit men and women during the night and subject them to sexual depravity, lust, and terrifying nightmares.

Encounters with evil sexual spirits are far more common than most people imagine. We don't hear about them often because such experiences are horribly disgusting and embarrassing. People don't want to admit being confronted by sexual spirits. And these encounters are so bizarre that most people are afraid no one will believe them. Being harassed by a sexual spirit today doesn't produce offspring, but it can result in sexual bondage. Thankfully, in Christ we have the authority to resist all of the devil's schemes.

Satan's assault on God's design of heterosexuality is evident in the account of Sodom and Gomorrah. When angels, appearing as men, visited Lot in Sodom, all the men of the city, young and old, clamoured to have them brought outside for a homosexual orgy. God cut off this evil seed-line by destroying the two cities by fire (Gen 19:1–29). Even today we use the term 'sodomy' to describe unnatural acts of sexual intercourse, such as oral and anal sex between males. The AIDS epidemic is a chilling reminder that sowing seeds in Satan's kingdom reaps a tragic harvest.

Israel continued to battle against idolatry — and the sexual immorality which always attends it — throughout Old Testament history. When Israel split into two kingdoms — Israel and Judah, both nations went down the tubes spiritually and morally, despite the commandments of the law and the warnings of the prophets. And both nations were judged for their sin. They were conquered by their enemies, and the survivors were deported.

The Old Testament ends on a sad note. Only a remnant of God's people returned from captivity to the land God had given them. For 400 years the stronger neighbour nations pushed them around like bullies. On the eve of Christ's birth the Jews were in political bondage to Rome and in spiritual bondage to their apostate leaders. The glory of God had departed from Israel. Satan had apparently foiled God's plan.

But even though the moral and spiritual fabric of Israel had been shredded, God miraculously preserved her and used her to provide the world's Redeemer. Abraham's seed — Jesus Christ — was about to make His entrance (Jn 1:14). The blessing of Abraham was soon to be extended to all the nations of the world in Christ.

The plan in the New Testament

What was God's plan for Christian marriage after the cross in a world still dark with sin? The answer is found in 1 Thessalonians 4:3–5: 'This is the will of God, your sanctification; that is, that you abstain from sexual immorality; that each of you know how to possess his own vessel in sanctification and honour, not in lustful passion, like the Gentiles who do not know God' (NASB).

The word 'possess' means to acquire or take for yourself. The word 'vessel' is rendered 'wife' in 1 Peter 3:7. Thus verse 4 can be translated, 'That each of you know how to take a wife for himself in sanctification and honour.' God's plan is the same in the New Testament as it was in the Old Testament: monogamous, heterosexual marriage under God which is free of sexual immorality. By following God's plan we sow seeds of righteousness in His kingdom for ourselves and future generations. By ignoring God's plan we propagate Satan's agenda in our lives and the lives of others.

My first attempt at discipling a young man in university failed miserably. No matter how I tried to help him, he couldn't seem to get his spiritual life together. I was baffled. During that time, he was seeing one of the nicest Christian young ladies in the university group. Finally he stopped coming to see me.

Two years later he confessed to me that, while I was trying to disciple him, he was sleeping with several classmates, though not with the nice girl he was dating. He admitted that he had written me off after he heard me talk about sexual purity. He wanted to be a growing Christian, but he wasn't about to give up his secret, sinful activities. No wonder the discipleship process wasn't going anywhere!

Any sexual activity outside God's design is forbidden because it is counterproductive to the process of sanctification. In other words, don't expect to reap the fruit of growth, victory, and fulfilment as a Christian if you are sowing seeds in Satan's kingdom through sexual impurity.

We can apply the instruction in 1 Thessalonians 4 to several specific areas of sexual temptation.

We are to abstain from premarital sex. As already noted, it is quite common in our culture for couples in love to sleep together and even live together before marriage or in lieu of marriage. We hear justifications such as, 'Love is what counts; who needs a marriage certificate?' or 'How can we know if we're sexually compatible unless we sleep together?' Our world places a high value on physical attraction and sexual compatibility in finding a partner. Christians are far from immune to this influence. During my early years of ministry, eighteen of the first twenty Christian couples I counselled prior to marriage admitted to me that they had slept together.

Premarital sexual activity is not God's way for us to seek a life partner. Outward appearance and sexual appeal may be part of the attraction to a potential mate, but neither has the power to hold a couple together. Physical attraction is like perfume. You smell the fragrance when you put it on, but within minutes your sense of smell is saturated and you barely notice the scent. Similarly, unless you go beyond physical attraction to know the real person, the relationship won't last.

Christian dating is not like shopping for a good-looking, comfortable pair of shoes. Shoes get scuffed and worn and dated, and you have to replace them every year or two. Christian dating is the process of finding God's will for a lifetime marriage partner. Commitment to Christ and beauty of character far outweigh physical attraction and sex appeal in importance.

We are to abstain from extramarital sex. Doug and Katy came to see me years ago because they were having marital problems. In an angry moment Doug had told his wife that she didn't satisfy him sexually as a previous girlfriend had. In tears Katy told me how hard she tried to be like that other girl, something which was impossible for her. The couple left my office without resolution.

One day some time later, Doug came home to find Katy sitting on the couch with a pillow on her lap. She asked him if he loved her. Doug said he did. Katy replied, 'Then I'm going to make you pay for what you said about me for the rest of your life.' She pulled his handgun from under the pillow and shot herself to death.

Marital unfaithfulness is rooted in comparison, which is wrong. You may have been attracted to your mate by his or her appearance, personality, and other qualities. Of all the people you knew, this person seemed made just for you, and you seemed made for him or her. So you committed yourselves to each other 'till death do us part'.

Once you are married, all comparisons must end. You may meet someone who looks more like a movie star than your spouse, who seems more sensitive and caring, or who may exhibit deeper spiritual fervour. It doesn't matter. You're with the person God gave you. The best-possible-mate contest is over, and you and your spouse both won! As Christians, our first commitment is to Christ, and this is the most important relationship we have. Your marriage is a picture of that union, and no other relationship must be allowed to deface that picture. The pathway to marital happiness and fulfilment is found in pouring yourself into loving, serving, and fulfilling that person, not in looking for someone you think may bring you greater happiness.

Many people who end up in extramarital affairs say that they were bored with their spouses sexually. They're not bored with their partners; they're bored with sex because they have depersonalised it. When the focus is on the sex act, the partner as a sex object, and personal sexual satisfaction, boredom is likely. But when the focus is on nurturing the total relationship and fulfilling the dreams and expectations of your mate, marital life — including sex — remains an exciting and rewarding experience.

We are not to violate the conscience of our spouse. Several years ago I conducted a one-day conference entitled 'For Women Only'. The participants were invited to ask me questions on any topic. Embarrassing questions were written out and dropped in a basket. Most of the written questions were about sex, and most of those centred on the question, 'Must I submit to anything my husband wants me to do sexually?'

If the real question is, 'Should I submit to anything my husband *needs* sexually?' the answer is yes. And the husband should submit to meet his wife's sexual needs also. The definitive passage is 1 Corinthians 7:3–5: 'The husband should fulfil his marital duty to his wife, and likewise the wife to her husband. The wife's body does not belong to her alone but also to her husband. In the same way, the husband's body does not belong to him alone but also to his wife. Do not deprive each other except by mutual consent for a time, so that you may devote yourselves to prayer. Then come together again so that Satan will not tempt you because of your lack of self-control.'

You are not to withhold sex from your spouse or use it as a weapon against him or her. To do so gives Satan an opportunity to tempt your spouse in areas where he or she lacks self-control.

But should a wife submit to anything her husband *wants* her to do sexually? No. Neither spouse has the right to violate the conscience of the other. If a sexual act is morally wrong for one, it is morally wrong for both. One man protested to me, 'But Scripture says that the wedding bed is undefiled.' I told him to read the whole verse: 'Marriage should be honoured by all, and the marriage bed kept pure, *for God will judge the adulterer and all the sexually immoral*' (Heb 13:4).

Demanding that your spouse violate his or her conscience to satisfy your lust violates the wedding vow of loving one another and destroys the intimacy of a relationship built on trust. A person can and should meet the legitimate sexual needs of his or her marriage partner. But in no way should your spouse be used to fulfil your lust. It is terribly degrading to demand that your spouse satisfy your lust. The more you feed lustful desires, the more they grow. Only Christ can break that cycle of bondage and give you the freedom to love your wife as Christ loved the church.

We are to abstain from sexual fantasy. There it was again, the thought to pull off the motorway and rent a sexually explicit video. Even though Scott was married with two children still living at home, he still battled the urge to fantasise sexually. He had prayed repeatedly against the impulse, but as he sped closer to the slip-road a conflict raged within him. He knew his actions wouldn't be pleasing to God. He knew he would feel ashamed when it was all over. He knew he would be embarrassed if his wife or children came home unexpectedly and found him acting out his fantasy. But he was propelled to the video store like a heroin addict to a fix.

Scott had found many ways to satisfy his secret craving for sexual excitement and release: pornographic paperback novels and magazines, textbooks on the subject of sexuality, sexual fantasies while in the shower, and steamy videos featuring nudity and sex (he avoided more obvious X-rated films, reasoning that the R-rated ones were easier to explain if he got caught).

Once he was off the motorway Scott was hooked again. He made his selection in the video shop and headed home for an afternoon of self-pleasure. But after watching the movie, he was again flooded with shame and guilt. 'How did I get sucked into this pattern again?' he cried. 'Lord, what am I going to do?' He had told no one about his ongoing struggle and repeated failure in this area, not his wife, not his pastor, and not the two Christian counsellors he had seen in the past for other problems. He felt weak and alone. Even God seemed distant and unavailable.

So Scott did what he always did: He stuffed his feelings and guilt deep inside and went on with the charade of the pure, successful Christian man. Eventually his despair would dissipate and he could relax until the old urges returned and pulled him under again.

The problem of sexual fantasy has surfaced in literally hundreds of Christian men and women I have counselled. These people are not usually physically involved in premarital or extramarital sex. But in their minds they play out an endless variety of sexual adventures with people they know, characters in a raunchy book or magazine or on the video screen, or phantom lovers they dream up on their own. Some sexual fantasy addicts make love to their spouses while secretly imagining that they are with someone else.

Others find release in masturbation. Still others seek out illicit affairs.

Sexual fantasy may be regarded by many as harmless self-pleasuring. But Christians are to abstain from it for at least three different reasons.

First, under Jesus' guideline for adultery in Matthew 5:27,28, sexual immorality in the mind carries the same weight as sexual immorality in the flesh: 'You have heard that it was said, "Do not commit adultery." But I tell you that anyone who looks at a woman lustfully has already committed adultery with her in his heart.' You may be able to avoid the personal embarrassment, public scandal, or potential diseases of a physical affair. But in God's eyes an affair in the mind is the same as the real thing. It is a violation of moral purity.

Some people think that looking is what constitutes the act of mental adultery. But the passage teaches that looking only gives evidence that adultery has already been conceived in the heart. We need to heed the instruction of Proverbs 4:23: 'Above all else, guard your heart, for it is the wellspring of life.'

Second, according to James 1:14,15, sexual immorality in the mind precipitates a sexually immoral act: 'Each one is tempted when, by his own evil desire, he is dragged away and enticed. Then, after desire has conceived, it gives birth to sin; and sin, when it is full-grown, gives birth to death.' You may think your secret is safe inside you, but 'out of the overflow of the heart the mouth speaks' (Mt 12:34). What is sown and nurtured as a seed in the heart will eventually flower as a deed.

Third, sexual fantasy depersonalises sex and devalues people. For the person caught up in sexual fantasy, sex is not a facet of mutual joy and sharing in the marital relationship but an avenue for personal pleasure. When sex becomes boring in this person's marriage — which it certainly will with the mentality of all take and no give, he or she must find a more exciting partner, such as a risqué picture or story, a steamy video, or an imagined lover.

One man assured me that his sexual fantasising was not a sin because he visualised girls without heads! I told him, 'That's precisely the problem. You have depersonalised sex.' This is what pornography does. Sex objects are never regarded as persons created in God's image, much less someone's daughter or son. Treating someone as an object for personal gratification goes against everything the Bible teaches about the dignity and value of human life.

Masturbation question

That brings us to the topic of masturbation, a point at which the fantasy world and the physical world meet for many in sexual bondage. Masturbation is seen by some as a harmless, pleasurable means of releasing sexual pressure. Those who practice it, condone it, or recommend it say masturbation is a private, readily available avenue for fully gratifying one's sexual needs without fear of disease or pregnancy.

The Bible is virtually silent on the topic of masturbation, and Christians are widely divided in their opinions about it. Some believe that masturbation is a God-given gift to release pent-up sexual energy when one is unmarried or when one's mate is unavailable. At the other extreme are Christians who condemn masturbation as a sin. Those in favour remind us that it is nowhere condemned in the Bible, that it poses no health risks, and that it may help prevent acts of sexual immorality. Those opposed state that it is sex without a marriage partner and therefore wrong, that it is self-centred, that it often accompanies sexual fantasies, and that it is an uncontrollable habit.

I certainly don't want to add any restrictions that God doesn't intend, nor do I want to contribute to the legalistic condemnation that is already being heaped on people. But why do so many Christians feel guilty after masturbating? Is it because the church or their parents have said it is wrong, and therefore the guilt is only psychological? If so, the condemnation springs from a conscience that has developed improperly. The condemnation may also come from the accuser of the brethren, Satan (Rev 12:10).

To understand how masturbation may be contributing to your sexual bondage, ask yourself the following questions:

1. Do you employ masturbation as the physical release for your sexual fantasies? If you masturbate as you fantasise about having sex with models in a magazine, characters in a novel or on the screen, or real or imagined persons in your mind, you are only underscoring the mental adultery Jesus condemned.

2. Does masturbation cause you to withhold yourself from your spouse? Paul wrote, 'The husband should fulfil his marital duty to his wife, and likewise the wife to her husband. The wife's body does not belong to her alone but also to her husband. In the same way, the husband's body does not belong to him alone but also to his wife' (1 Cor 7:3,4). If through masturbation you are depleting your sexual energy at the expense of your spouse's enjoyment, you are not fulfilling your marital duty.

3. Can you stop masturbating if you want to? If you can't, you may have elevated masturbation, and perhaps your secret life of sexual fantasy, to become a god in your life. God does not tolerate any pretenders to His throne. All idols must be removed.

4. Can you masturbate without visual stimulation (video, magazines, books, etc.) or fantasising sexually in such a way that you reach orgasm while focusing on someone other than your spouse? I believe such activity constitutes adultery in the mind.

5. Do you sense the Holy Spirit's conviction when you masturbate? Perhaps you are able to masturbate apart from fantasies and from depriving your spouse. Maybe you are not chained to the act by habit; you can stop at will. But if you sense God's urging to stop, that's reason enough.

There is encouraging hope for you if you are trapped in the web of sexual fantasy and uncontrolled masturbation. Scott spent many years struggling against his sexual bondage. But when he recognised that Satan was behind his bondage, he decided to get right with God. Scott walked through the Steps to Freedom in Christ and, over a period of months, established a pattern of truth for living his life. The same way of escape is available to you.

As you struggle to gain your freedom in Christ, remember that 'there is now no condemnation for those who are in Christ Jesus' (Rom 8:1). Guilt and shame do not produce good mental health; love and acceptance do. God loves you, and He will not give up on you. You may despair in confessing again and again, but His love and forgiveness are unending.

We are to abstain from homosexuality. God's view of homosexuality hasn't changed, even though society seems to be more accepting of this 'alternate lifestyle'. The New Testament places homosexuality in the same category as other sexual sins we must avoid: 'Do not be deceived: Neither the sexually immoral nor idolaters nor adulterers nor male prostitutes nor homosexual offenders nor thieves nor the greedy nor drunkards nor slanderers nor swindlers will inherit the kingdom of God' (1 Cor 6:9,10).

Some argue, 'But I was born this way. I have always had homosexual tendencies. I can't help it; this is the way God created me.' God did not create anyone to be a homosexual. He created us male and female. Homosexuality is a lie. There is no such thing as a homosexual; there is only homosexual behaviour. Nor did God create paedophiles, adulterers, or alcoholics. If one can rationalise homosexual behaviour, why can't another rationalise adultery, fornication, paedophilia, etc.?

There may be events or influences in your past which have predisposed you to homosexual behaviour, just as other seemingly unbidden addictive behaviours, such as alcoholism, can be traced to hereditary, environmental, or spiritual causes beyond the individual's control. But God never commands us to do something we cannot do. He has commanded us to abstain from homosexuality, and He has provided a way of escape. This way of escape from homosexuality and other sexual bondages is covered in the last four chapters of this book and the Steps to Freedom in Christ.

For some sick reason, our culture is bent on finding the ultimate sexual experience without regard for whether it is right or wrong. But when they think they've found it, it satisfies only for a season, so the quest must continue. Unfortunately, Christians are negatively influenced by the world's obsession with sex, and such a focus carries painful consequences, as the next chapter describes.

Instead, we should be bent on finding the ultimate personal relationship: 'Blessed are those who hunger and thirst for righteousness, for they will be satisfied' (Mt 5:6). Are you willing to pursue the greatest of all relationships, one that every child of God can have with his heavenly Father? If so, you will be satisfied.

16
The Harvest
of Sinful Deeds

Consequences. What goes up must come down. Every action has an equal but opposite reaction. If you jump off a tall building without the benefit of a parachute, hang glider, or bungee cord, you will drop to the pavement like a rock. If you plant water-melon seeds in the spring, you'll have water-melons in your garden by summer. Everything we do and every choice we make has built-in consequences. Every seed sown produces a crop.

The same is true of our response to God's plan for sex and marriage. If we sow seeds of sexual purity in our marriages, we will reap the benefits and blessings which come from obedience to God's order. If we sow seeds of sexual immorality, we will reap a dark harvest of negative personal and spiritual consequences. Paul said it this way: 'The one who sows to his own flesh shall from the flesh reap corruption, but the one who sows to the Spirit shall from the Spirit reap eternal life' (Gal 6:8 NASB).

What are the consequences of sowing to the flesh in the area of sexual conduct? What kind of corruption is Paul talking about? First there are the more obvious outward or physical and relational consequences, which we will deal with in this chapter. Second, there are the inward or spiritual consequences, which we will explore in the next chapter. Perhaps one or more of these consequences in your life has arrested your attention and prompted you to turn from sowing to the flesh to finding your freedom and sowing in the Spirit.

The outward harvest of sexual immorality

Perhaps the most obvious and alarming consequences of ignoring God's design for sex are the physical and relational consequences. Physical pain, the threat of disease and death, and the breakup of a relationship get our attention quickly.

Free sex isn't free, and those who pursue it aren't living in freedom. Sexual promiscuity leads to disgusting forms of bondage, and the potential price tag in terms of health is staggering. Dr Joe McIlhaney, a gynaecologist, states that thirty per cent of single, sexually active Americans have herpes. Another thirty per cent have venereal wart virus. As many as thirty to forty per cent have chlamydia, which is rampant among teenagers and university students. Cases of gonorrhoea and syphilis are increasing at an alarming rate.[1] Medical health experts insist that sexually transmitted diseases (STD's) are by far the most prevalent of communicable diseases. The problem is no longer epidemic but pandemic.

The most frightening aspect of STD's is that they can be passed on without the carrier exhibiting any symptoms. This is especially true for those who test positive for HIV. Victims may go for years without showing signs of illness, unknowingly passing on the disease to their sexual partners who in turn pass it on to other unsuspecting victims. Without medical testing, a person cannot be sure that his or her sexual partner is free of all STD's. Indeed, the partner may not even know he is infected. The rapid spread of STD's in our culture illustrates the chilling truth that a sexual encounter involves more than two people. If you have sex with a promiscuous person, as far as STD's are concerned, you are also having sex with every one of that person's previous sex partners, and you are vulnerable to the diseases carried by all of them.

People who have violated God's design for sex also pay a price in their marriage relationships. Those who have had unholy sex don't seem to enjoy holy sex. I have counselled many women who can't stand to be touched by their husbands due to past illicit sexual experiences. Incredibly, their feelings change almost immediately after finding their freedom in Christ from sexual bondages. One pastor had been snubbed sexually by his wife for ten years because of bondage which had blocked her from sexual intimacy. To their mutual surprise, the couple was able to come together sexually after she found her freedom at one of our conferences.

Promiscuity before marriage seems to lead to lack of sexual fulfilment after marriage. The fun and excitement of sex outside God's will leaves the participant in bondage to illicit encounters and unable to enjoy a normal sexual relationship. If the past sins were consensual, the bondages only increase as the individual attempts to satisfy his or her lust in the marriage bed. If the sins were not consensual, meaning that the person went along with the acts but didn't really want to, he or she is not able to enjoy wholesome marital sex until the past is resolved. These persons lack the freedom to enter into mutual expressions of love and trust.

In cases where persons were victims of severe sexual abuse such as rape or incest, their bodies were used as unwilling instruments of unrighteousness. Tragically, these victims became one flesh with their abusers and have great difficulty relating to their spouses in a normal, healthy way. It's not fair that these people were violated against their will. It's sick, and the sickness pollutes what should be a beautiful and fulfilling marriage relationship. The good news is that people can be set free from the bondage of such violations. They can renounce the unrighteous uses of their body, submit to God, resist the devil, and forgive those who abused them.

In extreme cases of bondage such as satanic ritual abuse, I regularly encounter demonic spirits who claim to be the husbands of their female victims. These women cannot function in a marriage relationship because they have been deceived into believing that they are married to Satan. Rituals that wed a person to Satan are a mockery of Christ's church, because the Bible declares that we are the bride of Christ. When satanic rituals are renounced, the victims are free to grow in their relationships with God and with their spouses.

Defilement of a family

One of the most heart-rending consequences of sexual sin relates to the effect such activities have on the children of the offender. The affair between King David of Israel and Bathsheba, wife of Uriah the Hittite, is a sad case study of the downward steps of personal defilement and its effect on his family. Even though David is called a man after God's own heart (Acts 13:22), he had one dark blot on his life. First Kings 15:5 summarises his life: 'David had done what was right in the eyes of the Lord and had not failed to keep any of the Lord's commands all the days of his life — except in the case of Uriah the Hittite.' And because of his moral failure, David's family paid a steep price. Let's consider his steps to defilement and their tragic consequences.

'One evening David got up from his bed and walked around on the roof of the palace. From the roof he saw a woman bathing. The woman was very beautiful, and David sent someone to find out about her' (2 Sam 11:2,3). There was nothing wrong with the woman, Bathsheba, being beautiful, and there was nothing wrong with David being attracted to her. That's the way God made us. Bathsheba may have been wrong for bathing where others could see her, and David was definitely wrong for continuing to look at her. God provided a way of escape — David could have turned and walked away from the tempting sight. But he didn't take it.

When David sent messengers to get Bathsheba, he was too far down the path of immorality to turn around. They slept together, and she became pregnant. David tried to cover up his sin by calling Uriah, Bathsheba's husband, home from the battlefield to sleep with her. The pregnancy could then be attributed to him. But noble Uriah wouldn't co-operate, so David sent him back to the battle and arranged for him to be killed. Now David the adulterer is also a murderer! Sin has a way of compounding itself. If you think living righteously is hard, try living unrighteously. Cover-up, denial, and guilt make for a very complex life.

After a period of mourning her dead husband, Bathsheba became David's wife. David lived under the guilt and covered his shame for nine months. He apparently suffered physical consequences because of his sin. In Psalm 32:3 he describes his torment: 'When I kept silent, my bones wasted away through my groaning all day long. For day and night your hand was heavy upon me; my strength was sapped as in the heat of summer.'

The Lord allowed plenty of time for David to come to terms with his sin. The king didn't confess, so God sent the prophet Nathan to confront him. God won't let His children live in darkness for long, because He knows it will eat them alive. One pastor with a pornography addiction travelled to a pastor's conference where colleagues asked for copies of his ministry materials. When the pastor opened the briefcase with a crowd around him, he suddenly realised he had brought the wrong case. His stack of smutty magazines was there for all to see! 'There is nothing concealed that will not be disclosed, or hidden that will not be made known' (Mt 10:26).

Sadly, the public lives of many Christians are radically different from their private lives. As long as they think the façade can continue, they will not deal with their own issues. Ironically, these people are often the ones who are the most critical of others. People who haven't dealt with their own guilt often seek to balance the internal scales by projecting blame on others. But the Lord says in Matthew 7:1–5:

> Do not judge, or you too will be judged. For in the same way you judge others, you will be judged, and with the measure you use, it will be measured to you.
>
> Why do you look at the speck of sawdust in your brother's eye and pay no attention to the plank in your own eye? How can you say to your brother, 'Let me take the speck out of your eye,' when all the time there is a plank in your own eye? You hypocrite, first take the plank out of your own eye, and then you will see clearly to remove the speck from your brother's eye.

Forgiveness and consequences

David finally acknowledged his sins, both of which were capital offences under the law. Then Nathan said, 'The Lord has taken away your sin. You are not going to die. But because by doing this you have made the enemies of the Lord show utter contempt, the son born to you will die' (2 Sam 12:13,14).

The enemies of the Lord are Satan and his angels. We have little idea of the moral outrage our sexual sins cause in the spiritual realm. Satan, the accuser of the brethren, throws them into God's face day and night (Rev 12:10). Our private, secret sins are committed openly before the god of this world and his fallen angelic horde! Far worse, our sexual sins are an offence to God, who is grieved by our failure and who must endure the utter contempt of Satan.

The Lord spared David, but his son by Bathsheba had to die. Why? God's law states, 'I, the Lord your God, am a jealous God, visiting the iniquity of the fathers on the children, on the third and fourth generations of those who hate Me' (Ex 20:5 NASB). Is it possible that God had to cut off the rebellious seed that was sown by David so that the male offspring of this adulterous relationship did not receive the birthright? Remember, this is the throne of David upon which the Messiah would eventually reign. Also remember that God is merciful. He took the infant home, and David had the assurance that he would be with the child in eternity (2 Sam 12:23).

Are succeeding generations guilty for the sins of their parents? Absolutely not! Such was the belief in Israel, but it required a correcting word from the Lord in Ezekiel 18:4: 'The soul who sins is the one who will die.' Everyone will account for his own sin, but we are all affected by the sins of others. Children are not guilty for their parents' sins, but because their parents sinned, judgement will fall upon them and their household according to the Mosaic covenant. Once a father has set himself against God, this propensity for self-will is likely to be passed to the next generation.

Additional judgement was meted out to David's household as a result of his sin. The prophet Nathan declared, 'This is what the Lord says: "Out of your own household I am going to bring calamity upon you. Before your very eyes I will take your wives and give them to one who is close to you, and he will lie with your wives in broad daylight. You did it in secret, but I will do this thing in broad daylight before Israel"' (2 Sam 12:11). The Lord's word was fulfilled when Absalom, one of David's sons, 'lay with his father's concubines in the sight of all Israel' (2 Sam 16:22).

Amnon, another son of David, followed his father's

example to an even more despicable level of sexual immorality (2 Sam 13). His lust for his virgin half-sister Tamar, Absalom's sister, provoked him to ply her sympathies with a feigned illness. When Tamar came to his room to take care of him, Amnon tried to seduce her. When she refused, he raped her. Apparently Amnon could have gone through legitimate channels to take Tamar as his wife. But his lust demanded to be satisfied *now*. Additional calamity came upon David as a result of his sin. Four of his sons died prematurely. Bathsheba's son died at birth, Amnon was killed by his brother Absalom in retaliation for the rape of Tamar, and Absalom and Adonijah were both killed attempting to take the throne from David. All this came upon David because he failed to turn away from the tempting sight of a woman bathing. How important it is to us and our loved ones to take every thought captive to the obedience of Christ (2 Cor 10:5).

Is sin inherited?

Do we inherit a specific bent toward sin from our parents? And if we do, is this transmission genetic, environmental, or spiritual? I believe the correct answers are *yes* and *all three!* First, there is plenty of evidence to show that we are genetically predisposed to certain strengths and weaknesses. However, genetics cannot be blamed for all bad choices. For example, it has been clearly shown that some people are genetically predisposed to alcoholism. Yet no one is born an alcoholic. People become alcoholics by drinking irresponsibly.

Similarly, some boys possess higher levels of testosterone than other boys, as evidenced by facial hair, body musculature, and obvious masculine traits. Other boys with lower levels of testosterone appear more effeminate. This does not make them homosexuals, but they may be more vulnerable to the possibility, especially if they are severely taunted and teased about their appearance by their peers or parents.

Second, environmental factors also contribute to sinful behaviour being passed on from one generation to the next. For example, if you were raised in a home where pornography was readily available and sexual promiscuity was modelled, you would certainly be influenced in this direction. Unless parents deal with their sins, they unwittingly set up the next generation to repeat their moral failures. 'A student is not above his teacher, but everyone who is fully trained will be like his teacher' (Lk 6:40).

Third, there seems to be an inherited spiritual bent toward sin as well. For instance, Abraham lied about his wife, calling her his sister. Later his son Isaac did exactly the same thing. Then Isaac's son Jacob lied in order to steal his brother's birthright. After Abraham's falsehood, his offspring appear to be spiritually predisposed to falsehood.

We are not just up against the world and the flesh in our struggle to find our freedom in Christ. Scripture tells of a third unwanted contributor to our make-up: Satan. Jeremiah 32:17,18 declares, 'Ah, Lord God! Behold, Thou hast made the heavens and the earth by Thy great power and by Thine outstretched arm! Nothing is too difficult for Thee, who showest lovingkindness to thousands, but repayest the iniquity of the fathers into the bosom of their children after them, O great and mighty God.'

Notice that the sins of the fathers are repaid into the bosom of their children. This is not an environmental or genetic factor; this is an intergenerational factor based on the disobedience of ancestors. This unholy inheritance cannot be dealt with passively. We must consciously take our place in Christ and renounce the sins of our ancestors. We are not guilty of our parents' sins, but because they sinned, their sins may be passed on to us. That is why we are told in Leviticus 26:40 to confess our own sin and the sin of our

forefathers 'in their unfaithfulness which they have committed against Me, and also in their acting with hostility
against Me'. The opposite is to cover up and defend the sins
of our parents, grandparents, etc. and continue in the cycle
of bondage.

The possibility of overcoming generational sins is evidenced in the life of Joseph, one of Jacob's sons. Joseph was
given every opportunity to lie to protect himself from his
jealous brothers. In fact, the more he told the truth, the
more trouble he endured. If he was predisposed to lying, he
chose not to comply. Eventually he was totally vindicated
for his honesty.

I frequently minister to people who repeat the sins of
their parents and grandparents. Are they forced to do these
things? No! But they will repeat them if they continue to
hold iniquity in their hearts, which can be visited to the
third and fourth generations.

No matter what our ancestors have done, if we repent
and believe in Christ, God rescues us from the dominion of
darkness and brings us into the kingdom of His dear Son
(Col 1:13). We are under a new covenant which promises,
'Their sins and lawless acts I will remember no more' (Heb
10:17).

Repentance breaks the chain

Repentance is God's answer to iniquity, whether ours or our
ancestors'. To repent means to have a change of mind about
sin, from active or passive participation to renunciation.
Repentance is far more than mental acknowledgement,
however. It means to turn from our wicked ways and trust
in God. It means to no longer hold iniquity in our hearts.
The early church began their public profession of faith by
declaring, 'I renounce you, Satan, and all your works and
ways.' This would be a good statement to add to our daily
confession of faith in Christ. The idea is to reclaim any

ground we or our forefathers have given to Satan. Then we commit all we have and all we are to God. In this way we are being faithful stewards of everything God has entrusted to us (1 Cor 4:1,2).

Such a commitment should include our possessions, our ministries, our families, and the activity of our physical bodies, including sexual activity. As we renounce any previous use of these for the service of sin and then dedicate them to the Lord, we are saying that the god of this world no longer has any right over them. They now belong to God, and Satan can't have them or use them.

It is important to understand that God forgives us when we repent, but He doesn't necessarily take away the consequences of our sin. If He did, it wouldn't take us long to figure out that we can sin all we want and then turn to God for cleansing without any repercussions.

It is also important to realise that when a parent repents there is no guarantee that his or her children will. Even if they were influenced genetically, environmentally, or spiritually in the direction of your sin, your children are responsible for their own choices. They may choose to repeat or not to repeat your failures. If they do follow you into sin, they may choose or not choose to follow your example of repentance.

Bad health is contagious, but unfortunately good health isn't. Paul wrote, 'Do not be misled: "Bad company corrupts good character"' (1 Cor 15:33). Your children may have 'caught' your bad habits from you, but they won't necessarily catch repentance from you. However, your repentant, healthy, God-fearing lifestyle may influence them to make their own choice to renounce sin and trust Christ.

David's sexual sin and murderous cover-up was tragic, and the consequences of sin in his own life and in the lives of his children were painful and long-lasting. But his story has a happy ending. David responded to his sin correctly and went on to shepherd Israel with integrity of heart and lead them with skilful hands (Ps 78:72). And his seed-line provided the human component to the Satan-crushing Redeemer promised in Genesis 3:15.

David's confession of sin in Psalm 51 is a model prayer for those who violate God's plan for sex:

> Have mercy on me, O God, according to your unfailing love; according to your great compassion blot out my transgressions. Wash away all my iniquity and cleanse me from my sin. For I know my transgressions, and my sin is always before me. Against you, you only, have I sinned and done what is evil in your sight, so that you are proved right when you speak and justified when you judge.... Create in me a pure heart, O God, and renew a steadfast spirit within me. Do not cast me from your presence or take your Holy Spirit from me. Restore to me the joy of your salvation and grant me a willing spirit, to sustain me (vv 1–4,10–12).

But what if we sin and don't confess? What if we get caught up in pornography, lust, sexual fantasy, or illicit affairs and keep it a secret instead of exposing it to the light? What kind of consequences can we expect?

In addition to exacerbating the physical and relational consequences described in this chapter, continued sexual sin leads us down a dark path to the dead end of sexual bondage. The next chapter describes this process and prepares us for finding the way of escape.

NOTE

1.   Joe McIlhaney, *Sexuality and Sexually Transmitted Diseases* (Grand Rapids, MI: Baker Book House, 1990), p 14.

17
The Dark Dead End
of Bondage

A second look at the story of Amnon's rape of his half sister Tamar, briefly described in the last chapter, introduces the most sobering of all consequences of sexual sin: bondage.

Before the act, 'Amnon son of David fell in love with Tamar.... Amnon became frustrated to the point of illness on account of his sister Tamar, for she was a virgin, and it seemed impossible for him to do anything to her' (2 Sam 13:1,2). What Amnon called love was really lust, as evidenced by his selfish behaviour.

Solomon warned in Proverbs 6:25,26, 'Do not lust in your heart after her beauty or let her captivate you with her eyes, for the prostitute reduces you to a loaf of bread, and the adulteress preys upon your very life.' Tamar was not a prostitute, but the sexual fantasy in Amnon's mind had been replayed so many times that he was physically sick. He had looked lustfully once too often. The way of escape was gone. He had probably slept with her in his mind many times. This kind of lust screams for expression. So Amnon and his friend Jonadab concocted a plan to get Tamar into Amnon's bed.

Once a plan to fulfil the demands of lust is set in motion, it can seldom be stopped. Amnon had lost control, and where there is no self-control all reason is gone. Amnon's sick desire had reduced him to a loaf of bread — powerless to stop the runaway train of his desires. Tamar's description .

was correct: Amnon was 'like one of the wicked fools in Israel' (2 Sam 13:13).

Ironically, right after the act, 'Amnon hated her with intense hatred. In fact, he hated her more than he had loved her. Amnon said to her, "Get up and get out!"' (2 Sam 13:15). It's clear that Amnon wasn't in love; he was trapped in a cycle of sexual addiction. All people in bondage hate the things that control them. The alcoholic craves a drink, then when he's had his fill he smashes the bottle against the wall in remorse, only to go and buy another when the craving returns. The pornography addict burns his magazines, tosses his X-rated videos into the garbage, or tells his secret lover he never wants to see her again. But when his lust rekindles, as it always does, he's back to his old haunts looking for a sexual fit. The most debilitating consequence of repeatedly yielding to sexual temptation and sin is the cycle of sexual addiction it leads to.

The addiction cycle

The addiction cycle is basically the same for every form of bondage, including sexual bondage. The cycle involves an individual's baseline experience of sexual behaviour. Activities above the baseline are acceptable or right in the eyes of the individual. Activities below the line are considered questionable or wrong. For the Christian, the area above the baseline represents God's plan for sexual purity, and the area below the line represents sexual impurity.

Each loop of the cycle represents a sexual thought or action with several stages. The emotional or physical rush prompted by the experience surges to an euphoric high, followed by a decline. For example, Joe, a teenaged boy, notices a new girl in class, Mary, a real beauty. Joe feels a rush of emotion just looking at Mary. When Mary returns his glance with a smile, Joe's face flushes warm and his

The Addiction Cycle

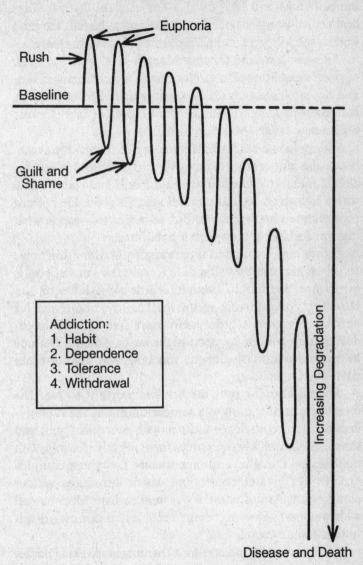

Euphoria

Rush

Baseline

Guilt and
Shame

Addiction:
1. Habit
2. Dependence
3. Tolerance
4. Withdrawal

Increasing Degradation

Disease and Death

heart races with excitement. He's never felt so high. When the bell rings and Mary walks out of class, Joe's feelings decline. It's over for now, but he liked what he felt. He can't wait to see Mary again and repeat the sensational high.

All week long Joe watches Mary in class with the same wonderful, exciting results. Now, Joe is a nice Christian boy, and he has his standards of sexual purity. He has Mary's best interests at heart. But Joe craves more of that glorious high. So he invites Mary on a date.

Riding in the car with Mary brings a tremendous rush. When she innocently reaches over and touches his leg, Joe almost flies out the top! They hold hands and end the date with a light hug. Joe is in love. So far, so good. He has not compromised his standards. But he begins to imagine what it might feel like if they went a little farther.

Before long a hug and then a kiss from Mary don't give Joe the same rush they first did. To have the same euphoric experience, Joe has to become a little more adventurous. However, going farther means he has to compromise his moral convictions a little. Joe is more free with his hands during their passionate good-night kisses. When he's alone he begins to fantasise about touching and kissing other parts of Mary's body.

At first stepping over the line was worth it to Joe. The immediate gratification was wonderful. But as the euphoria declines, Joe's conscience kicks in with twinges of guilt and shame. So he quickly overcomes these negative feelings with more sexual thoughts and experiments. Every new compromise brings greater conviction, which introduces greater compromise. At this point, Joe — and perhaps Mary as well — is well on his way to being locked into a downward-spiralling addictive cycle.

The same cycle operates for other forms of sexual addiction: pornography, sexual fantasy, homosexuality. Like a drug, seemingly harmless injections of euphoria wear off and call for greater doses. As lust grows, more experience is required to quench it. But it can't be satisfied. The more a fleshly desire is fed, the larger it grows. Normal sexual experiences don't seem to bring the euphoria that a simple touch once did. So other experiences must be tried to get that same high. Self-centred thinking begins to dominate. The conviction to not violate another's conscience or moral boundaries is replaced by 'How far can I get her to go?'

As the decline continues, a sexual habit brings an increasing sense of dependence on the experience. The pleasurable act becomes a means of releasing stress and tension. There is an increased tolerance for sin as the mind is repeatedly filled with pornographic images and actual experiences. Most people in sexual bondage begin to withdraw from people and from God as the degradation continues. The unchecked cycle of sexual addiction eventually opens the door to sexually transmitted diseases and even death. Addicts with a strong conscience against violating others will turn to self-gratification. Pornography and uncontrolled masturbation become a vicious cycle of habitual experience.

Fear and danger replace love and trust in the search for greater sexual highs. A married man shared that he filled his craving for 'exciting' sex by carrying on an adulterous affair in a motel. He and his girlfriend liked to perform sex with the curtains open or late at night in the motel swimming pool. For this man, sex with his Christian wife had become unexciting because his lust was reinforced by fear and danger.

A spiritual battle

The shameful decline of sexual addiction is depicted in Romans 1:24–28:

> Therefore God gave them over in the sinful desires of their
> hearts to sexual impurity for the degrading of their bodies

with one another. They exchanged the truth of God for a lie, and worshipped and served the created things rather than the Creator — who is forever praised. Amen.

Because of this, God gave them over to shameful lusts. Even their women exchanged natural relations for unnatural ones. In the same way the men also abandoned natural relations with women and were inflamed with lust for one another. Men committed indecent acts with other men, and received in themselves the due penalty for their perversion.

Furthermore, since they did not think it worthwhile to retain the knowledge of God, he gave them over to a depraved mind, to do what ought not to be done.

If you find yourself in this downward spiral, realise that your degradation began when you exchanged the truth of God for a lie and began worshipping created things rather than the Creator. In a moment of temptation, you chose to follow lustful desires instead of God's plan for sexual purity. With every repeated negative choice, the lie became more deeply entrenched. Satan, the 'father of lies' (Jn 8:44), couldn't be more pleased.

There are many ways by which we are tempted to exchange the natural for the unnatural in the area of sexual behaviour. One is the fascination with oral and anal sex. Before the so-called sexual revolution of the '60s, those acts were considered to be sodomy in almost every state in America. Even today the media uses the term 'sodomy' for forced oral sex. Our young people are experimenting with oral sex because they consider it 'safe', that is, they can't get pregnant. But it's not safe in a time when sexually transmitted diseases are rampant.

Can oral and anal sex be considered natural uses of our bodies? Is that how God designed those body parts to be used? From the standpoint of hygiene only, is it natural to put the mouth so close to the orifices for bodily elimination? Scripture is silent on this specific issue. We are left to determine what is natural and unnatural based on the Holy Spirit's guidance. If a Christian couple mutually agrees that oral sex is a holy use of your body, so be it.

Ignorance of the truth is no excuse. God has designed us with a built-in tracking system that directs us toward appropriate moral conduct (Rom 1:18–20). If we stubbornly ignore this system, God permits the kingdom of darkness to further blind us to the truth. This results in the overthrow of God the Creator as King in favour of 'almighty self', the creature.

Operating on the basis of a lie, the individual denies that his unrighteous behaviour is wrong. Every conscious choice against the truth numbs the soul's awareness of it. Behaviours that were once seen as unnatural and indecent are passionately accepted as normal. The conscience becomes seared and any knowledge of God is gradually blotted out.

God brings judgement upon those who will not honour Him. He gives them over to their degrading passions. When the church at Corinth condoned an incident of sexual perversion, Paul instructed them, 'Hand this man over to Satan, so that the sinful nature may be destroyed and his spirit saved on the day of the Lord' (1 Cor 5:5).

Throughout this degenerative process, God graciously provides a way of escape through Christ. No matter where a person may be in his or her flight from the truth into darkness, there is a way out. The serial rapist and murderer on death row is just as welcome to God's forgiveness and deliverance as the child who lies about stealing a biscuit. In God's economy, sin is not measured in quality or quantity. Jesus paid the price for all of it. Freedom from sexual bondage is available to everyone.

Notice the progression that Paul gives in Romans 1: from shameful lusts to homosexuality to a depraved mind. As a nation, America is probably between stages two and three. Homosexuality is accepted as an alternative lifestyle and protected by our courts. Our minds are becoming increasingly depraved. The frightening thing is that a depraved mind is devoid of logic. It can no longer reason morally. We are well on our way to sliding completely off our moral foundation as a nation.

Is there hope for those who haven't gone too far? Can we repent of our sinful ways and return to God? Of course we can, and we can have victory over sin if we understand and appropriate our position in Christ, as the last remaining chapters in this book explain.

Strongholds in the mind

Another way to view the dark, dead-end consequence of sexual bondage is to understand how strongholds are erected in the mind. Remember: A stronghold is an established, habitual pattern of thinking and behaving against which the individual is virtually powerless to choose or act. The formation of these strongholds occurs in two ways, often beginning early in life.

The first avenue is through the *prevailing experiences* in our lives, such as families, friends, churches, neighbourhoods, jobs, etc. As children, our attitudes and actions were partially shaped by each of these influences. For example, friends who shared their pornographic magazines with you may have encouraged you into a fascination with or addiction to pornography. Or if a relative sexually abused you as a child, those experiences have influenced your thinking and behaviour. Even into adulthood our day-to-day environment helps shape how we live.

Environment isn't the only prevailing experience which determines how we develop. Two children can be raised in the same home by the same parents, eat the same food, play with the same friends, and attend the same church and still respond differently to life. We are individually created expressions of God's workmanship (Ps 139:13,14; Eph 2:10). Despite similarities in genes and upbringing, our particular differences make our responses to the world around us unique.

The second great contributor to the development of strongholds in our mind is *traumatic experiences*. Whereas prevailing experiences are assimilated by the mind over time, one traumatic experience can be instantly burned into our memory because of its intensity. For example, one bad encounter with a nest of hornets may leave a child with a deep fear of all flying, stinging insects as an adult. Perhaps you were raped as a child or teenager. Or maybe your parents were divorced, or one of them died suddenly. All of these traumatic experiences are stored in our memory bank and influence our thinking.

As we struggle to reprogramme our minds against the negative input of past experiences, we are also confronted daily with an ungodly world system. Paul warned us, 'Do not conform any longer to the pattern of this world' (Rom 12:2). As Christians we are not immune to worldly values; we can allow them to affect our thinking and behaviour. But Paul insisted, 'Don't let them influence you!' He also instructed, 'See to it that no one takes you captive through hollow and deceptive philosophy, which depends on human tradition and the basic principles of this world rather than on Christ' (Col 2:8).

Since we live in this world, we will continuously face the temptation to conform to it. It is not a sin to be tempted. If it were, Christ was the worst sinner who ever lived, because He was 'tempted in every way, just as we are — yet was without sin' (Heb 4:15). We sin when we consciously choose to give in to temptation.

All temptation is an attempt by Satan to get us to live our lives independently of God, to walk according to the flesh rather than according to the Spirit (see Gal 5:16–23).

Satan knows exactly which buttons to push when tempting us. He knows your weaknesses and your family history. He's aware of the prevailing experiences and traumatic experiences which have made you vulnerable to certain temptations. And based on your past behaviour, he knows how to tantalise you to entertain impure thoughts and deeds.

Each temptation begins with a seed thought planted in our minds by the world, the flesh, or the devil himself. Since we live in Satan's world, we must learn how to stand against the temptations he throws at us. Since sex is used in the media to entertain and to sell everything from beer to deodorant to toothpaste to cars, we are constantly bombarded with seed thoughts perverting God's plan for sex. Many people can be tempted to sexual sin without much prompting from the external world, because they have programmed so much junk into their minds through television, movies, books, and magazines. They can fantasise for years without leaving their homes.

That's why sexual strongholds are so difficult to overcome. Once they are formulated in the mind, the mental pictures are there for instant recall. An alcoholic can't get drunk by fantasising about a bottle. A drug addict can't get high by imagining himself snorting cocaine. A habitual overeater isn't soothed thinking about a giant chocolate cake. But some victims of sexual bondage can get a rush, a high, and even a self-induced orgasm without any external props. Of course, pornography and illicit sexual activities serve to reinforce and strengthen sexual strongholds.

Understanding the strongholds

If we continue to act on wrong choices in response to temptation, a habit can be formed in about six weeks. If the habit persists, a stronghold will be developed in the mind. My friend Ed Silvoso says, 'A stronghold is a mindset impregnated with hopelessness that causes one to accept as unchangeable something known to be contrary to the will of God.'

Strongholds are mental habit patterns that have been burned into our minds over time or by the intensity of traumatic experiences. They are evident in temperament and behaviour that is less than Christlike, as illustrated by three common strongholds: inferiority, alcoholism, and homosexuality.

Inferiority is a major stronghold that many Christians struggle with. We don't develop an inferiority complex overnight; it is burned into our minds over time. If you are plagued by feelings of inferiority, chances are you were raised under a harsh performance code. No matter how hard you tried, you couldn't please your parents, your teachers, your pastor, or God. Your efforts were never quite good enough.

As a redeemed child of God, you understand that you are inferior to no other person. But the deeply ingrained feelings of the past won't let you act on the truth. You feel trapped on a dead-end street. So you are constantly searching for the acceptance that eluded you as a child. That's a stronghold. It must be demolished for you to walk in the freedom of who you are in Christ.

Look at the strongholds that come from living in an alcoholic home. Three boys are raised by a father who becomes an alcoholic after years of drinking. The man comes home drunk and abusive every night. His oldest boy is strong enough to stand up to Dad. There is no way he is going to take anything from this drunk. The middle boy doesn't think he can stand up to Dad, so he accommodates the man, tries to comfort him. The youngest boy is terrorised. When Dad comes home he heads for the cupboard or hides under the bed.

Twenty years later the father is gone and these three boys are now adults. When they are confronted with a hostile situation, how do you think they respond? Of course, the older one fights, the middle one accommodates, and the younger one runs and hides. Those are strongholds in the mind — mental habit patterns of thought that have developed over time.

Similarly, sexual strongholds are the dark end of sexual temptation, sexual sin, and impure habit patterns. You may *know* about God's plan of sexual purity and even *agree* with it. But, try as you might, you can't *conform* to it. You are likely trapped in one of the following sexual strongholds.

Homosexuality is a major stronghold, probably one of the most resistant to normal treatment. Those who are caught in the web of this stronghold weren't born that way. Homosexuality itself is a lie. There is no such thing as a homosexual. God created us male and female. There is only homosexual behaviour, which the Lord condemns. Condemning those who struggle with this behaviour, however, will prove counterproductive. They don't need any more condemnation. They suffer from an incredible identity crisis already. Overbearing authoritarianism is what drove many to this lifestyle in the first place.

Most of those who struggle with homosexual tendencies or behaviours have had poor developmental upbringing. Sexual abuse, dysfunctional families (often where the roles of mother and father are reversed), exposure to homosexual literature before they had an opportunity to fully develop their own sexual identity, playground teasing, and poor relationships with the opposite sex all contribute to their mental and emotional development. Mixed messages lead to mixed emotions.

Charles, a 52-year-old pastor, admitted to me that he had struggled with homosexual tendencies for as long as he could remember. More than once he had given in to those urges. He begged God to forgive him and take the feelings away. He had attended healing services and self-help groups for those with sexual bondages. Nothing worked. To his credit, Charles never once got mad at God. He was married and somehow had kept his struggle a secret from his family. Most people in sexual bondage struggle privately. It is an extremely lonely battle.

I asked Charles what his earliest childhood memory was. He went right back to the age of two. His birth father left before he was born, and his Christian mother raised him. She had a boyfriend who occasionally came over and spent the night. On those nights two-year-old Charles had to share a bed with this man. Charles' earliest childhood memory was of this man, whom he admired so much, turning his back to him and going to sleep. The little boy was desperately looking for affirmation from a male figure, wanting so much to be loved, accepted, and appreciated. As an adult he found that affection in homosexual men.

As I walked him through the Steps to Freedom in Christ, Charles broke down and cried. He forgave his birth father for abandoning him and forgave the man who slept in his bed for rejecting him. Then he renounced every sexual use of his body as an instrument of unrighteousness and gave himself and his body to the Lord. I also encouraged him to renounce the lie that he was a homosexual and declare the truth that God had created him to be a man. As he finished the Steps, the bondage to homosexuality was broken.

I didn't cast a demon of homosexuality out of him. I don't believe there is a demon of homosexuality or a demon of lust. That kind of simplistic thinking has hurt the credibility of the church. I have seen Christianity mocked on prime-time television by a parade of homosexuals and lesbians who have left the church because well-meaning Christians have tried to cast a demon of homosexuality out of them.

Don't get me wrong: There is no question that Satan is behind their problem, and his demons will tempt, accuse, deceive, and take advantage of any ground that is given to them. Focusing on the demonic only deals with part of the problem. It doesn't take into consideration all the other factors, and I personally don't think that method of dealing with the demonic is best.

We have identified God's beautiful design for sex and marriage. We have seen how Satan attempts to pervert God's design and direct our attention away from the Creator to self and its desires. We have considered the contributing factors to sexual bondage and listed the steps which lead to this dark dead end. Hopefully you have gained insight into the reasons for your struggles in the area of sexual purity.

But that's only half the story. The best is yet to come. There is a way out of the dark, suffocating prison of sexual bondage. That way out is Jesus Christ. His provision for our freedom is the theme of the rest of this book.

18
Beliefs that
Open Prison Doors

So if God's Word so clearly and strongly commands people not to live in sexual bondage, why don't we just obey God and stop doing what He forbids? Because telling people that they are doing wrong does not give them the power to stop doing it. Paul declared, 'If a law had been given that could impart life, then righteousness would certainly have come by the law. But the Scripture declares that the whole world is a prisoner of sin' (Gal 3:21,22). The law is powerless to eliminate the problem and give life. Something more is needed.

Even more discouraging is Paul's statement, 'The sinful passions aroused by the law were at work in our bodies' (Rom 7:5). The law not only can't help us do right, it actually has the capacity to provoke what it is trying to prohibit. Forbidden fruit always appears more desirable. If you don't believe it, tell your child he can go *here* but he can't go *there*. Where does he immediately want to go? *There!* Laying down the law does not remove sinful passions. The core problem is the basic sinful nature of people, not their behaviour.

The Pharisees were the most law-abiding people of Jesus' day, but they were far from righteous. Jesus told His disciples, 'Unless your righteousness surpasses that of the Pharisees and the teachers of the law, you will certainly not enter the kingdom of heaven' (Mt 5:20). Jesus' Sermon on the Mount confronts the issue of genuine righteousness which is determined by the condition of the heart. For example, He taught, 'You have heard that it was said, "Do not commit adultery." But I tell you that anyone who looks at a woman lustfully has already committed adultery with her in his heart' (Mt 5:27,28). A person doesn't commit adultery when he or she looks; the looking just gives evidence that adultery was already committed in the heart.

Jesus goes on to say, 'If your right eye causes you to sin, gouge it out.... If your right hand causes you to sin, cut it off' (vv 29,30). Do our eyes and hands cause us to sin? Not really. Getting rid of them may be necessary if our only option is to live under the law. But if we keep cutting off body parts to stop sinning, we will end up as dismembered torsos rolling down the street — and we will still have to deal with lust in our hearts. No, taking cold showers to put out the fires of lust and walking blindfolded on a sunbathers' beach may bring temporary relief, but it does not deal with the condition of the heart.

Trying to live a righteous life externally when we are not righteous internally will only result in us becoming 'whitewashed tombs, which look beautiful on the outside but on the inside are full of dead men's bones and everything unclean' (Mt 23:27). The focus must be on what is inside: 'For from within, out of men's hearts, come evil thoughts, sexual immorality, theft, murder, adultery, greed, malice, deceit, lewdness, envy, slander, arrogance, and folly. All these evils come from inside and make a man "unclean"' (Mk 7:20–23).

The secret of victory

If trying harder to break the bonds of lustful thoughts and behaviour and to live in sexual purity doesn't work, what will? Two verses in the Bible succinctly state what must happen in order for us to live righteously in Christ: 'The reason the Son of God appeared was to destroy the devil's work. No one who is born of God will continue to sin, because

God's seed remains in him' (1 Jn 3:8,9). If you are going to be set free from sexual bondage and walk in that freedom, your basic nature must be changed, and you must have a means for overcoming the evil one.

For those of us who are Christians, these conditions have already been met. God has made us partakers of His divine nature (2 Pet 1:4) and provided the means by which we can live in victory over sin and Satan.

Before we knelt at the cross, the following words described us: 'You were dead in your trespasses and sins, in which you formerly walked according to the course of this world, according to the prince of the power of the air, of the spirit that is now working in the sons of disobedience. Among them we too all formerly lived in the lusts of our flesh, indulging the desires of the flesh and of the mind, and were by nature children of wrath' (Eph 2:1–3 NASB). Before Christ, we were dead in our sins and subject to the control of Satan.

But a change took place at salvation. Paul wrote, 'You were once darkness, but now you are light in the Lord' (Eph 5:8). Our old nature in Adam was darkness; our new nature in Christ is light. We have been transformed at the core of our being. We are no longer 'in the flesh'; we are 'in Christ'. Paul wrote, 'Those who are in the flesh cannot please God. However you are not in the flesh but in the Spirit, if indeed the Spirit of God dwells in you' (Rom 8:8,9 NASB).

Furthermore, before we became Christians we were under the dominion of the god of this world, Satan. But at salvation God 'rescued us from the dominion of darkness and brought us into the kingdom of the Son he loves, in whom we have redemption, the forgiveness of sins' (Col 1:13,14). We no longer have to obey the evil prompting of the world, the flesh, and the devil. We 'have been given fullness in Christ, who is the head over every power and authority' (Col 2:10). We are free to obey God and walk in righteousness and purity.

There is no way we can fix the failure and sin of the past, but by the grace of God we can be free from it. God's Word promises, 'If anyone is in Christ, he is a new creation; the old has gone, the new has come!' (2 Cor 5:17). Furthermore, we are seated with Christ in the heavenlies, far above Satan's authority (Eph 2:4–6; Col 2:10,11), paving the way for us to live in victory and freedom over sin and bondage. But we also have a responsibility. We must *believe* the truth of who we are in Christ and change how we *walk* as children of God to conform to what is true.

Paul writes in Ephesians 1:18,19, 'I pray also that the eyes of your heart may be enlightened in order that you may know the hope to which he has called you, the riches of his glorious inheritance in the saints, and his incomparably great power for us who believe.' We already share in Christ's rich inheritance, and we already have the power to live victoriously in Christ. God has provided these glorious benefits for us. The problem for most Christians struggling in bondage is that they just don't see it.

As you work through the rest of this book, my prayer is that the eyes of your heart will be opened to see the inheritance and power God has provided for you in Christ. In this chapter you will discover what you must *believe* to find the way of escape from sexual bondage. In Chapter 19 you learn how to *walk* in accordance with that liberating belief.

Alive in Christ and dead to sin

Before examining our position in Christ from the book of Romans, let me clarify some basic principles of Bible interpretation. When you come to a command in the Bible, the only proper response is to obey it. But when Scripture is expressing something that is true, the only proper response is to believe it. It's a simple concept, but people often get it twisted by trying to do something God only expects them to believe and accept as truth before living accordingly by faith.

Nowhere is this more likely to occur than in Romans 6:1–11, which is explored in this chapter. Many Christians read this section and ask, 'How do I do that?' Romans 6:1–11 is not something you can do; it's only something you can believe. But believing it will totally affect your walk by faith. It is the critical first step to finding the way of escape from sexual bondage.

Another principle of Bible interpretation to understand is that the New Testament Greek language is very precise, especially when it comes to verb tenses. You can know when a verb is past, present, or future tense, and whether the verb is describing continuous action or an action which occurred at a point in time. However, you don't have to know the Greek language to appreciate what the Word of God is saying. The English translations bring this out fairly well, although sometimes the verb tenses are not quite as obvious.

Applying these principles to Romans 6:1–11, we discover several specific truths we are called to believe about ourselves, sin, and God. These beliefs form the foundation for the believer's hope in overcoming sin and bondage, including sexual bondage.

You are dead to sin

'What shall we say, then? Shall we go on sinning so that grace may increase? By no means! We died to sin; how can we live in it any longer?' (Rom 6:1,2). The defeated Christian asks, 'How do I do that? How do I die to sin, including the sexual sins which have me bound?' The answer is, 'You can't do it!' Why not? Because you have already died to sin at salvation. 'We died to sin' is past tense;

it has already been done. This is something you must believe, not something you must do.

'I can't be dead to sin,' you may respond, 'because I don't *feel* dead to sin.' You will have to set your feelings aside for a few verses, because it's what you believe that sets you free, not what you feel. God's Word is true whether you choose to believe it or not. Believing the Word of God doesn't make it true; His Word is true, therefore you must believe it even if your emotions don't co-operate.

A pastor stopped by my office one day and said, 'I have been struggling for twenty-two years in my Christian experience. It's been one trial after another, and I think I know what my problem is. I was doing my devotions the other day when I came across Colossians 3:3, "For you died, and your life is now hidden with Christ in God." That's the key to victory, isn't it?' I assured him that I agreed. Then he asked, 'How do I do that?'

I was surprised by his question, so I asked him to look at the passage again and read it just a little slower. So he read it again: 'For you died, and your life is hidden with Christ in God.' Again he asked in desperation, 'I know I need to die with Christ, but how do I do it?' This dear man has been desperately trying for twenty-two years to do something that has already been done, to become someone he already is. He's not alone. Many Bible-believing Christians are bogged down in their maturity and victory because they are trying to become something they already are.

You were baptised into Christ's death

'Don't you know that all of us who were baptised into Christ Jesus were baptised into his death?' (Rom 6:3). You may still be wondering, 'How do I do that?' The answer is the same: You can't do it, because you have already been baptised into Christ Jesus. It happened the moment you placed your faith in Jesus Christ as Saviour and Lord. It is futile to seek something which the Bible affirms we already have: 'We were all baptised by one Spirit into one body' (1 Cor 12:13). 'We were' is past tense. It's done, so it must be believed.

The ordinance of water baptism is understood by most Christians to be the symbolic representation of what has already been done. Augustine called baptism a visible form of an invisible grace. It is a public identification with the death, burial, and resurrection of the Lord Jesus Christ. Those who practice infant baptism understand the ordinance to identify with the Holy Spirit coming upon Christ. They sprinkle water on the infant's head instead of immersing the body. Both look to Scripture for the basis of their practice, and both see it as an identification with Christ. The passage we are looking at, however, deals with our spiritual baptism into Christ, of which the external ordinance practiced by most of our churches is a symbol.

When Christ died on the cross and was buried, as pictured by a baptismal candidate being immersed in water, you died and were buried to sin. And when you placed your faith in Jesus Christ as Saviour and Lord, your death and burial was activated. You died then; you can't do it again. You can only believe it.

You were raised to new life in Christ

'We were therefore buried with him through baptism into death in order that, just as Christ was raised from the dead through the glory of the Father, we too may live a new life. If we have been united with him like this in his death, we will certainly also be united with him in his resurrection' (Rom 6:4,5). Have we been united with Him? Absolutely! 'If we have been united with him' is described by those who study the original languages as a first class conditional clause. It can literally be read: 'If we have become united with Him in the likeness of His death — and we certainly have — we shall also be united with him in the likeness of His resurrection.'

Paul's argument in this passage is twofold. First, you cannot have only part of Jesus. You cannot identify with the death and burial of Christ without also identifying with His resurrection and ascension. You will live in defeat if you believe only half the gospel. You have died with Christ, *and* you have been raised with Him and seated in the heavenlies (Eph 2:6). From this position you have the authority and power you need to live the Christian life.

Every child of God is spiritually alive and therefore 'in Christ'. Paul clearly identifies every believer with Christ:

In His death	Romans 6:3,6; Galatians 2:20; Colossians 3:1–3
In His burial	Romans 6:4
In His resurrection	Romans 6:5,8,11
In His ascension	Ephesians 2:6
In His life	Romans 5:10,11
In His power	Ephesians 1:19,20
In His inheritance	Romans 8:16,17; Ephesians 1:11,12

The second part of Paul's argument is that death no longer has any power over you, and therefore neither does sin. We will see how and why this is true when we get to those verses.

Jesus didn't come only to die for our sins; He also came that we might have life (Jn 10:10). We celebrate the resurrection of Jesus Christ on Easter, not just His death on

Good Friday. It is the resurrected life of Christ that God has given to us.

Notice how Paul develops this truth in Romans 5:8–11. 'God demonstrates his own love for us in this: While we were still sinners, Christ died for us' (v 8). Isn't that great, Christian? God loves you! But is that all? No! 'Since we have now been justified by his blood, how much more shall we be saved from God's wrath through him!' (v 9).

Isn't that great, Christian? You're not going to hell! But is that all? No! 'For if, when we were God's enemies, we were reconciled to him through the death of his Son, how much more, having been reconciled, shall we be saved through his life!' (v 10).

Isn't that great, Christian? You have been saved by His life. Eternal life isn't something you get when you die. You are alive in Christ right now. But is that all? No! 'Not only is this so, but we also rejoice in God through our Lord Jesus Christ, through whom we have now received reconciliation' (v 11). This reconciliation assures us that our souls are in union with God, which is what it means to be spiritually alive.

Peter also affirms this incredible truth: 'His divine power has given us everything we need for life and godliness through our knowledge of him who called us by his own glory and goodness. Through these he has given us his very great and precious promises, so that through them you may participate in the divine nature and escape the corruption in the world caused by evil desires' (2 Pet 1:3,4). Are you beginning to see a glimmer of hope for overcoming sexual bondage? You should be, because you have already died to it and been raised to new and victorious life in Christ.

Your old self was crucified with Christ

'For we know that our old self was crucified with him so that the body of sin might be done away with, that we should no longer be slaves to sin' (Rom 6:6). The text does not say 'we do' but 'we know'. Your old self was crucified when Christ was crucified. The only proper response to this marvellous truth is to believe it. Many people are desperately trying to put to death the old self with all its tendencies to sin, but they can't do it. Why not? Because it is already dead! You cannot do what God alone can and has already done for you.

Christians who continually fail in their Christian experience begin to question incorrectly, 'What experience must I undergo in order for me to live victoriously?' There is none. The only experience that was necessary for this verse to be true occurred nearly 2,000 years ago on the cross. And the only way we can enter into that experience today is by faith. We can't save ourselves, and we can't by human effort overcome the penalty of death or the power of sin. Only God can do that for us, and He has already done it.

As I was explaining this truth during a conference, a man raised his hand and said, 'I've been a Christian for thirteen years. Why hasn't someone told me this before?' Maybe no one shared with him, or maybe he wasn't listening. Some have asserted that this is just 'positional truth', implying that there is little or no present-day benefit for being in Christ. What a tragic conclusion! This is not pie-in-the-sky theology. There is a powerful application of this truth to daily life. If we choose to believe it and walk accordingly by faith, the truth of this passage works out in our experience. Trying to make it true by our experience will only lead to defeat.

We don't live obediently hoping that God may someday accept us. We are already accepted by God, so we live obediently. We don't labour in God's vineyard hoping that He may someday love us. God already loves us, so we joyfully labour in His vineyard. It is not what we do that determines who we are; it is who we are and what we believe that determines what we do.

You have been freed from sin

'Anyone who has died has been freed from sin' (Rom 6:7). Have you died with Christ? Then you are free from sin. You may be thinking, 'I don't feel free from sin.' If you only believe what you feel, you will never live a victorious life. In all honesty, I wake up quite a few mornings and feel very alive to sin and dead to Christ. But that's just the way I feel. If I believed what I feel and walked that way the rest of my day, what kind of a day do you think I would have? It would be a pretty bad day!

Rather, I have learned to get up in the morning and say, 'Thank You, Lord, for another day. I deserved eternal damnation, but You gave me eternal life. I ask You to fill me with Your Holy Spirit, and I choose to walk by faith regardless of how I feel. I realise that I will face many temptations today, but I choose to take every thought captive to the obedience of Christ and to think upon that which is true and right.'

One seminary student heard me teaching this concept and responded, 'Are you telling me I don't have to sin?'

I said, 'Where did you ever get the idea that you have to sin?' Then I read 1 John 2:1 to him: 'My dear children, I write this to you so that you will not sin. But if anybody does sin, we have one who speaks to the Father in our defence — Jesus Christ, the Righteous One.' God does not refer to us in Scripture as sinners but saints who can choose to sin. Obviously, Christian maturity is a factor in our ability to stand against temptation. But what an incredible sense of defeat must accompany the belief that we are bound to sin when God commands us not to sin! Many people in sexual bondage are caught in this hopeless web.

They think, 'God, You made me this way, and now You condemn me for it. Unfair!'

Others say, 'The Christian life is impossible.' Then when they fail, they proclaim, 'I'm only human!' Those who struggle with sexual sins lead the parade in this category. They believe the lie that the gospel isn't big enough to cover sexual bondage. This attitude reflects a faulty belief system. We have been saved, not by how we *behave*, but how we *believe*. This is a paradox and often a stumbling-block to the natural mind. But to biblically informed Christians it is the basis for our freedom and conquest — our union with God and our walk by faith.

There is no greater sin than the sin of unbelief. On more than one occasion the Lord made statements like, 'According to your faith will it be done to you' (Mt 9:29). Paul wrote, 'Everything that does not come from faith is sin' (Rom 14:23). If we choose to believe a lie, we will live a lie, but if we choose to believe the truth, we will live a victorious life by faith in the same way that we were saved.

Death is no longer your master

'If we died with Christ, we believe that we will also live with him. For we know that since Christ was raised from the dead, he cannot die again; death no longer has mastery over him' (Rom 6:8,9). Does death have mastery over you? Absolutely not! Why? Because death could not master Christ, and you are in Him. '"Death has been swallowed up in victory." "Where, O death, is your victory? Where, O death, is your sting?" The sting of death is sin, and the power of sin is the law. But thanks be to God! He gives us the victory through our Lord Jesus Christ' (1 Cor 15:54–57).

Since Christ has triumphed over death by His resurrection, death has no mastery over us who are spiritually alive in Christ Jesus. Jesus said, 'I am the resurrection and the life. He who believes in me will live [spiritually], even though he dies [physically]; and whoever lives and believes in me will never die [spiritually]. Do you believe this?' (Jn 11:25,26). Do you believe? Be it done to you according to how you believe!

Sin is no longer your master

Paul argues that if death has no mastery over us, then neither does sin. 'The death he died, he died to sin once for all; but the life he lives, he lives to God' (Rom 6:10). This was accomplished when 'God made him who had no sin to be sin for us, so that in him we might become the righteousness of God' (2 Cor 5:21). When Jesus went to the cross, all the sins of the world were upon Him. When they nailed those spikes into His hands and feet, all the sins of the world were upon Him. But when He was resurrected, there were no sins upon Him. They stayed in the grave. As He sits at the right hand of the Father today, there are no sins upon Him. He has triumphed over sin and death. And since you are in Him, you are also dead to sin.

Many Christians accept the truth that Christ died for the sins they have already committed. But what about the sins they commit in the future? When Christ died for all your sins, how many of your sins were then future? All of them, of course! This is not a licence to sin, which leads to bondage, but a marvellous truth on which to stand against Satan's accusations. It is something we must know in order to live free in Christ.

You are dead to sin and alive in Christ

How are we to respond to what Christ has accomplished for us by His death and resurrection? Paul summarises it in Romans 6:11: 'In the same way, count yourselves dead to sin but alive to God in Christ Jesus.' We do not make ourselves dead to sin by considering it to be so. We consider ourselves dead to sin because God says it is already so. The old King James Version reads, 'Reckon yourselves to be dead unto sin.' If you think that your reckoning makes you dead to sin, you will reckon yourself into a wreck! We can't make ourselves dead to sin; only God can do that — and He has already done it. Paul is saying that we must keep on choosing to believe by faith what God says is true even when our feelings scream the opposite.

The verb 'consider' is present tense. In other words, we must continuously believe this truth, daily affirming that we are dead to sin and alive in Christ. This activity is parallel to abiding in Christ (Jn 15:1–8) and walking by the Spirit (Gal 5:16). As we take our stand in the truth of what God has done and who we are in Christ, we will not easily be deceived or carry out the desires of the flesh.

Has sin disappeared because we have died to it? No. Has the power of sin diminished? No, it is still strong and still appealing. But when sin makes its appeal, we have the power to say no to it because our relationship with sin ended when the Lord 'rescued us from the dominion of darkness and brought us into the kingdom of the Son he loves' (Col 1:13). Paul explains how this is possible in Romans 8:1,2: 'Therefore, there is now no condemnation for those who are in Christ Jesus, because through Christ Jesus the law of the Spirit of life set me free from the law of sin and death.'

Is the law of sin and death still operative? Yes, because it is a law. But it has been overcome by a greater law — the law of the Spirit of life. It's like flying. Can you fly by your own power? No, because the law of gravity keeps you bound to earth. But you *can* fly if you buy an airline ticket and apply a law greater than gravity: jet propulsion. As long as you stay in that aircraft and operate according to the greater law, you will soar. But if you cease to operate under that law by stepping out the door in mid-flight, the law of gravity will quickly take effect and down you will go!

Like gravity, the law of sin and death is still here, still operative, still powerful, and still making its appeal. But you don't need to submit to it. The law of the Spirit of life is a greater law. As long as you live by the Spirit, you will not carry out the desires of the flesh (Gal 5:16). You must 'be strong in the Lord and in his mighty power' (Eph 6:10). The moment you think you can stand on your own, the moment you stop depending on the Lord, you are headed for a fall (Prov 16:18).

All temptation is an attempt by the devil to get us to live our lives independently of God. 'So, if you think you are standing firm, be careful that you don't fall! No temptation has seized you except what is common to man. And God is faithful; he will not let you be tempted beyond what you can bear. But when you are tempted, he will also provide a way out so that you can stand up under it' (1 Cor 10:12,13). When we succumb to temptation or are deceived by the father of lies, we should quickly repent of our sin, renounce the lies, return to our loving Father, who cleanses us, and resume the walk of faith.

Perhaps you have struggled in defeat against sexual sin and bondage while vainly trying to work out what you must do to get free. Hopefully the truth of Romans 6:1–11 has blown away the prison doors in your understanding. It's not what you do that sets you free; it's what you believe. God has done everything that needs to be done through the death and resurrection of Jesus Christ. Your vital first step to freedom is to consider it so, affirm it, and stand on it.

Having taken that step, there are some follow-up steps you must take to apply what God has done to your experience with temptation, sin, and bondage. In the next chapter we will begin to look at these steps.

19
Behaving Must Follow Believing

In the previous chapter we examined Romans 6:1–11 to discover what God has done for us, how we must accept His provision, and how we must live by faith in accordance with the truth. The key thought is this: It's not what you do that sets you free from sexual bondage, it's what you believe.

However, according to Romans 6:12,13, there is also something we must do in response to what God has already done. But beware: What God calls you to do in verses 12 and 13 will not be effective in your life if you're not believing what God has called you to believe in verses 1–11. It is the truth that sets us free, and believing the truth must precede and determine responsible behaviour.

Give yourself as an offering

Paul continues his instruction in Romans 6 with a specific assignment for all believers: 'Therefore do not let sin reign in your mortal body so that you obey its evil desires' (v 12). According to this verse, whose responsibility is it not to allow sin to reign in our bodies? Clearly, it is ours as believers. This means we cannot say, 'The devil made me do it.' God never commands us to do something we cannot do or that the devil can prevent us from doing. In Christ you have died to sin, and the devil can't *make* you do anything. He will tempt you, accuse you, and try to deceive you. But if sin reigns in your body, it is because you allowed it to happen. You are responsible for your own attitudes and actions.

How then do we prevent sin from reigning in our bodies? Paul answers in verse 13: 'Do not offer the parts of your body to sin, as instruments of wickedness, but rather offer yourselves to God, as those who have been brought from death to life; and offer the parts of your body to him as instruments of righteousness.' Notice that there is one negative action to avoid and two positive actions to practice.

Don't offer your body to sin. We are not to use our eyes, hands, feet, etc. in any way that would serve sin. When you run across a sexually explicit programme on television and linger lustfully to watch it, you are offering your body to sin. When you get inappropriately 'touchy-feely' with a colleague of the opposite sex, you are offering your body to sin. When you fantasise sexually about someone other than your spouse and act out your desires through masturbation, you are offering your body to sin. Whenever you choose to offer yourself to sin, you invite sin to rule in your physical body, something God has commanded us not to do.

Offer yourself and your body to God. Notice that Paul makes a distinction between 'yourselves' and 'the parts of your body'. What is the distinction? Self is who we are on the inside, the immortal, eternal part of us. Our bodies and their various parts are who we are on the outside, the mortal, temporal part of us. Someday we are going to jettison these old earth suits. At that time we will be absent from our mortal bodies and present with the Lord in immortal bodies (2 Cor 5:8). As long as we are on planet Earth, however, our inner selves are united with our outer physical bodies. We are to offer the complete package — body, soul, and spirit — to God.

Paul wrote, 'The body that is sown is perishable, it is raised imperishable; it is sown in dishonour, it is raised in glory; it is sown in weakness, it is raised in power; it is sown a natural body, it is raised a spiritual body' (1 Cor 15:42–44). Our inner man will live forever with our heavenly

Father, but our bodies won't. Paul continues, 'Flesh and blood cannot inherit the kingdom of God, nor does the perishable inherit the imperishable' (v 50). That which is mortal is corruptible.

Is our physical body evil? No, it's amoral and neutral. So what are we to do about the neutral disposition of our bodies? We are instructed to present them to God 'as instruments of righteousness.' To 'present' means to place at the disposal of. An instrument can be anything the Lord has entrusted to us, including our bodies. For example, your car is another amoral, neutral instrument for your use. You can use your car for good or bad purposes as you choose to drive people to church or to deliver drugs. Similarly, your body is yours to use for good or evil purposes as you choose. You have opportunities every day to offer your eyes, your hands, your brain, your feet, etc. to sin or to God. The Lord commands us to be good stewards of our bodies and use them only as instruments of righteousness. But ultimately it's our choice.

Your body, God's temple

In 1 Corinthians 6:13–20, Paul applies these instructions about the body specifically to the topic of sexual immorality:

> The body is not meant for sexual immorality, but for the Lord, and the Lord for the body. By his power God raised the Lord from the dead, and he will raise us also. Do you not know that your bodies are members of Christ himself? Shall I then take the members of Christ and unite them with a prostitute? Never! Do you not know that he who unites himself with a prostitute is one with her in body? For it is said, 'The two will become one flesh.' But he who unites himself with the Lord is one with him in spirit.
>
> Flee from sexual immorality. All other sins a man commits are outside his body, but he who sins sexually sins against his own body. Do you not know that your body is a

temple of the Holy Spirit, who is in you, whom you have received from God? You are not your own; you were bought at a price. Therefore honour God with your body.

This passage teaches that we have more than a spiritual union with God. Our bodies are members of Christ Himself. Romans 8:11 declares, 'If the Spirit of him who raised Jesus from the dead is living in you, he who raised Christ from the dead will also give life to your mortal bodies through his Spirit, who lives in you.' Our bodies are actually God's temple, because His Spirit dwells in us. To use our bodies for sexual immorality is to defile the temple of God.

It is hard for us to fully appreciate the moral outrage felt in heaven when one of God's children misuses His temple through sexual sin. It compares to the despicable act of Antiochus Epiphanes in the second century before Christ. This godless Syrian ruler overran Jerusalem, declared Mosaic ceremonies illegal, erected a statue of Zeus in the Temple, and slaughtered a pig — an unclean animal — on the altar. Can you imagine how God's people must have felt to have their holy place so thoroughly desecrated? God must feel the same way when we desecrate His temple — our bodies — through sexual immorality.

As a Christian, aren't you offended when people suggest that Jesus was sexually intimate with Mary Magdalene? This is how God must feel when a member of His pure Son's bride, the church, commits sexual immorality. Jesus was fully God, but He was also fully man. He was tempted in every way we are, including sexually, but He never sinned. His earthly body was not meant for sexual immorality, and neither is ours. If our eyes were fully open to the reality of the spiritual world and we understood the scandal felt in heaven when we sin against our own bodies, we would more quickly obey the Scripture's command to flee from sexual immorality.

Can you think of any way that you could commit a sexual sin and not use your body as an instrument of unrighteousness? I can't. And when we do commit sexual sin, we allow sin to reign in our mortal bodies! Does that mean we are still united with the Lord? Yes, because He will never leave us nor forsake us. We don't lose our salvation, but we certainly lose a degree of freedom. Paul urged, 'You were called to freedom, brethren; only do not turn your freedom into an opportunity for the flesh, but through love serve one another' (Gal 5:13 NASB).

What happens when a child of God who is united with the Lord and one spirit with Him also 'unites himself with a prostitute' through sexual immorality? The Bible says he becomes one flesh with the object of his sin. Somehow they bond together. Bonding is a positive thing in a wholesome relationship, but in an immoral union bonding only leads to bondage.

How many times have you heard of a nice Christian young woman who becomes involved with an immoral man, has sex with him, and then continues in a sick relationship for two or three years? He takes advantage of her and abuses her. Friends and relatives tell her, 'He's no good for you.' But she won't listen to them. Even though her boyfriend treats her badly, the girl won't leave him. Why? Because a spiritual and emotional bond has formed. They have become one flesh. Such bonds must be broken. That's one reason why God instructs us not to become entangled in immoral activities and relationships in the first place.

This spiritual and emotional bond can occur even as a result of heavy petting. At one of my conferences, a colleague and I counselled a young husband and wife who were experiencing marital problems. Even though they were deeply committed to each other and highly respected each other, their sexual relationship had been lifeless and dull since their wedding. Both husband and wife had been very romantically involved before marriage with other partners, but without intercourse.

During our counselling session, both husband and wife admitted for the first time that they were still emotionally attached to their 'first loves'. At our encouragement, they renounced petting and romantic involvement with their previous partners and recommitted their lives and their bodies to the Lord. They further committed to reserve the sexual use of their bodies for each other only. The next day they shared with me that they had a joyful, intimate encounter with each other that night — a first for their marriage. Once the sexual bonds were broken, they were free to enjoy each other the way God intended.

The beauty of offering yourself to God

Wonderful things happen when we determine to offer our bodies to God as instruments of righteousness instead of offering our bodies to sin. The Bible's sacrificial system provides a beautiful illustration.

The sin offering in the Old Testament was a blood offering. Blood was drained from the sacrificial animal, and the carcass was taken outside the camp and disposed of. Only the blood was offered to God for the forgiveness of sin. Hebrews 9:22 states, 'Without the shedding of blood there is no forgiveness.'

At the cross, the Lord Jesus Christ became our sin offering. After He shed His blood for us, His body was taken down and buried outside the city, but unlike the slain lamb of the Old Testament, the Lamb of God did not stay buried for long.

There was also a burnt offering in the Old Testament. Unlike the sin offering which involved only blood, the burnt offering was totally consumed on the altar — blood, carcass, everything. In the Hebrew, 'burnt' literally means 'that which ascends'. In the burnt offering, the whole sacrificial animal ascended to God in flames and smoke from the altar. It was 'an aroma pleasing to the Lord' (Lev 1:9).

Jesus is the sin offering, but who is the burnt offering? We are! Paul writes, 'I urge you, brothers, in view of God's mercy, to offer your bodies as living sacrifices, holy and pleasing to God — this is your spiritual act of worship' (Rom 12:1). It's wonderful that our sins are forgiven; Christ did that for us when He shed His blood. But if you want to live victoriously in Christ over the lust and sin which plagues you, you must present yourself to God and your body as an instrument of righteousness. Such a sacrifice is 'pleasing to God' as the aroma of the burnt offering was in the Old Testament.

A tremendous spiritual revival under King Hezekiah is recorded in 2 Chronicles 29. First, he cleaned out the temple and prepared it for worship by purifying it. What a beautiful picture of repentance from past sins! Then he ordered the blood offering for the forgiveness of sins. Nothing really extraordinary happened during the blood offering, but according to God's law, the sins of the people were forgiven. Then 'Hezekiah gave the order to sacrifice the burnt offering on the altar. As the offering began, singing to the Lord began also.... All this continued until the sacrifice of the burnt offering was completed' (2 Chron 29:27,28). The burnt offering was such a significant and worshipful event that it was surrounded by music. The account concludes, 'Hezekiah and all the people rejoiced at what God had brought about for his people' (v 36). Great joy results when believers obediently and whole-heartedly present themselves to God.

Ephesians 5:18–20 gives us a similar picture of the beauty of offering ourselves completely to God. 'Do not get drunk on wine, which leads to debauchery. Instead, be filled with the Spirit' (v 18). In other words, don't defile the temple of God, but let the Spirit of God rule in your hearts.

Guess what happens when you do? You will be prepared to
fulfil verses 19,20: 'Speak to one another with psalms,
hymns, and spiritual songs. Sing and make music in your
heart to the Lord, always giving thanks to God the Father
for everything.' Music fills the temple when we yield ourselves to God.

Winning the struggle with sin

Sadly, the music ringing inside many Christians today is
more of a funeral dirge than a song of joy. They feel
defeated instead of victorious. They have offered their bodies as instruments of sexual sin and feel hopelessly trapped
in sexual bondage. They may experience occasional periods
of relief and success at saying no to temptation. But since
sin has been allowed to reign in their bodies, they continue
to crash in defeat. Perhaps you find yourself in this discouraging condition.

Paul clearly describes this struggle and its solution in
Romans 7:15–25. The discussion which follows is based on
many counselling sessions I have had with Christians struggling with temptation, sin, and bondage, including the sexual arena. You may find yourself identifying with Dan as I
talk through Romans 7:15–25 (NASB) with him. I trust you
will also identify with the liberating truth of God's Word.[1]

> *Dan:* Neil, I can't keep going on like this. I have been
> sexually promiscuous in the past, and I'm really sorry
> about it. I have confessed it to the Lord, but I can't
> seem to get victory over it. I sincerely commit myself to
> avoid pornography. But the temptation is overwhelming
> and I give into it. I don't want to live like this! It's ruining
> my marriage.

> *Neil:* Dan, let's look at a passage of Scripture that
> seems to describe what you are experiencing. Romans

7:15 reads: 'That which I am doing, I do not understand; for I am not practicing what I would like to do, but I am doing the very thing I hate.' Would you say that pretty well describes your life?

Dan: Exactly! I really desire to do what God says is right, and I hate being in bondage to this lust. I sneak down at night and call one of those sex hot-lines. Afterward I feel disgusted with myself.

Neil: It sounds like you would identify with verse 16 as well: 'But if I do the very thing I do not wish to do, I agree with the law, confessing that it is good.' Dan, how many persons are mentioned in this verse?

Dan: There is only one person, and it is clearly 'I'.

Neil: It is very defeating when we know what we want to do but for some reason can't do it. How have you tried to resolve this conflict in your own mind?

Dan: Sometimes I wonder if I'm even a Christian. It seems to work for others, but not for me. I sometimes question if the Christian life is possible or if God is really here.

Neil: You're not alone, Dan. Many Christians believe that they are different from others, and most think they are the only ones who struggle with sexual temptations. If you were the only player in this battle, it would stand to reason that you would question your salvation or the existence of God.

But look at verse 17: 'So now, no longer am I the one doing it, but sin which indwells me.' Now how many players are there?

Dan: Apparently two, 'I' and 'sin'. But I don't understand.

Neil: Let's read verse 18 and see if we can make some sense out of it: 'I know that nothing good dwells in me, that is, in my flesh; for the wishing is present in me, but the doing of the good is not.'

Dan: I learned that verse a long time ago. It has been easy for me to accept that I'm no good for myself and no good for my wife. Sometimes I think it would be better if I just wasn't here.

Neil: That's not true, because that's not what the verse says. In fact it says the opposite. The 'nothing good' that is dwelling in you is not you. It's something else. If I had a wood splinter in my finger it would be 'nothing good' dwelling in me. But the 'nothing good' isn't me; it's a splinter. It is important to note that the 'nothing good' is not even my flesh, but it dwells in my flesh. If we see only ourselves in this struggle, living righteously will seem hopeless. These passages are going to great lengths to tell us that there is a second party involved in our struggle whose nature is evil and different from ours.

You see, Dan, when you and I were born, we were born under the penalty of sin. And we know that Satan and his emissaries are always working to keep us under that penalty. When God saved us, Satan lost that battle, but he didn't curl up his tail or pull in his fangs. He is now committed to keeping us under the power of sin. But in Christ we have died to sin and are no longer under its power.

In 1 John 2:12–14, John writes to little children because their sins are forgiven. In other words, they have overcome the penalty of sin. He writes to young men because they have overcome the evil one. In other words, they have overcome the power of sin. We have the authority in Christ to overcome the penalty and power of sin despite Satan's lies that we are still under them. The passage we are looking at also says that this evil is going to work through the flesh, which remained with us after our salvation. It is our responsibility to crucify the flesh and to resist the devil.

Let's continue in the passage to see if we can learn more about how the battle is being waged. Verses 19–21 state: 'For the good that I wish, I do not do; but I practice the very evil that I do not wish. But if I am doing the very thing I do not wish, I am no longer the one doing it, but sin which dwells in me. I find then the principle that evil is present in me, the one who wishes to do good.'

Dan: Sure, it is clearly evil and sin. But isn't it just my own sin? When I sin, I feel guilty.

Neil: There's no question that you and I sin, but we are not 'sin' as such. Evil is present in us, but we are not evil per se. This does not excuse us from sinning, because Paul wrote in Romans 6:12 that we are responsible not to let sin reign in our mortal bodies. When you came under conviction about your sexual sin, what did you do?

Dan: I confessed it to God.

Neil: Dan, confession literally means to agree with God. It is the same thing as walking in the light or living in moral agreement with Him about our present condition. We must confess our sin if we are going to live in harmony with our heavenly Father, but it doesn't go far enough. Confession is only the first step to repentance. The man that Paul is writing about agrees with God that what he is doing is wrong, but it didn't resolve his problem. You have confessed your sin to God, but you are still in bondage to lust. It has to be very frustrating for you. Have you ever felt so defeated that you just wanted to lash out at someone or yourself?

Dan: Almost every day!

Neil: But when you cool down, do you again entertain thoughts that are in line with who you really are as a child of God?

Dan: Always, and then I feel terrible about lashing out.

Neil: Verse 22 explains why: 'For I joyfully concur with the law of God in the inner man.' When we act out of character with who we really are, the Holy Spirit immediately brings conviction because of our union with God. Out of frustration and failure we think or say things like, 'I'm not going back to church any more. Christianity doesn't work. It was God who made me this way, and now I feel condemned all the time. God promised to provide a way of escape. Well, where is it? I haven't found it!' But soon our true nature begins to express itself. 'I know what I'm doing is wrong, and I know God loves me, but I'm so frustrated by my continuing failure.'

Dan: Someone told me once that this passage was talking about a non-Christian.

Neil: I know some good people who take that position, but that doesn't make sense to me. Does a natural man joyfully concur with the law of God in the inner man? Does an unbeliever agree with the law of God and confess that it is good? I don't think so! In fact, they speak out rather strongly against it. Some even hate us Christians for upholding such a moral standard.

Now look at verse 23, which describes the nature of this battle with sin: 'But I see a different law in the members of my body, waging war against the law of my mind, and making me a prisoner of the law of sin which is in my members.' According to this passage, Dan, where is the battle being fought?

Dan: The battle appears to be in the mind.

Neil: That's precisely where the battle rages. Now if Satan can get you to think you are the only one in the battle, you will get down on yourself or God when you sin, which is counterproductive to resolving the problem. Let me put it this way: Suppose you opened a door that you were told not to open, and a dog came through the door and wrapped his teeth around your leg. Would you beat on yourself or would you beat on the dog?

Dan: I suppose I would beat on the dog.

Neil: Of course you would. On the other side of the door, another dog — Satan — is tempting you with thoughts like, 'Come on, open the door. I have an exciting video to show you. Everybody else is doing it. You'll get away with it.' So you open the door and the dog comes in and grabs hold of your leg. You feel the pain of conviction and the sting of sin. Then the tempter switches to being the accuser. Your mind is pummelled with his accusations: 'You opened the door. You're a miserable excuse for a Christian. God certainly can't love someone as sinful as you.'

So you cry out, 'God, forgive me!' And He does. But the dog is still clinging to your leg! You go through the cycle repeatedly: sin, confess, sin, confess, sin, confess. You beat on yourself continuously for your repeated failure.

People get tired of being on themselves, so they walk away from God under a cloud of defeat and condemnation. Paul expressed this feeling in verse 24: 'Wretched man that I am! Who will set me free from the body of this death?' He doesn't say he's wicked or sinful, but that he's miserable. This man is not free. His attempts to do the right thing are met in moral failure because he has submitted to God but has not resisted the devil (James 4:7). There is nobody more miserable than someone who knows what is right and wants to do what is right but can't.

Dan: That's me — miserable!

Neil: Wait a minute, Dan. There is victory. Jesus will set us free. Look at verse 25: 'Thanks be to God through Jesus Christ our Lord! So then, on the one hand I myself with my mind am serving the law of God, but on the other, with my flesh the law of sin.' Let's go back to the dog illustration. Why isn't crying out to God enough to solve your ongoing conflict with sexual sin?

Dan: Well, like you said, the dog is still there. I guess I have to chase off the dog.

Neil: You will also have to close the door. What have you done to resolve your sexual sins and temptations?

Dan: Like I said, I have confessed them to God and asked His forgiveness.

Neil: But as you have already found out, that didn't quite resolve the problem. Here are the steps you must take.

First, realise that you are already forgiven. Christ died once for all your sins. You were right in confessing your sin to God, because you need to own up to the fact that you opened the door when you knew it was wrong.

Second, to make sure that every door is closed, you need to ask the Lord to reveal to your mind every sexual use of your body as an instrument of unrighteousness. As the Lord brings them to your mind, renounce them. Your body belongs to God and it is not to be used for sexual immorality.

Third, present your body to God as a living sacrifice and reserve the sexual use of your body for your spouse only.

Finally, resist the devil and he will flee from you.

Dan: I think I'm getting the picture. But every sexual use of my body! That will take a long time. But even if it took a couple of hours, I guess it would be a lot easier than living in bondage for the rest of my life. I've been condemning myself for my inability to live the Christian life. I can also see why I have been questioning my salvation. I see that Paul was frustrated about his failure, but he didn't get down on himself. He accepts his responsibility. More important, he expresses confidence by turning to God, because the Lord Jesus Christ will enable him to live above sin.

Neil: You're on the right track. Condemning yourself won't help because there is no condemnation for those who are in Christ Jesus (Rom 8:1). We don't want to assist the devil in his role as the accuser. Most people who are in bondage question their salvation. I have counselled hundreds who have shared with me their doubts about God and themselves. Ironically, the very fact that they are sick about their sin and want to get out of it is one of the biggest assurances of their salvation. Non-Christians don't have those kinds of convictions.

Romans 7:15–25 contains truth you must believe about sin and Satan and implies steps of action you must take to resist him. There is one more important thing you need to know: No one particular sin, including sexual sin, is isolated from the rest of reality. To gain complete freedom, you need to walk through all the Steps to Freedom in Christ.

In further preparation for doing so, you also need to understand the battle which is raging for your mind. Satan is a defeated foe, but if he can get you to believe a lie, he can control your life. In the next chapter we will seek to understand how our minds function so that we can win this critical battle.

NOTE

1. Neil T. Anderson, *The Bondage Breaker* (Eugene, OR: Harvest House Publishers, 1990), adapted from pages 48–52.

20
Rethink
How You Think

Imagine that you have worked most of your adult life for the same boss, a cantankerous, unreasonable tyrant. The man is known throughout the company for bursting into employees' offices and chewing them out royally for even the slightest suspicion of a mistake. You learned early during your employment to walk on eggshells around the old grouch and avoid him as much as possible. Every time he appears at your door you automatically cringe in fear, expecting to get blasted, even if he has only come to borrow a paper clip.

One day you arrive at work to learn that the boss has been suddenly transferred to another branch. You are no longer under his authority, and your relationship with him has ended. Your new boss is a saint — mild-mannered, kind, considerate, affirming. He clearly has the best interests of his employees at heart. But how do you think you will behave around him? Whenever you see your new boss coming down the hall, you start looking for a place to hide, just like you did around the old boss. Whenever the man steps into your office, your heart jumps into your throat. You wonder what you're going to get reamed out for this time. The more you get to know your new boss the more you realise he is as different from your old boss as night is from day. But it will take time to get to know your new boss and to change the negative reaction you learned under the old authority in your life.

Old habits are hard to break. Once we become conditioned to a certain stimulus-response pattern, it can be difficult to reprogramme our minds. This is certainly true of established sexual thought patterns and habits which are contrary to God's Word, patterns which may have been ingrained in us long before we became Christians.

We learned from Romans 6:1–11 that we are no longer under the authority of sin and Satan, because our relationship with them has been severed. We are new creatures in Christ (2 Cor 5:17). Old thought patterns and habits of responding to temptations don't automatically go away. They are still with us. Some traumatic memories of abuse during childhood still cause us to recoil in pain after all these years. We have a new boss — Jesus Christ, but having lived under the domination of sin and Satan, we must adjust to the glorious freedom our new boss has provided for us.

How does that happen? Paul called the process *renewing our minds*. Having instructed us on what to believe about our relationship to sin and Satan (Rom 6:1–11) and challenging us to present ourselves and our bodies to God instead of to sin (Rom 6:12,13; 12:1), Paul urges, 'Do not conform any longer to the pattern of this world, but be transformed by the renewing of your mind. Then you will be able to test and approve what God's will is — his good, pleasing and perfect will' (Rom 12:2). Next to what you believe about your relationship to sin, the two most critical issues you face in overcoming sexual bondage are presenting your physical body to God and renewing your mind to line up with God's truth.

Why is renewing the mind so critical? Because no one can consistently live in a way that is inconsistent with how he thinks or perceives himself. What we do doesn't determine who we are; who we are determines what we do. If you continue to think and respond as if you are under the domination of your old boss, you will continue to live that way.

You must change your thinking if you're going to change your behaving.

Reprogramming the computer

Why do we need to have our minds renewed? Let's answer that question with a brief review of our spiritual history.

Because of the fall of Adam, we are all born physically alive but spiritually dead in our trespasses and sins (Eph 2:1). Before we placed faith in Jesus Christ, we had neither the presence of God in our lives nor the knowledge of God's ways. So during those formative years we learned how to live our lives independently of God and gratify our sinful desires. We had no other choice.

Then one day we heard the gospel and decided to invite Jesus into our lives. We were born again. We became new creations in Christ. But unfortunately, there is no erase feature in this tremendous computer we call our mind. Everything that was previously programmed into our memory banks before Christ is still there. Our brains recorded every experience we ever had, good and bad. We remember every sexual temptation and have stored away how gratifying it felt to yield to them. If we don't reprogramme our minds we will continue to respond to stimuli the way we learned to under our old boss, Satan.

The good news — literally, the gospel — is that we have at our disposal all the resources we need to renew our minds. The Lord has sent us the Holy Spirit, who is the Spirit of truth (Jn 14:16,17), and He will guide us into all truth (Jn 16:13). Because we are in Christ, 'we have the mind of Christ' (1 Cor 2:16). We have superior weapons to win the battle for our minds. Paul wrote, 'For though we live in the world, we do not wage war as the world does. The weapons we fight with are not the weapons of the world. On the contrary, they have divine power to demolish strongholds. We demolish arguments and every pretension that sets itself up against the knowledge of God, and we take captive every thought to make it obedient to Christ' (2 Cor 10:3–5). Paul is not talking about defensive armour, but about battering-ram weaponry that tears down strongholds in our minds which have been raised up against the knowledge of God.

Practice threshold thinking

If we are going to take the way of escape from sexual bondage that God has provided for us, we must avail ourselves of God's provision and change how we respond at the threshold of every sexual temptation. We must take those first thoughts captive and make them obedient to Christ. If we allow ourselves to ruminate on tempting thoughts, we will eventually act on them.

For example, suppose a man struggles with lust. One night his wife asks him to go to the store for milk. When he gets into the car, he wonders which store he should go to. He remembers that the local convenience store has a display of pornographic magazines within easy reach. He can buy milk at other stores which don't sell those magazines. But the memory of the seductive photos he has ogled before at the convenience store gives rise to a tempting thought. The more he thinks about it, the harder it is to resist. When he pulls out of the driveway, guess which way he turns.

On the way to the convenience store, all kinds of thoughts cross the man's mind. He prays, 'Lord, if You don't want me to look at the pornography, have my pastor be in the store buying milk or cause the store to be closed.' Since the store is open (do you know any convenience stores that ever close?!) and since the pastor isn't there, he decides it must be okay to take a look. The mind has an incredible propensity to rationalise, which is why tempting thoughts must be arrested before your mind can come up with a reason to act on them.

But the man's stolen pleasure doesn't last. Before he leaves the store, guilt and shame overwhelm him. 'Why did I do it?' he moans. He did it primarily because he ignored the way of escape available to him before he even pulled out of the garage. He failed to take that initial thought captive and make it obedient to Christ. Rare is the person who can turn away from sin once the initial tempting thought has been embraced.

Hardware and software

Why does our mind work this way? To answer this question we need to understand how our outer self — our physical body — relates to our inner self — our soul or spirit. Scripture declares that we have an outer self and an inner self (2 Cor 4:16). Our brain is part of the outer self. Our mind is a part of the inner self. There is something fundamentally different between our brain and our mind. Our brain is little more than meat. When we die physically our outer self, including our brain, will return to dust. Our inner self will be absent from the body. We will be brainless, but we will not be mindless.

God has obviously created the outer self to correlate with the inner self. The correlation between the mind and the brain is clear. The brain functions much like a digital computer. Neurons operate like little switches that turn on and off. Each neuron has many inputs — called dendrites — and only one output, which channels the neurotransmitters to other dendrites. Millions of these connections make up the computer hardware of our brain.

Our mind is the software. As the brain receives input from the external world through the five senses, the mind compiles, analyses, and interprets the data and chooses responses based on how the mind has been programmed.

Before we came to Christ, our minds were programmed by the world, the flesh, and the devil, and our choices were made without the knowledge of God or the benefit of His presence. When we became Christians nobody pressed the CLEAR button in our minds. We need to be reprogrammed by God's truth. We need our minds renewed.

The Western world tends to assume that mental problems are primarily caused by faulty hardware — the brain. There is no question that organic brain syndrome, Alzheimer's disease, and chemical imbalance can impede our ability to function mentally. The best programme (mind) won't work if the computer (brain) is unplugged or in disrepair. However, the Christian's struggle with sin and bondage is not primarily a hardware problem but a software problem. Renewing our mind is the process of reprogramming the software.

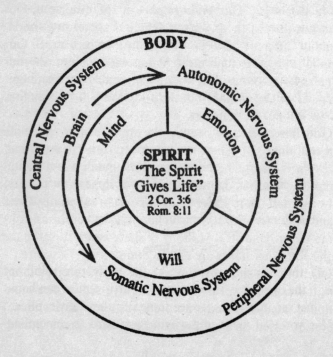

The brain and the spinal cord make up the central nervous system, which splits off into a peripheral nervous system comprised of two channels: the somatic and the autonomic. The somatic system regulates large and small motor movements over which we have volitional control. That's why we can think 'move' to an arm, a leg, or a toe, and it moves. The autonomic system regulates organs and glands over which we have no volitional control. We don't have to tell our heart to beat or our glands to secrete. They function automatically, thanks to the autonomic nervous system.

Sex glands are also part of the autonomic nervous system. That's why a woman has no volitional control over her menstrual cycle and a man has no volitional control over erections which occur during sleep. This is just the way God created our outer self to operate.

'But if I have no control over my sex glands,' someone may argue, 'how can God expect me to control my sexual behaviour?' Because self-control is not an action of the outer self but of the inner self. Our sex glands are not the cause of sexual immorality; they just operate based on how the mind is programmed. Sexual behaviour is primarily the result of our thought life, and we do have control over what we think. If you fill your mind with pornography, you will drive your autonomic nervous system into the stops. Your sex glands will begin to operate and set in motion behaviour you will later regret. You may not have control over what comes out, but you do have control over what you put in. Just like a computer: garbage in, garbage out!

The power of visual stimulation

One of the primary ways we programme our mind is through the eye-gate: visual input. Powerful things can happen in just seconds when we see something sexually explicit.

Have you ever wondered why it is so hard to remember

some things and forget others? In school we would study all night and then pray that the facts wouldn't leave us before we took the big exam. But just one glance at a pornographic image seems to stay in the mind for years. Why is that?

When we are stimulated emotionally — including being visually stimulated by sexually charged images — an autonomic signal is sent to the adrenal glands. A hormone called epinephrine is secreted into the bloodstream, which locks into the memory whatever stimulus is present at the time of the emotional excitement. This reaction causes us to involuntarily remember emotionally charged events, negative and traumatic ones as well as positive ones. It's too bad we didn't get more emotionally involved with some of our subjects in school; we would have remembered them better!

It has been said that three viewings of hard-core pornography have the same lasting effect on us as the actual illicit experience. A person can become emotionally excited and sexually stimulated just from entertaining thoughts of sexual activity. That's why an aroused man or woman will experience an emotional rush before any sexual contact is made. And that's why a man going to the store where pornography is sold will be sexually stimulated long before he even sees the magazines. It begins in his thoughts, which triggers his autonomic nervous system, which secretes epinephrine into the bloodstream.

The power of thoughts over emotions

Just as we can't control our glands, we can't control our emotions. If you think you can, try liking someone right now that you don't like! We can't order our emotions that way, nor are there any instructions in Scripture to do so. We must acknowledge our emotions, because we can't be right with God if we aren't real about how we feel. But we can't tell ourselves not to feel. What we do have control over is how we think, and how we think controls how we feel. And

Scripture does tell us to control our thinking: 'Brothers, stop thinking like children. In regard to evil be infants, but in your thinking be adults' (1 Cor 14:20).

Incidentally, this verse also reveals why our society's concept of 'adults only' is so ridiculous. The phrase implies that there are separate standards of morality for adults and children. Adults are mature enough not to allow their minds to be programmed with filth. Instead the television programme announces, 'The following content is suitable for "mature" audiences only. Viewer discretion is advised.' The content isn't suitable for anyone, and mature people should be the first to know that. In regard to evil, we should all be like infants: restricting ourselves only to wholesome entertainment. We have already been advised by God concerning sexual immorality in any form: 'Flee' (1 Cor 6:18).

Since we have no control over how we feel, plan to drop the following line from your repertoire, whether you use it in reference to yourself or to others: 'You shouldn't feel that way.' That's a subtle form of rejection, because we can't change how we feel. Our feelings are primarily a product of our thought life. What we believe, how we think, and how we perceive ourselves and the world around us determines how we feel. The following story illustrates the point.

Suppose you were paddling a canoe down a beautiful river in the wilderness, enjoying God's creation. As you round a bend in the river, the serenity is disturbed. Standing on the riverbank is someone of the opposite sex. The person is very attractive physically and beckons you to the shore. There is a blanket spread on the riverbank, and your mind and emotions suddenly go wild from the tempting possibilities. Your heart races and your palms are moist. 'What an incredible opportunity. We're all alone out here. I can get away with this.' Ignoring the conviction, you paddle toward the shore with your emotions up to 9.9 on a scale of 10.

But as you draw nearer the shore, you see an expression

of distress instead of seduction on the person's face, and you notice small sores revealing that the person may be suffering from AIDS. You suddenly realise that your initial impression of the stranger was all wrong, and your emotions quickly drop to a .1 — from sexual arousal to revulsion, fear, and then compassion for a person in need. You had a totally wrong perception, but your feelings responded to what you believed was the truth. It's clear that the person wasn't beckoning you to the shore for a romantic interlude but calling for help after becoming lost while in such poor health. You quickly confess your wrong thoughts and desires, and then assist the person.

Your first thoughts about that person were wrong, therefore what you felt was a distortion of reality. Our feelings can be distorted by what we choose to think or believe. If what we choose to believe does not reflect truth, then what we feel will not reflect reality. If what we see or mentally visualise is morally wrong, then our emotions are going to be violated. If you want to feel right you must think right.

Choose to think the truth

There is someone active in the world today who doesn't want you to think or believe the truth about God, yourself, Christian maturity, or sexual purity. Paul writes, 'The Spirit clearly says that in later times some will abandon the faith and follow deceiving spirits and things taught by demons' (1 Tim 4:1). I have counselled hundreds of people who struggle with their thoughts or literally hear voices. In every case the root problem has been a spiritual battle for their minds. No wonder Paul exhorts us, 'Finally, brothers, whatever is true, whatever is noble, whatever is right, whatever is pure, whatever is lovely, whatever is admirable — if anything is excellent or praiseworthy — think about such things' (Phil 4:8). What joy we would feel if we saw life from God's perspective and entertained only His thoughts!

If Satan can get us to believe a lie, he can control our lives. He is intent on destroying our proper perception of God, ourselves, members of the opposite sex — including our spouses, and the world we live in. Our problems don't just stem from what we believed in the past. Paul says we are to presently and continuously take every thought captive and make it obedient to Christ (2 Cor 10:5).

'Thought' is the Greek word *noema*. Notice how Paul uses this word elsewhere in 2 Corinthians. 'I have forgiven in the sight of Christ for your sake, in order that Satan might not outwit us. For we are not unaware of his schemes [noema]' (2:10,11). Unforgiveness is a thought that Satan plants in our minds. I believe the greatest access Satan has to the church is our unwillingness to forgive those who have offended us. It certainly has been true with the thousands I have been privileged to work with.

If you have been sexually abused and struggle with thoughts like, 'I can't forgive that person,' 'I hate that person,' or 'I don't want to forgive him, I want him to suffer as much as he made me suffer,' Satan has outwitted you. He has planted his thoughts in your mind. You must renounce those schemes and choose to believe and act on the truth.

Look at another passage in 2 Corinthians: 'The god of this age has blinded the minds [noema] of unbelievers, so that they cannot see the light of the gospel of the glory of Christ' (4:4). The one who raises up thoughts against the knowledge of God has a field day with the sexually abused. 'Where is your God now?' he taunts. 'If God is love, why does He allow the innocent to suffer? If God is all powerful, why didn't He stop that person from violating you?' Such is the smoke screen of lies Satan uses to blind us to the truth.

Look at one more verse: 'I am afraid that just as Eve was deceived by the serpent's cunning, your minds [noema] may somehow be led astray from your sincere and pure devotion to Christ' (2 Cor 11:3). I'm concerned too, because I see so many people living in bondage to those lies and wandering from devotion to Christ.

Satan is the father of lies, and he will work on our minds to destroy our concept of God and our understanding of who we are as children of God. People in bondage don't know who they are in Christ. That is the one common denominator in every person I have been privileged to help find freedom in Christ. Satan can't do anything about our position in Christ, but if he can get us to believe it isn't true, we will live as though it is not true, even though it is.

Satan preys on the minds of wounded people — the victim of a broken marriage, the child of an alcoholic, someone who was sexually abused as a child, etc. They are prime candidates for Satan's lies because their minds have already been pummelled with self-doubt, fear, anger, and hatred as a result of their circumstances. But you don't have to be the victim of a broken home or a painful childhood to be the target of the enemy's sexual temptations, accusations, and deceptions.

For example, suppose in a vulnerable moment a young woman has a tempting sexual thought toward someone of the same sex. At first she can't believe she could be tempted to homosexuality. She would probably be embarrassed and immediately flee from the tempting situation. But she might not tell anyone about it. Who would understand? Then if it happens again and again, she may begin to wonder, 'Why am I thinking like this? Could I be one of them?' Once the door of doubt is open, she may begin to seriously question her sexuality.

If her mind continues to dwell on those tempting thoughts, it will affect the way she feels. That's the way God made us — to feel on the basis of how we think. But if she believes what she feels and behaves accordingly, she will use her body as an instrument of unrighteousness. Sin will then reign in her mortal body. Unless she takes those thoughts captive and makes them obedient to Christ, she is on her way to sexual bondage.

Don't assume that all disturbing thoughts are from Satan. We live in a sinful world with tempting images and messages all around us. You have memories of hurtful experiences which prompt thoughts contrary to the knowledge of God. Whether the thought was introduced into your mind from the television set, your memory bank, the pit itself, or your own imagination doesn't matter much, because the answer is always the same: Choose to reject the lie and think the truth.

You can try to analyse the source of every thought, but it won't resolve the problem. Too much of the recovery movement is caught up in the paralysis of analysis. Someone may be able to give a brilliant analysis of what's wrong and still be mired in the problem. The answer is Christ. His truth will set us free.

Breaking the strongholds

Can strongholds of sexual bondage in the mind be broken? Yes! If our minds have been programmed wrongly, they can be reprogrammed. If we learned something the wrong way, we can learn it the right way. Will this take time? Yes, it will take the rest of our lives to renew our minds and to develop our character. We will never be perfect in our understanding on this earth, nor will our character be perfect like Christ's, but this is what we pursue.

Christian maturity cannot fully take place, however, unless we are free in Christ. When people aren't free in Christ they go from book to book, from pastor to pastor, and from counsellor to counsellor, but nothing seems to work. Watch how fast they can grow, however, when they are free in Christ!

After I had the privilege of helping a missionary find her freedom in Christ, she wrote, 'I'm firmly convinced of the significant benefits of finding our freedom in Christ. I was making some progress in therapy, but there is no comparison with the steps I am able to make now. My ability to 'process' things has increased manyfold. Not only is my spirit more serene, my head is actually clearer! It's easier to make connections now. It seems like everything is easier to understand now.'

As we set about demolishing sexual strongholds in our mind, we are not just up against the world — the godless system we were raised in. And we are not just up against the flesh — including those reprogrammed habit patterns of thought that have been burned into our minds over time or by intense traumatic experiences. We're up against the world, the flesh, and the devil. All three influences are at work to turn our minds away from the truth and set us on a path to sexual bondage.

The death and resurrection of Christ dealt a death-blow to Satan's kingdom. But the world system remained after the cross. Television programming, for instance, will never be totally cleaned up. And some of you work where pornography is displayed and people will use the Lord's name in vain. The world's influence is all around us. As Paul identified himself more with Christ and less with the world, he was able to say, 'May I never boast except in the cross of our Lord Jesus Christ, through which the world has been crucified to me, and I to the world' (Gal 6:14). We must consider ourselves dead to a world system which largely opposes God's truth and sexual purity.

The flesh also remains with the Christian after salvation, but as we bond to Christ we also crucify the flesh. 'Those who belong to Christ Jesus have crucified the sinful nature [flesh] with its passions and desires. Since we live by the Spirit, let us keep in step with the Spirit' (Gal 5:24,25).

Satan still exerts his power in the fallen world. But we are dead to sin and alive in Christ. When we resist the devil he will flee from us (James 4:7).

Cleaning up the mind

When I was a young Christian, I decided to clean up my mind. I had a very clean upbringing, for which I am thankful, and became a Christian in my twenties. But after four years in the Navy my mind was cluttered with a lot of junk. I had seen enough pornography to plague me for years. Images would dance in my mind for months after one look. I hated it. I struggled every time I went to a place where pornography was available.

When I made the decision to clean up my mind, do you think the battle got easier or harder? It got harder, of course. Temptation isn't much of a battle if you easily give in to it. But it is fierce when you decide to stand against it. I finally got the victory, however. The following illustration may be helpful as you set out to rid your mind of years of impure thoughts.

Think of your polluted mind as a pot filled to the brim with black coffee. Sitting beside the coffee-pot is a huge bowl of crystal-clear ice, which represents the Word of God. Your goal is to purify the contents in the pot by adding ice cubes to it. Every cube displaces some of the coffee and dilutes the rest, making it a little purer. You can only put in one or two cubes a day, so the process seems futile at first. But over the course of time the water begins to look less and less polluted and the taste and smell of coffee is greatly diminished. The process continues to work provided you don't add more coffee grounds.

Paul writes, 'Let the peace of Christ rule in your hearts, since as members of one body you were called to peace. And be thankful' (Col 3:15). How do we rid ourselves of evil thoughts, purify our mind, and allow the peace of Christ to reign? Shall we focus on rebuking all those tempting, accusing, and deceiving thoughts? If we do, we'll spend the rest of our lives doing nothing more. It would be as futile as trying to separate the coffee from the water after it has percolated.

The answer is found in Colossians 3:16: 'Let the word of Christ dwell in you richly.' The psalmist gave similar instruction: 'How can a young man keep his way pure? By living according to your word. I seek you with all my heart; do not let me stray from your commands. I have hidden your words in my heart that I might not sin against you' (Ps 119:9–11). Merely trying to stop thinking bad thoughts won't work. We must fill our minds with the crystal-clear Word of God. God has no alternative plan. We are not called to dispel the darkness, we are called to turn on the light. We overcome the father of lies by choosing the truth!

You may find that winning the battle for your mind will initially be a two-steps-forward, one-step-back process as you take on the world, the flesh, and the devil. But gradually it will become three steps forward, one step back, and then four and five steps forward as you learn to take every thought captive and make it obedient to Christ. You may despair with all your steps backward, but God won't give up on you. Remember, your sins are already forgiven. You only need to fight for your own personal victory over sin. This is a winnable war because you are alive in Christ and dead to sin. The bigger battle has already been won by Christ.

Freedom to be all that God has called you to be is the greatest blessing in this present life. This freedom is worth fighting for. As you learn more about who you are as a child of God and about the nature of the battle waging for your mind, the process becomes easier. Eventually it is twenty steps forward and one back, and finally the steps are all forward, with only an occasional slip in the battle for the mind.

21
Recovery in Christ

Nancy, a devoted wife and mother, attended my conference on resolving personal and spiritual conflicts. During the sessions I related several tremendous stories of persons who had experienced unspeakable atrocities and pain as victims of child abuse and who had found their freedom in Christ. As Nancy listened to the testimonies she felt nauseated, dizzy, and disgusted. Later in the week she confronted me with stern questions: 'Why are you telling these awful stories? Those poor children were not at fault. I'm so angry with you. Why are you doing this?'

I wasn't surprised by Nancy's response, because the conference often surfaces in people a lot of problems which haven't been dealt with. So I told her, 'These stories are not intended to cause pain; they are stories of victory and hope. I don't think your response has anything to do with me or the testimonies. The Lord is using this conference to bring to the surface something in your life that hasn't been resolved, and the evil one doesn't like it. He's behind your agitation. Please talk with one of our Freedom In Christ staff members, because there is something you need to face and resolve.' Indeed there was! Nancy spent the rest of that morning and part of the afternoon finding her freedom in Christ.

Two weeks later Nancy shared her testimony with me, which related to a bedtime story she had often read to her children, *The Bears on Hemlock Mountain*. She recounted how Jonathan, the main character in the short children's story, trudged up the mountain to fetch a large kettle for his mother. On the way he sang, 'There are no bears on Hemlock Mountain. No bears. No bears. No bears at all.'

He saw dark figures in the distance that looked like bears. But he knew they couldn't be bears, because he didn't want to believe there were bears on Hemlock Mountain. So he continued to climb and sing, 'There are no bears on Hemlock Mountain. No bears. No bears. No bears at all.' Then he saw a bear. He quickly scrambled under the kettle for safety. He remained hidden until his father and uncles arrived with their guns to rescue him from the bears.

Nancy said that she had been confronted with 'dark figures' from her past, but she would not allow her mind to accept the possibility that she had 'bears' in her life. It was as if she sang herself to sleep each night, 'There was no sexual molestation in my past, no sexual molestation at all.' But there were 'bear tracks' everywhere. Memories of sexual abuse flooded her mind, but she didn't want to admit it and face the truth. She hid under a kettle of denial.

Finally, during the conference, she understood that she no longer needed to be afraid, because her heavenly Father had overcome the painful threat of the bear of sexual abuse. He had already destroyed the bear, and facing the truth was her only way of escape. After she renounced the unrighteous use of her body and forgave her abuser, there was peace in her life and safety at last on her 'Hemlock Mountain'.

Perhaps your experience parallels that of Nancy. The truth and testimonies in the previous chapters of this book have brought into sharp focus your shame, failure, and pain in the area of sexual promiscuity, sexual disorientation, or sexual abuse. You may have been in denial for years, insisting, 'I don't have a problem.' But your lack of peace and victory regarding the sexual sin in your life has worn you down. Try as you might to avoid it, you keep falling into the same thoughts and behaviours again and again. You're too tired to run away any more. You're ready to take the way of escape from sexual bondage Christ has provided for you.

As I have indicated throughout this book, a key element to finding your freedom in Christ is taking the specific Steps to Freedom in Christ found in the Appendix. In this chapter we will prepare you for that experience.

Take the initiative

A prerequisite to finding your freedom from sexual bondage is to face the truth, acknowledge the problem, and assume responsibility to change. It's likely that few people know you're in bondage, so you can't count on your family members or friends to urge you into action. Compared to many forms of substance abuse which leave tell-tale evidence on the body, sexual bondage is relatively easy to hide. For example, someone who is secretly hooked on pornography or illicit sex can lead a Jekyll-and-Hyde existence for many years without being detected. Many people I counsel tell me that they are tired of living a lie. Nothing will happen until you choose to honestly face your problem and initiate the process for resolving it. God holds each of us responsible for confessing and repenting of our own sin. No one can do that for you.

Inherent in this process is your willingness to submit to God completely without trying to hide anything from Him. Adam and Eve were created to live in a completely transparent relationship with God. They walked with God daily in the garden, naked and unashamed. When they sinned, Adam and Eve covered their nakedness and tried to avoid God. It is ridiculous to try to hide from the all-knowing God. Yet we are often guilty of the same self-deceptive ploy. We mistakenly think that if we go about our daily business, God won't notice that we are hiding in the darkness.

We are spiritually alive in Christ as Adam and Eve were before the fall. God wants us to live before Him 'naked and unashamed', completely honest about who we are and what we have done. We must give up our defensive, self-protective posture and determine to walk in the light of His presence.

If we are going to walk as children of light (Eph 5:8), we must first understand who we are as children of light. Right belief determines right behaviour. If you knew who you were as a child of God, would it affect the way you live? The apostle John sure thought so. 'How great is the love the Father has lavished on us, that we should be called children of God! Dear friends, now we are children of God!... Everyone who has this hope in him purifies himself, just as he is pure' (1 Jn 3:1,3). Walking in the light as God's children promises the reward of purity, which perhaps is a quality you have sought in your life for years. You need to know how Christ meets your deepest needs, which is the topic of my book, *Living Free in Christ*. Every chapter describes another facet of who we are in Christ.

Repentance is another aspect of coming clean before God. Repentance means to have a change of mind. It is far more than just mental acknowledgement. It means to turn from our self-centred and self-indulging ways and trust in God. It means no longer to hold iniquity in our hearts. The early church exercised repentance by opening their public profession of faith with the words, 'I renounce you, Satan, and all your works and all your ways.' The idea is to take back any ground you or your parents or your grandparents have given to Satan.

Repentance involves not only what we turn *from* but what we turn *to*. We must commit all we have and all we are to God. We are to be faithful stewards of everything that God has entrusted to us (1 Cor 4:1,2). Such a commitment should include our properties, our ministries, our families, and our physical bodies. As we renounce any previous use of our lives and our possessions in the service of sin and then dedicate ourselves to the Lord, we are saying that the god of this world no longer has any right over us because we now belong to God.

Taking steps to reclaim your heritage

The Steps to Freedom in Christ were developed to assist believers in taking back the land that is rightfully theirs. This 'land' is our heritage in Christ, the freedom which was purchased on the cross and fully deeded over to us by the resurrected Christ. The Steps to Freedom cover seven critical areas affecting our relationship with God, areas where you may have allowed the prince of darkness to establish strongholds in your life. God has done everything necessary to set us free. It is your responsibility to appropriate what He has done and then to stand firm and resist being lulled back into subjection.

How you view this experience will greatly determine what you gain from it. If you see the Steps simply as a means to rid yourself of bad habits, like employing a counselling technique to move from one life-stage to another, you will receive only limited benefits. There is nothing magical about reading through the steps. The Steps to Freedom in Christ do not set people free; Jesus does. He is the bondage breaker and the way of escape. You will only find your freedom in Him and in response to what He has done. The steps are merely an instrument to help you apply Christ's victory to your need for freedom.

Gearing up for the journey

You will find great benefit in going through the Steps in one sitting with a mature Christian friend or leader present to provide accountability and objectivity. Allow plenty of time for the process. It may require many hours to break through the spiritual strongholds which have been erected in your life. When the process is fragmented over two or more appointments, you will miss out on the impact of dealing with each issue in the immediate context of the others, which are often related to the most troublesome area in your life. Furthermore, it may be difficult to bring painful emotions to the surface without resolving them in the same session.

Before going through the steps with your helper, review your personal history with him or her so that specific areas of need can be addressed in the prayers you will pray. The following points will lead you through the process of sharing your life experiences.

- Describe the religious history of your family (parents and grandparents).

- Describe your home life from childhood through high school.

- Describe your relationship with any adoptive parents, foster parents, or legal guardians.

- Discuss any history of physical or emotional illness in your family's background.

- Identify any bad eating habits (bulimia, binging and purging, anorexia, compulsive eating, etc.).

- Identify any substance addictions (alcohol, drugs).

- Identify any prescription drugs you are taking and the reasons for taking them.

- Discuss your sleep patterns, problems with insomnia or nightmares, etc.

- Discuss any sexual, physical, or emotional abuse you may have suffered.

- Identify problems with your thought life (obsessive, blasphemous, condemning, or distracting thoughts in church or during prayer and Bible study; poor concentration; fantasies; etc.).

- Describe your general emotional state and any problems you may have with anger, anxiety, depression, bitterness, fear, etc.

- Describe your personal spiritual journey (when and how you found Christ, your level of assurance of salvation, etc.).

Not without a struggle

As you process through the Steps to Freedom, you may experience feelings of fear or other physical sensations such as heart palpitations, pain in the pit of your stomach, or extreme headaches. These distractions must be acknowledged aloud to God, and to the person helping you. The only way you can lose control in this process is if you become distracted and believe a lie. The mind is the battleground, but it is also the control centre. It doesn't matter if the thought in your mind is from a speaker on the wall or from the pit. The only way it can have any control over you is if you choose to believe it. Keeping your feelings and fears hidden gives power to the enemy. Getting them into the open and renouncing them breaks his power.

You may experience mental resistance or interference as the steps are being processed. The intensity for some is so great that they want to run out of the room. Others fear that Satan will retaliate when they get home. I regularly hear people say, 'This isn't going to work' or 'I'm getting a sharp, piercing headache behind my eyes' or 'I'm going to throw up.' Profane or obscene language may flood the mind. The 'f-word' seems to be Satan's favourite. These thoughts and feelings are Satan's schemes to distract you from resolving the conflicts in your life.

To counteract these attacks, I often tell the person I'm helping, 'Thank you for letting me know what's happening. I will certainly not force you to go beyond what you think is safe. You have the freedom to leave, but would you be willing to check if this is from the enemy or not? Why don't you again affirm that you are God's child. Then, as His child, commit yourself and your body to Him as a living sacrifice, and by the authority of Christ command Satan and all his evil workers to leave your presence.' This simple truth of submitting to God and resisting the devil is effective (James 4:7). When people realise the nature of the battle and where those lies are coming from, they usually respond, 'I want to keep going so I can finish this!'

If the feelings or physical sensations persist, ask God to reveal the causes behind them. You may be on the edge of a painful memory that Satan doesn't want you to deal with. Ask God to show you what else you need to do to overcome Satan and to find your freedom. As God brings something to mind, address it openly and deal with it.

If it's a sin, confess it and renounce it. God did not bring it up to badger you, shame you, or condemn you. He is your loving heavenly Father. He is *for* you in this process, not *against* you. Call on Him to help you navigate through the enemy's opposition. He will answer!

If you are being harassed by negative feelings, look for the lie behind them and expose it by declaring the truth. Condemning feelings are almost always the product of false beliefs based on lies. We must learn to recognise these lies and reject them, and then reaffirm and declare the truth of being in Christ. The feelings are real, but when they are lined up with the truth, the lies behind them are exposed. Knowing the truth sets us free from the powerful pull of painful memories.

Important steps for sexual victims

There are two Steps to Freedom in Christ which will be extremely critical for you if you have been victimised by rape, incest, or other forms of sexual abuse: forgiving those who have offended you and breaking bonds that were formed when you were violated sexually.

The area of forgiveness can be most difficult for anyone who has suffered severely at the hands of a sexual offender. If you fall into this category, you may be in special need of finding a trustworthy individual to help you through this process. To forgive those who offended you means to let go of that person's offence. As difficult as it may be, forgiving the offender actually sets you free from their offence. It is an act of your will, not your feelings. You must choose to forgive for your own sake. It is the only way to be free of the bitterness that may have filled your heart.

As you take this step, Satan may try to convince you that forgiving the offender somehow makes what he or she did right. That's a lie. What the offender did to you can never be justified. You were stripped of your safety and used for someone else's pleasure. That person owes you a debt that can never be paid. But that's between God and the offender. The wrongs of the past do not become right when you forgive, but by forgiving you can be free of them.

Another tactic Satan may employ to keep you from forgiving is to convince you that you will be relinquishing your only defence against future violations from the offender: your anger. But our emotions were not designed to be a defence. The are only an internal warning system about what is happening to us. Your anger is a signal that you have been threatened or hurt and that you need to take action. The proper action is to forgive and then to take appropriate steps so the offender cannot hurt you again. When you deal with the offence, the anger will dissipate.

Satan may also insist that you have a right to revenge for

what the offender did to you. But only God can deal with that person justly. You must leave vengeance to God.

Others protest, 'Why should I forgive? You don't know how badly that person hurt me.' But they are still hurting you! How do you stop the pain? The only way is to break the bondage and forgive from your heart. When you choose to forgive by facing all the painful memories connected with your abuse — the hate, the hurt, the absolute ugliness of what the offender did to you — you can and will be free. Step 3 in the Steps to Freedom in Christ will guide you through this important process.

Another vital step to gaining freedom from past offences is to ask God to break the spiritual bonds that were formed when you were violated sexually. When a husband and wife consummate their marriage physically, they become one. A physical, emotional, and spiritual bond is formed. When your body was used for unrighteous sexual purposes, a bond was formed — not the holy bond God ordained for marriage, but an unholy bond. You may have been an unwitting or unwilling participant in this union, but a bond was formed nevertheless.

I have learned through much experience to encourage everyone who comes to us for help to ask the Lord to reveal every sexual use of their body as an instrument of unrighteousness. Many people will openly share one or two experiences, but when they sincerely pray this prayer, I hear all the other sexual experiences they had forgotten or didn't want to mention. Once the experiences are brought to light and renounced the bonds can be broken. Step 6 in the Steps to Freedom in Christ will guide you through the process of breaking spiritual bonds which have been formed in the past.

Beth is a classic example of the bondage that results from sexual promiscuity and abuse. She was a Christian girl who had so many problems that her parents made an appointment for her to see me. Her behaviour was tearing up her parents and destroying their Christian home. Usually nothing good comes from appointments made by parents for children who don't want to be helped. But Beth's parents assured me that the girl wanted to see me.

Beth's opening statement was, 'I don't want to get right with God or anything like that.' Hiding my own frustration, I said, 'I can accept that. But since you're here, maybe we could try to resolve some of the conflicts in your life.' Beth thought that would be okay. She told me the story of being date-raped by the campus hero at her high school. At the time she was too embarrassed to tell anyone about it, and she had no idea how to resolve it. Having lost her virginity, she became sexually promiscuous, living off and on with a real loser.

I asked Beth's permission to lead her through the Steps to Freedom in Christ, and she agreed. When I invited her to ask the Lord to reveal to her mind every sexual use of her body as an instrument of unrighteousness, she said, 'That would be embarrassing.' So I stepped out of the room while my female partner helped her through the process. That night she was singing in church for the first time in years. She was free.

After years of helping people find their freedom in Christ we have observed several generalities. First, if people have had 'unholy' sex, they don't seem to enjoy 'holy' sex. I have counselled many wives who can't stand to be touched by their husbands. In hard cases they are actually repulsed by the idea until they break the bondages that come from sex outside the will of God. Incredibly, their feelings toward their spouse change almost immediately after finding their freedom in Christ.

We have also noticed that promiscuity before marriage seems to lead to a lack of fulfilment after marriage. The fun and excitement of sex outside the will of God leaves one in bondage. If it was consensual, the bondages only increase as they attempt to satisfy their lust. If it wasn't consensual (they were forced to submit), they shut down and remain in bondage to their past until it is resolved. They lack the freedom to enter into a loving relationship where there is mutual expression of love and trust. We have them renounce those previous sexual uses of their body, commit their bodies to God as a living sacrifice, and reserve the sexual use of their bodies for their spouses only.

In the cases of rape and incest, someone has used their bodies as instruments of unrighteousness. Tragically, they have become one flesh. I want to scream 'not fair' when some sick person defiles another person's 'temple' against the will of that person who is trying to use it to glorify God. It's not fair! It's sick, but we live in a sick world. It is no different than Antiochus defiling the Temple against the will of those who died trying to save it. The good news is we can be free from such violations. We can renounce those uses of our body, submit to God, and resist the devil (James 4:7). We can and must forgive those who have abused us.

Ideally, you should read my books *Victory over the Darkness* and *The Bondage Breaker* before going through the Steps to Freedom in Christ. You need to know who you are as a child of God and how to walk by faith. You must understand how to renew your mind and realise the spiritual nature of the battle that is taking place there. You must understand the spiritual authority and protection every believer possesses in Christ.

The Steps to Freedom in Christ are not an end in themselves. They really offer a new beginning. For some people, the first time through the steps will represent the first major victory in a war that continues on. The following testimony from a man who was formerly trapped in nearly every form of sexual bondage mentioned in this book, illustrates the process of securing freedom in Christ one victory at a time.

My dad left our home when I was four years old. Every day I cried out to God to bring my daddy home. But he never came back. So my mother, my brother, and I moved in with my grandparents. I disconnected from God early in life because no one tried to explain why He never answered my pleas.

One night my grandfather undressed in front of me and my grandmother. He had an erection. Although he wouldn't have done anything to hurt me, my grandfather's act of indiscretion left a terrible mark in my mind which surfaced years later.

I thought my grandfather loved me. It didn't matter to me that he had been unfaithful to my grandmother, that he had sexually abused my mother, and that he was becoming an alcoholic. In the absence of my father, as a young boy I bonded with my grandfather. When my mother remarried and we moved away, I felt like I lost my father for a second time. But I didn't bother to ask God for help because I felt He had let me down.

We moved every year as I grew up. Every time I made a friend, we moved again, keeping the wounds of abandonment and loneliness painful. I grieved over every loss and did everything to protect myself from being hurt again.

I believed that I was different from most boys. I started playing sexually with some of my male friends during grade school. Voices in my head told me it was okay because I was born that way. I had a terrible male void in my life and my heart burned with desire. The memory of seeing my grandfather with an erection prompted a fascination with seeing boys and men naked. Voyeurism became a way of life for me.

Meanwhile, my own family was being ripped apart by conflict. The squabbles and fights mortified me. I was a loyal and sensitive child who carried a deep concern for everyone in my family. I tried to convince my friends' parents to adopt me in order to escape the turmoil, but it didn't work. I finally detached completely from my mother and brother.

As an adolescent and young adult, I threw myself into the gay world. I was addicted watching men in public toilets and visited gay bars almost every night. When I found a gay lover, I thought I had finally met a man who would love me and stay with me forever. I was emotionally co-dependent on him. When the relationship ended after three years, I fell into a deep depression. I was emotionally bankrupt and lost. News of my brother's death added to my sense of despair and abandonment.

At his funeral I purchased a Bible, but I didn't know why. I kept it on my bedside table with a cross someone gave me. I didn't dare move them. I was terrified at night. I felt a horrifying dark presence around me at night. Someone told me to hold the cross and yell, 'I bind you in the name of Jesus Christ of Nazareth!' I did so night after night with the covers pulled up to my neck. But something kept tormenting me night after night.

I finally started reading the Bible and attending church. I accepted the Lord at a baptism service and left the gay lifestyle completely. I studied the Word seriously, but with my background it was easy to fall into legalism. I didn't understand grace and forgiveness. The Bible talked a lot about sexual immorality and clearly forbade homosexual behaviour. I asked myself, 'If I am a Christian, why do I still feel the same homosexual tendencies?' The more I tried to do what the Bible said and what others expected of me, the more guilty I felt. I didn't dare tell anyone what I was feeling.

The voyeurism became intense and triggered an uncontrollable bondage to masturbation.

As I began teaching a Sunday School class, the voices in my head condemned me daily and accused me of being a hypocrite. I believed them. I was tormented. The more I fought back by reading my Bible and serving the Lord, the greater the oppression became. My mind was ruled by immoral thoughts. I experienced intense sexual dreams. I was out of control and backsliding quickly. I found myself back in public toilets. I talked to Christian counsellors and pastors, but no one seemed to offer a workable solution to my problem. I wanted so badly to know and serve the Lord.

A friend who was aware of my struggle gave me a copy of *Victory over the Darkness* by Neil Anderson. As I began reading it, the book seemed to be written about me. For the first time I understood how I got into my horrible condition and how I could get out of it. No one had ever told me that I was a child of God, that God had chosen me as His friend, and that He loved me specifically. I had learned about God intellectually, but through reading this book I finally met my gentle and loving heavenly Father personally.

When I read *The Bondage Breaker*, I knew I was spiritually oppressed. I had been involved in almost everything in the non-Christian spiritual experience inventory at the end of the book. I began to understand my oppressive thought life, rampant voyeurism, and low sense of worth. I discovered that realising I am a child of God was the answer to breaking the destructive cycle that had been present in my family for generations.

I learned that Jesus is the bondage breaker and that I have authority over the kingdom of darkness because I am seated with Christ in the heavenlies. However, the more I embraced these truths, the more I was attacked. I was falling apart emotionally. I had to see Neil Anderson.

I attended one of his conferences and my entire life was changed. One of his staff met with me in a four-hour session. No one has ever wanted to spend that much time with me. I felt free for the first time in my life. Still, my desperate need for affirmation prevented me from being totally honest in the counselling session.

Two days later Neil talked about forgiving others. I asked him if a person has to cry when they forgive someone. He didn't answer. He made me think about it. On the way back to the motel, I told the Lord that I really wanted to forgive my dad and stepdad for not validating me. Then the Lord let me feel the pain of not being validated. He gave me a glimpse of His pain on the cross. I cried so hard I could hardly drive. Then I thought of the women in my life that had hurt me so badly. The floodgates opened as I forgave each person from my heart.

I was free, but Neil shared with me that people who have been in bondage a long time are more like onions than bananas. You peel a banana once, and that's it. But an onion has many layers. He cautioned me that I had successfully worked through at least one layer of my problem. Other layers may surface, but at least I knew how to respond when they did.

After a couple of months, the glow of my freedom subsided. I started to backslide and return to voyeurism. I read Neil's books, *Released from Bondage* and *Walking in the Light*. I fought back against the attack and worked through the issues. Another layer of the onion was peeled away. I felt renewed again, but also worn out from the battle. I wasn't reading the Word or praying much. I didn't feel like doing it.

So I started reading Neil and Joanne's devotional, *Daily in Christ*. I was filled with guilt because of my mental lapses into voyeurism and masturbation. How could I teach Sunday School and be such a hypocrite? I told the Lord that I really loved Him and wanted to serve Him. Then I decided to prove it. I was always fearful of vows, but I made one. I told the Lord that I was His child and that I was going to be baptised again. I knew I didn't have to and that baptism didn't save me, but I wanted to erect a milestone for the Lord like the Israelites did when they crossed the Jordan.

I made the vow and the Lord honoured it beyond my wildest anticipation. He confirmed in me that I was a child of God and that He loved me. Once I submitted myself completely to Him and stopped trying to fix myself, He could do it for me.

The masturbation stopped instantaneously and has never come back. The voyeurism has also stopped. I have learned what it means to take every thought captive in obedience to Christ. Now I measure everything that comes into my mind against what the Lord says in His Word, and the truth has set me free.

Now that I know I am a child of God, there is no more low self-worth, inferiority, obsessive, negative, or perverse thoughts, or secret behaviour. I busted through that last layer of the onion like a rocket. There may be more layers ahead, but this time I am armed with the Lord's belt of truth.

Staying free

Your experience of going through the Steps to Freedom in Christ and being set free from bondages may be different from anyone else's. Why? Because each individual is unique, and each has his or her own unique set of conflicts to resolve. Some people are elated at the overwhelming sense of peace they feel for the very first time. Others may have to work through many layers yet to come. God graciously doesn't hurry us through everything at once, especially if the process is difficult. Getting free and staying free in Christ are two different issues.

Paul write, 'It was for freedom that Christ set us free' (Gal 5:1). Once we have tasted freedom in Christ, how do we keep it? It is nurtured and maintained by continuing to stand in the truth of who we are in Christ. Paul completes the verse by encouraging, 'Stand firm, then, and do not let yourselves be burdened again by the yoke of slavery.' Freedom is our inheritance, but we must not turn our freedom in Christ into ritualistic rules and regulations — legalism — or an opportunity to indulge our fleshly nature — licence (Gal 5:13). The steps you take to find your freedom are not the end of a journey but the beginning of a walk in the Spirit. Paul instructed, 'Live by the Spirit, and you will not gratify the desires of the old nature' (Gal 5:16).

Important relationships

Staying free also involves being in positive relationships with others. We absolutely need God, but we also desperately need the loving fellowship of the body of Christ. There are different kinds of relationships, and we need each of them. If you are married, God will use your spouse, even if he or she is not a believer, to help conform your life to His image. No other human knows you better than the members of your family. Giving your marriage partner access to your heart through honest communication makes your relationship vulnerable to change and intensifies healthy intimacy. In our homes and churches, we must speak the truth in love (Eph 4:25) and walk in the light (1 Jn 1:6–8). There is always the possibility of discord in any human relationship, but if interaction is founded on seeking the truth, conflicts will be minimised and resolvable. The fewer the restrictions there are to intimacy in your marriage, the closer you will come to marital harmony at every dimension — physically, emotionally, and spiritually.

Another important relationship for you to cultivate is with a spiritually mature believer of your gender — a big brother or big sister in the faith. Ask this person to disciple you and spur you on in your Christian life. A mature Christian will be your spiritual reference point to help you maintain your walk before the Lord, providing accountability and modelling for your walk of faith. Ask God to direct you to the individual whom He has chosen to fill this role at this time in your life.

You also need to be involved in a group of Christian peers who have taken the Steps to Freedom in Christ and understand your journey. You may be able to meet this need by joining a small Bible study group at your church where others can come alongside you to provide objectivity, to encourage you to grow, and to keep you on track. You will discover with others that maturity is not instantaneous but gradual. Together you will help pace each other and stimulate forward motion in your daily walk.

Consider also getting involved in a Bible-based support group with others who have struggled with sexual bondage, people who understand exactly what you have been through and what you face every day. There are a variety of support groups in nearly every community, and many large churches sponsor such groups. Seek out a group whose central focus is Jesus Christ.

Support groups can provide a positive, supportive atmosphere as you mature emotionally, physically, socially, and spiritually. Relationships formed and nurtured in the safety of a support group can be a springboard into other positive relationships.

Beware of the attitude, fostered by some support groups,

that you will be in recovery from spiritual bondage for life. Recovery may take time and effort. But inferring that the process has no end can seriously hamper the process of maturity. My colleague, Russ, talked to someone recently who illustrates this problem.

Years ago, Byron attended a support group Russ co-led. Byron came to the group for help in overcoming dependency on certain addictive behaviours. At the same time he continued to attend two other recovery groups.

As Russ talked to Byron during a meeting, it was clear that he had achieved only minimal progress over the years in mastering his negative thoughts and behaviours. Jesus had indeed become a significant part of Byron's recovery experience, but he continued to struggle with the same destructive behaviours. In tearful voice he told Russ, 'I don't feel like I'm making any headway. I'm frustrated that the process is taking so long, even though I know I will always be in a process of recovery from my addictions.' Byron appeared to be stuck in the recovery process with no hope of moving on to further personal growth and spiritual maturity. Some support groups seem to validate the slow and tedious process that they believe necessary to eventually overcome addictive behaviours.

This is certainly not everyone's experience with support or recovery groups. Many people have taken advantage of biblically based support groups and have reoriented their lives to the truth of God's Word, and I certainly encourage that.

Freedom in Christ from sexual bondage and other captivating behaviours is a gift that God offers to all His children. This gift is available in abundance and is completely satisfying. It is my prayer that, as you walk through the Steps to Freedom in Christ, you will revel in the truth of God's forgiveness and His freeing grace. He alone is the way of escape.

APPENDIX
Steps to Freedom in Christ

If you have received Christ as your personal Saviour, He has set you free through His victory over sin and death on the cross. If you are not experiencing freedom, it may be because you have not stood firm in the faith or actively taken your place in Christ. It is the Christian's responsibility to do whatever is necessary to maintain a right relationship with God. Your eternal destiny is not at stake; you are already secure in Christ. But your daily victory is at stake if you fail to claim and maintain your position in Christ.

You are not the helpless victim caught between two nearly equal but opposite heavenly superpowers; Satan is a deceiver. Only God is omnipotent (all-powerful), omnipresent (always-present), and omniscient (all-knowing). Sometimes the reality of sin and the presence of evil may seem more real than the presence of God, but that is part of Satan's deception. Satan is a defeated foe, and we are in Christ. A true knowledge of God and our identity in Christ are the greatest determinants of our mental health. A false concept of God, a distorted understanding of who we are as children of God, and the misplaced deification of Satan (attributing God's attributes to Satan) are the greatest contributors to mental illness.

As you prepare to go through the Steps to Freedom in Christ, you need to remember that the only power Satan has is the power of the lie. As soon as you expose the lie, Satan's power is broken. The battle is for your mind. If

Satan can get you to believe a lie, he can control your life. But you don't have to let him control you. If you are going through the steps by yourself, don't pay attention to any lying, intimidating thoughts in your mind, such as, 'This isn't going to work,' 'God doesn't love me,' 'I'm just going to fall back into the same traps of sexual sin,' etc. Such thoughts are lies from the pit. They can only control you if you believe them, so don't.

If you are going through the steps with a pastor, counsellor, or prayer partner (which we strongly recommend if there has been severe trauma in your life), share any thoughts you have which are in opposition to what you are attempting to do. As soon as you expose the lie, the power of Satan is broken. You must co-operate with the person trying to help you by sharing what is going on inside.

Knowing the nature of the battle for our minds, we can pray authoritatively to stop any interference. The steps begin with a suggested prayer and declaration. If you are going through the steps by yourself, you will need to change some of the personal pronouns ('I' instead of 'we', etc.).

Prayer

Dear heavenly Father, we acknowledge Your presence in this room and in our lives. You are the only omniscient (all-knowing), omnipotent (all-powerful), and omnipresent (always-present) God. We are dependent upon You, for apart from Christ we can do nothing. We stand in the truth that all authority in heaven and on earth has been given to the resurrected Christ, and because we are in Christ, we share that authority in order to make disciples and set captives free. We ask You to fill us with Your Holy Spirit and lead us into all truth. We pray for Your complete protection and ask for Your guidance. In Jesus' name we pray. Amen.

Declaration

In the name and authority of the Lord Jesus Christ, we command Satan and all evil spirits to release (name) in order that (name) can be free to know and choose to do the will of God. As children of God seated with Christ in the heavenlies, we agree that every enemy of the Lord Jesus Christ is bound and gagged to silence. We say to Satan and all his evil workers that he cannot inflict any pain or in any way prevent God's will from being accomplished in (name).

The following seven specific steps will help you experience the full freedom and victory that Christ purchased for you on the cross. These steps will help you walk free of many areas of bondage, but in this book specific application is made to areas of sexual bondage. Realising your freedom will be the result of what you choose to believe, confess, forgive, renounce, and forsake. No one can do it for you. The battle for your mind can only be won as you personally choose truth.

As you go through these Steps to Freedom, remember that Satan will be defeated only if you confront him verbally. He cannot read your mind, and he is under no obligation to obey your thoughts. Only God has complete knowledge of your mind. As you take each step, it is important that you submit to God inwardly and resist the devil by reading aloud each prayer, verbally renouncing Satan, confessing sin, forgiving offenders, etc.

You will be taking a fierce moral inventory and making a rock-solid commitment to truth. If your problems stem from a source other than those covered in these steps, you have nothing to lose by going through them. If you are sincere, the only thing that can happen is that you will get right with God on these issues.

Step 1: Counterfeit Versus Real

Many roots of sexual perversion and bondage are found in false teaching and the occult. So the first step to freedom in Christ is to renounce your previous or current involvements with satanically inspired occult practices and false religions. You need to renounce any activity and group which denies Jesus Christ, offers guidance through any source other than the absolute authority of the written Word of God, or requires secret initiations, ceremonies, or covenants.

In order to help you assess your spiritual experiences, begin this step by asking God to reveal false guidance and counterfeit religious experiences.

Dear heavenly Father, I ask You to guard my heart and my mind and reveal to me any and all involvement I have had either knowingly or unknowingly with cultic or occult practices, false religions, and false teachers. In Jesus' name I pray. Amen.

Using the 'Non-Christian Spiritual Experience Inventory' shown below, circle any activities in which you have been involved in any way. This list is not exhaustive, but it will guide you in identifying non-Christian experiences. Add any other involvements you have had. Even if you 'innocently' participated in something or watched someone do it, you should write it on your list to renounce, just in case you unknowingly gave Satan a foothold.

Non-Christian
Spiritual Experience Inventory

Astral projection
Automatic writing
Bahaism
Black and white magic
Black Muslim
Blood pacts or cut yourself in a
　destructive way
Christian Science
Clairvoyance
Dungeons and Dragons

Eckankar
Father Divine
Fetishism (worship of objects)
Fortune-telling
Ghosts
Hare Krishna
Herbert W. Armstrong
Hinduism
Incubi and succubi (sexual spirits)
Islam
Jehovah's Witnesses
Magic eight ball
Masons
Materialisation
Mental suggestions or attempts to swap minds
Mormonism
New Age
Ouija board
Rod & pendulum (dowsing)
Rosicrucianism
Roy Masters
Science of Creative Intelligence
Science of the Mind
Seance
Self-hypnosis
Silva Mind Control
Speaking in trance
Spirit guides
Swedenborgianism
Table-lifting
Tarot cards
Telepathy
Theosophical Society
Transcendental Meditation
Unification Church
Unitarianism
The Way International
Yoga
Zen Buddhism
Other

Ask yourself

1. Have you ever been hypnotised, attended a New Age or parapsychology seminar, or consulted a medium, spiritist, or channeler? Explain.

2. Do you now have or have you ever had an imaginary friend or spirit guide offering you guidance or companionship? Explain.

3. Have you ever heard voices in your mind or had repeating and nagging thoughts condemning you or that were foreign to what you believe or feel, like there was a dialogue going on in your head? Explain.

4. What other spiritual experiences have you had that would be considered out of the ordinary?

5. Have you ever been involved in satanic ritual of any form? Explain.

When you are confident that your list is complete, confess and renounce each involvement, whether active or passive, by praying aloud the following prayer, repeating it separately for each item on your list:

Lord, I confess that I have participated in (activity). I ask your forgiveness, and I renounce (activity).

If you have had any involvement in satanic ritual or heavy occult activity (or you suspect past involvement because of blocked memories, severe nightmares, or sexual dysfunction or bondage), you need to state aloud the special renunciations which follow. Read across the page, renouncing first the item in the column for the Kingdom of Darkness and then affirming its counterpart in the Kingdom of Light. Continue down the page in this manner.

Renounce all satanic rituals, covenants, and assignments as the Lord allows you to remember them. Some people who have been subjected to satanic ritual abuse have developed multiple personalities in order to survive. Nevertheless, continue through the Steps to Freedom in order to resolve all you can remember. It is important that you resolve the demonic strongholds first. Eventually every personality must be accessed, and each one must resolve his or her issues and agree to come together in Christ. You may need someone who understands spiritual conflict to help you with this.

Special Renunciations
for Satanic Ritual Involvement

Kingdom of Darkness	Kingdom of Light
I renounce ever signing my name over to Satan	I announce that my name is now written in the Lamb's Book of Life.

I renounce any ceremony where I may have been wed to Satan.

I announce that I am the bride of Christ.

I renounce any and all covenants that I made with Satan.

I announce that I am a partaker of the New Covenant with Christ.

I renounce all satanic assignments for my life, including duties, marriage, and children.

I announce and commit myself to know and do only the will of God and accept only His guidance.

I renounce all spirit guides assigned to me.

I announce and accept only the leading of the Holy Spirit.

I renounce ever giving of my blood in the service of Satan.

I trust only in the shed blood of my Lord Jesus Christ.

I renounce ever eating of flesh or drinking of blood for satanic worship.

By faith I eat only the symbolic flesh and drink only the symbolic blood of Jesus in Holy Communion.

I renounce any and all guardians and Satanist parents that were assigned to me.

I announce that God is my Father and the Holy Spirit is my Guardian by whom I am sealed.

I renounce any baptism in blood or urine whereby I am identified with Satan.

I announce that I have been baptised into Christ Jesus and my identity is now in Christ.

I renounce any and all sacrifices that were made on my behalf by which Satan may claim ownership of me.

I announce that only the sacrifice of Christ has any hold on me. I belong to Him. I have been purchased by the blood of the Lamb.

Step 2: Deception Versus Truth

Truth is the revelation of God's Word, but we need to acknowledge the truth in the inner self (Ps 51:6). When David lived a lie after committing adultery and murder, he suffered greatly. When he finally found freedom by acknowledging the truth, he wrote, 'How blessed is the man...in whose spirit is no deceit' (Ps 32:2). We are to lay aside falsehood and speak the truth in love (Eph 4:15,25). A mentally healthy person is one who is in touch with reality and relatively free of anxiety. Both qualities should characterise the Christian who renounces deception and embraces the truth.

You doubtless became trapped in sexual bondage because you believed Satan's lies about sex and/or your sexuality. Begin this critical step by expressing aloud the following prayer regarding deceit and truth. Don't let the enemy accuse you with thoughts such as 'I wish I could believe this, but I can't' or any other lies in opposition to what you are proclaiming. Even if you have difficulty doing so, you need to pray the prayer and read the doctrinal affirmation which follows.

Dear heavenly Father, I know that You desire truth in the inner self and that facing this truth is the way of liberation (Jn 8:32). I acknowledge that I have been deceived by the father of lies (Jn 8:44) and that I have deceived myself (1 Jn 1:8). I pray in the name of the Lord Jesus Christ that You, heavenly Father, will rebuke all deceiving spirits by virtue of the shed blood and resurrection of the Lord Jesus Christ. By faith I have received You into my life and I am now seated with Christ in the heavenlies (Eph 2:6). I acknowledge that I have the responsibility and authority to resist the devil, and when I do so, he will flee from me. I now ask the Holy Spirit to guide me into all truth (Jn 6:13). I ask You to 'search me, O God,

and know my heart; try me and know my anxious thoughts; and see if there be any hurtful way in me, and lead me in the everlasting way' (Ps 139:23,24 NASB). In Jesus' name I pray. Amen.

You may want to pause at this point to consider some of Satan's deceptive schemes. In addition to false teachers, false prophets, and deceiving spirits, you can deceive yourself. Now that you are alive in Christ and forgiven, you never have to live a lie or defend yourself. Christ is your defence. How have you deceived or attempted to defend yourself according to the following?

Self-deception

____ Being a hearer and not a doer of the Word (James 1:22; 4:17).

____ Saying you have no sin (1 Jn 1:8).

____ Thinking you are something when you are not (Gal 6:3).

____ Thinking you are wise in this age (1 Cor 3:18,19).

____ Thinking you will not reap what you sow (Gal 6:7).

____ Thinking the unrighteous will inherit the kingdom of God (1 Cor 6:9).

____ Thinking you can associate with bad company and not be corrupted (1 Cor 15:33).

Self-defence (defending ourselves instead of trusting in Christ)

____ Denial (conscious or subconscious).

____ Fantasy (escape from the real world).

____ Emotional insulation (withdrawal to avoid rejection).

____ Regression (reverting back to a less threatening time).

____ Displacement (taking out frustrations on others).

____ Projection (blaming others).

____ Rationalisation (defending self through verbal excursion).

For the self-deceiving attitudes and actions which have been true of you, pray aloud:

Lord, I agree that I have been deceived in the area of (attitude or action). Thank You for forgiving me. I commit myself to know and follow Your truth. Amen.

Choosing the truth may be difficult if you have been deceived and living a lie for many years. You may need to seek professional help to weed out the defence mechanisms you have depended upon to survive. Knowing that you are forgiven and accepted as God's child is what sets you free to face reality and declare your dependence on Him.

Faith is the biblical response to the truth, and believing the truth is a choice. When someone says, 'I want to believe God, but I just can't,' he is being deceived. Of course you can believe God! Faith is something you *decide to do*, not something you *feel like doing*. Believing the truth doesn't make it true. It's true; therefore we believe it. The New Age movement is distorting the truth by saying we create reality through what we believe. We can't create reality with our minds; we face reality. It's what or who you believe in that counts. Everybody believes in something, and everybody walks by faith according to what he or she believes. But if what you believe isn't true, then how you live won't be right.

Historically, the church has found great value in publicly declaring its beliefs. The Apostles' Creed and the Nicene Creed have been recited for centuries. Read aloud the following affirmation of faith, and do so again as often as necessary to renew your mind. Read it daily for several weeks.

Doctrinal Affirmation

I recognise that there is only one true and living God (Ex 20:2,3) who exists as the Father, Son, and Holy Spirit, and that He is worthy of all honour, praise, and glory as the Creator, Sustainer, and Beginning and End of all things (Rev 4:11; 5:9,10; Is 43:1,7,21).

I recognise Jesus Christ as the Messiah, the Word who became flesh and dwelt among us (Jn 1:1,14). I believe that He came to destroy the works of Satan (1 Jn 3:8), that He disarmed the rulers and authorities and made a public display of them, having triumphed over them (Col 2:15).

I believe that God has proven His love for me because when I was still a sinner, Christ died for me (Rom 5:8). I believe that He delivered me from the domain of darkness and transferred me to His kingdom, and in Him I have redemption, the forgiveness of sins (Col 1:13,14).

I believe that I am now a child of God (1 Jn 3:1–3) and that I am seated with Christ in the heavenlies (Eph 2:6). I believe that I was saved by the grace of God through faith, that it was a gift and not the result of any works on my part (Eph 2:8).

I choose to be strong in the Lord and in the strength of His might (Eph 6:10). I put no confidence in the flesh (Phil 3:3), for the weapons of our warfare are not of the flesh (2 Cor 10:4). I put on the whole armour of God (Eph 6:10–20), and I resolve to stand firm in my faith and resist the evil one.

I believe that apart from Christ I can do nothing (Jn 15:5), so I declare myself dependent on Him. I choose to abide in Christ in order to bear much fruit and glorify the Lord (Jn 15:8). I announce to Satan that Jesus is my Lord

(1 Cor 12:3), and I reject any counterfeit gifts or works of Satan in my life.

I believe that the truth will set me free (Jn 8:32) and that walking in the light is the only path of fellowship (1 Jn 1:7). Therefore, I stand against Satan's deception by taking every thought captive in obedience to Christ (2 Cor 10:5).

I declare that the Bible is the only authoritative standard (2 Tim 3:15,16). I choose to speak the truth in love (Eph 4:15).

I choose to present my body as an instrument of righteousness, a living and holy sacrifice, and I renew my mind by the living Word of God in order that I may prove that the will of God is good, acceptable, and perfect (Rom 6:13; 12:1,2).

I put off the old self with its evil practices and put on the new self (Col 3:9,10), and I declare myself to be a new creature in Christ (2 Cor 5:17).

I ask You, heavenly Father, to fill me with Your Holy Spirit (Eph 5:18), lead me into all truth (Jn 16:13), and empower my life that I may live above sin and not carry out the desires of the flesh (Gal 5:16). I crucify the flesh (Gal 5:24) and choose to walk by the Spirit.

I renounce all selfish goals and choose the ultimate goal of love (1 Tim 1:5). I choose to obey the two greatest commandments: to love the Lord my God with all my heart, soul, and mind, and to love my neighbour as myself (Mt 22:37–39).

I believe that Jesus has all authority in heaven and on earth (Mt 28:18) and that He is the head over all rule and authority (Col 2:10). I believe that Satan and his demons are subject to me in Christ because I am a member of Christ's body (Eph 1:19–23). Therefore I obey the command to submit to God and to resist the devil (James 4:7), and I command Satan in the name of Christ to leave my presence.

Step 3: Bitterness Versus Forgiveness

You may have been mildly encouraged or strongly influenced into sexual sin and bondage by other persons. Perhaps a relative or neighbour sexually abused you as a child, or a sibling or schoolmate introduced you to pornography, or a boyfriend or girlfriend used you for sexual experimentation. You may harbour strong feelings against these people for their thoughtless, selfish, and sinful deeds — anger, hatred, bitterness, resentment.

You need to forgive others so that Satan cannot take advantage of you (2 Cor 2:10,11). As Christians, we are to be merciful just as our heavenly Father is merciful (Lk 6:36). We are to forgive as we have been forgiven (Eph 4:31,32). Use the following prayer to ask God to bring to your mind the names of people you need to forgive:

Dear heavenly Father, I thank You for the riches of Your kindness, forbearance, and patience, knowing that Your kindness has led me to repentance (Rom 2:4). I confess that I have not extended that same patience and kindness toward others who have offended me, but instead I have harboured bitterness and resentment. I pray that during this time of self-examination You will bring to my mind the people I have not forgiven in order that I may do so (Mt 18:35). I ask this in the precious name of Jesus. Amen.

As names come to mind, make a list of only the names. Include at the end of your list 'myself'. Forgiving yourself is accepting God's cleansing and forgiveness. Also, write 'thoughts against God'. Thoughts raised up against the knowledge of God will usually result in angry feelings toward Him. Technically, we don't forgive God because He cannot commit any sin. But you need to specifically renounce false expectations and thoughts about God and agree to release any anger you have toward Him.

Before you pray to forgive the people on your list, stop and consider what forgiveness is, what it is not, what decision you will be making, and what the consequences will be.

Forgiveness is not forgetting. People who try to forget find that they cannot. God says He will remember our sins no more (Heb 10:17), but God, being omniscient, cannot forget. 'Remember our sins no more' means that God will never use the past against us (Ps 103:12). Forgetting may be the result of forgiveness, but it is never the means of forgiveness. When we bring up the past against others, we are saying we haven't forgiven them.

Forgiveness is a choice, a crisis of the will. Since God requires us to forgive, it is something we can do. But forgiveness is difficult for us because it pulls against our concept of justice. We want revenge for offences suffered. However, we are told never to take our own revenge (Rom 12:19). You say, 'Why should I let these people off the hook?' That is precisely the problem. You are still hooked to them, still bound by your past. You will let them off your hook, but they are never off God's hook. He will deal with them fairly, something we cannot do.

You say, 'You don't understand how much these people hurt me!' By not forgiving them, you are still being hurt by them. How do you stop the pain? Forgive. You don't forgive others for their sake; you do it for your sake, so you can be free. Your need to forgive isn't an issue between you and the offender; it's between you and God.

Forgiveness is agreeing to live with the consequences of another person's sin. Forgiveness is costly. You pay the price of the evil you forgive. You're going to live with those consequences whether you want to or not; your only choice is whether you will do so in the bitterness of unforgiveness or the freedom of forgiveness. Jesus took the consequences of your sin upon Himself. All true forgiveness is substitutionary, because no one really forgives without bearing the consequences of the other person's sin. God the Father 'made Him who had no sin to be sin for us, so that in him we might become the righteousness of God' (2 Cor 5:21).

Where is the justice? It is the cross of Christ that makes forgiveness legally and morally right: 'The death he died, he died to sin once for all' (Rom 6:10).

How do you forgive from your heart? You acknowledge the hurt and the hate. If your forgiveness doesn't visit the emotional core of your life, it will be incomplete. Many people feel the pain of interpersonal offences, but they won't or don't know how to acknowledge it. Let God bring the pain to the surface so He can deal with it. This is where the healing takes place.

Decide that you will bear the burdens of their offences by not using the past against them in the future. This doesn't mean you must tolerate sin; you must always take a stand against sin.

Don't wait to forgive until you feel like forgiving; you will never get there. Feelings take time to heal after the choice to forgive is made and Satan has lost his place (Eph 4:26,27). Freedom is what will be gained, not a feeling.

As you pray, God may bring to mind offending people and experiences you have totally forgotten. Let Him do it even if it is painful. Remember, you are doing this for your sake. God wants you to be free. Don't rationalise or explain the offender's behaviour. Forgiveness is dealing with your pain and leaving the other person to God. Positive feelings will follow in time; freeing yourself from the past is the critical issue right now.

Don't say, 'Lord, please help me to forgive,' because He is already helping you. Don't say, 'Lord, I want to forgive,' because you are bypassing the hard-core choice to forgive, which is your responsibility. Stay with each individual until you are sure you have dealt with all the remembered pain — what the offender did, how he or she hurt you, how he or she made you feel (rejected, unloved, unworthy, dirty, etc.).

You are now ready to forgive the people on your list so that you can be free in Christ, with those people no longer having any control over you. For each person on your list, pray aloud:

Lord, I forgive (name) for (specifically identify all offences and painful memories or feelings).

Step 4: Rebellion Versus Submission

We live in a rebellious generation. Many people believe it is their right to sit in judgement of those in authority over them. But rebelling against God and His authority gives Satan an opportunity to attack. As our General, the Lord commands us to get into ranks and follow Him. He will not lead us into temptation, but He will deliver us from evil (Mt 6:13).

You may have a problem with authority figures because someone you looked up to or followed was instrumental in your moral downfall. Perhaps a teacher or coach abused you. Perhaps an employer or spiritual leader took advantage of you sexually. You may not trust or want to submit to other leaders because of what happened to you.

We have two biblical responsibilities in regard to authority figures: Pray for them and submit to them. The only time God permits us to disobey earthly leaders is when they require us to do something morally wrong before God or attempt to rule outside the realm of their authority.

Pray the following prayer:

Dear heavenly Father, You have said that rebellion is as the sin of witchcraft and insubordination is as iniquity and idolatry (1 Sam 15:23). I know that in action and attitude I have sinned against You with a rebellious heart. I ask Your forgiveness for my rebellion and pray that by the shed blood of the Lord Jesus Christ all ground gained by evil spirits because of my rebelliousness will be cancelled. I pray that You will shed light on all my ways that I may know the full extent of my rebelliousness. I now choose to adopt a submissive spirit and a servant's heart. In the name of Christ Jesus, my Lord, I pray. Amen.

Being under authority is an act of faith. You are trusting God to work through His established lines of authority. There are times when employers, parents, and husbands violate the laws of civil government which are ordained by God to protect innocent people against abuse. In those cases you need to appeal to the state for your protection. In many states, the law requires such abuse to be reported.

In difficult cases, such as continuing abuse at home, you may need further counsel. In some cases, when earthly authorities have abused their position and require disobedience to God or a compromise in your commitment to Him, you need to obey God rather than man.

We are all admonished to submit to one another as equals in Christ (Eph 5:21). However, there are specific lines of authority in Scripture for the purpose of accomplishing common goals:

- Civil government (Rom 13:1–7; 1 Tim 2:1–4; 1 Pet 2:13–17);

- Parents (Eph 6:1–3);

- Husband (1 Pet 3:1–4);

- Employer (1 Pet 2:18–23);

- Church leaders (Heb 13:17);

- God (Daniel 9:5,9).

Examine each area and ask God to forgive you for those times you have not been submissive:

Lord, I agree I have been rebellious toward (name or position). Please forgive me for this rebellion. I choose to be submissive and obedient to Your Word. In Jesus' name I pray. Amen.

Step 5: Pride Versus Humility

Pride is a killer. Pride says, 'I can do it! I can get myself out of this mess of immorality without God or anyone else's help.' But we can't! We absolutely need God, and we desperately need each other. Paul wrote, 'We…worship in the Spirit of God and glory in Christ Jesus and put no confidence in the flesh' (Phil 3:3 NASB). Humility is confidence properly placed. We are to be 'strong in the Lord and in His mighty power' (Eph 6:10). James 4:6–10 and 1 Peter 5:1–10 reveal that spiritual conflict follows pride.

Use the following prayer to express your commitment to live humbly before God:

Dear heavenly Father, You have said that pride goes before destruction and an arrogant spirit before stumbling (Prov 16:18). I confess that I have lived independently and have not denied myself, picked up my cross daily, and followed You (Mt 16:24). In so doing, I have given ground to the enemy in my life. I have believed that I could be successful and live victoriously by my own strength and resources. I now confess that I have sinned against You by placing my will before Yours and by centring my life around self instead of You. I now renounce the self-life and by so doing cancel all the

ground that has been gained in my members by the enemies of the Lord Jesus Christ. I pray that You will guide me so that I will do nothing from selfishness or empty conceit, but with humility of mind I will regard others as more important than myself (Phil 2:3). Enable me through love to serve others and in honour prefer others (Rom 12:10). I ask this in the name of Christ Jesus my Lord. Amen.

Having made that commitment, now allow God to show you any specific areas of your life where you have been prideful, such as:

____ Stronger desire to do my will than God's will.

____ More dependent upon my strengths and resources than God's.

____ Sometimes believe that my ideas and opinions are better than others'.

____ More concerned about controlling others than developing self-control.

____ Sometimes consider myself more important than others.

____ Tendency to think I have no needs.

____ Find it difficult to admit I was wrong.

____ Tendency to be more of a people-pleaser than a God-pleaser.

____ Overly concerned about getting the credit I deserve.

____ Driven to obtain the recognition that comes from degrees, titles, positions.

____ Often think I am more humble than others.

____ Other ways that you may have thought more highly
of yourself than you should.

For each of these that has been true in your life, pray
aloud:

Lord, I agree I have been prideful in the area of _____
_____. **Please forgive me for this pridefulness.
I choose to humble myself and place all my confidence in You.
Amen.**

Step 6: Bondage Versus Freedom

The next step to freedom deals with habitual sin. People
who have been caught in the trap of sin-confess-sin-confess
may need to follow the instructions of James 5:16: 'Confess
your sins to each other and pray for each other so that you
may be healed. The prayer of a righteous man is powerful
and effective.' Seek out a righteous person who will hold
you up in prayer and to whom you can be accountable.
Others may need only the assurance of 1 John 1:9: 'If we
confess our sins, he is faithful and just and will forgive us
our sins and purify us from all unrighteousness.'
Confession is not saying 'I'm sorry'; it's saying 'I did it.'
Whether you need the help of others or just the accountability of God, pray the following prayer:

**Dear heavenly Father, You have told us to put on the Lord
Jesus Christ and make no provision for the flesh in regard to
its lust (Rom 13:14). I acknowledge that I have given in to
fleshly lusts which wage war against my soul (1 Pet 2:11). I
thank You that in Christ my sins are forgiven, but I have
transgressed Your holy law and given the enemy an opportunity to wage war in my members (Rom 6:12,13; Eph 4:27;
James 4:1; 1 Pet 5:8). I come before Your presence to**

acknowledge these sins and to seek Your cleansing (1 Jn 1:9) that I may be freed from the bondage of sin. I now ask You to reveal to my mind the ways that I have transgressed Your moral law and grieved the Holy Spirit. In Jesus' precious name I pray. Amen.

The deeds of the flesh are numerous. You may want to open your Bible to Galatians 5:19–21 and pray through the verses, asking the Lord to reveal the ways you have specifically sinned.

It is our responsibility not to allow sin to reign in our mortal bodies by not using our bodies as an instrument of unrighteousness (Rom 6:12,13). If you are struggling with habitual sexual sins (pornography, masturbation, sexual promiscuity) or experiencing sexual difficulty and lack of intimacy in your marriage, pray as follows:

Lord, I ask You to reveal to my mind every sexual use of my body as an instrument of unrighteousness. In Jesus' precious name I pray. Amen.

As the Lord brings to your mind every sexual use of your body, whether it was done to you (rape, incest, or any sexual molestation) or willingly by you, renounce every occasion:

Lord, I renounce (name the specific use of your body) with (name the person) and ask You to break that bond.

Now commit your body to the Lord by praying:

Lord, I renounce all these uses of my body as an instrument of unrighteousness and by so doing ask You to break all bondages Satan has brought into my life through that involvement. I confess my participation. I now present my body to

You as a living sacrifice, holy and acceptable unto You, and I reserve the sexual use of my body only for marriage. I renounce the lie of Satan that my body is not clean, that it is dirty or in any way unacceptable as a result of my past sexual experiences. Lord, I thank You that You have totally cleansed and forgiven me, that You love and accept me unconditionally. Therefore, I can accept myself. And I choose to do so, to accept myself and my body as cleansed. In Jesus' name I pray. Amen.

Special prayers for specific needs

Homosexuality

Lord, I renounce the lie that You have created me or anyone else to be homosexual, and I affirm that You clearly forbid homosexual behaviour. I accept myself as a child of God and declare that You created me to be a (your sex). I renounce any bondages of Satan that have perverted my relationships with others. I announce that I am free to relate to the opposite sex in the way that You intended. In Jesus' name I pray. Amen.

Abortion

Lord, I confess that I did not assume stewardship of the life You entrusted to me, and I ask Your forgiveness. I choose to accept Your forgiveness by forgiving myself, and I now commit that child to You for Your care in eternity. In Jesus' name I pray. Amen.

Suicidal tendencies

I renounce the lie that I can find peace and freedom by taking my own life. Satan is a thief, and he comes to steal, kill, and destroy. I choose life in Christ, who said He came to give me life and to give it abundantly.

Eating disorders or cutting on yourself

I renounce the lie that my worthiness is dependent upon my appearance or performance. I renounce cutting myself, purging, or defecating as a means of cleansing myself of evil, and I announce that only the blood of the Lord Jesus Christ can cleanse me from my sin. I accept the reality that there may be sin present in me because of the lies I have believed and the wrongful use of my body, but I renounce the lie that I am evil or that any part of my body is evil. I announce the truth that I am totally accepted by Christ just as I am.

Substance abuse

Lord, I confess that I have misused substances (alcohol, tobacco, food, prescription or street drugs) for the purpose of pleasure, to escape reality, or to cope with difficult situations. The result has been the abuse of my body, the harmful programming of my mind, and the quenching of the Holy Spirit. I ask Your forgiveness, and I renounce any satanic connection or influence in my life through my misuse of chemicals or food. I cast my anxiety onto Christ, who loves me, and I commit myself to no longer yield to substance abuse but to the Holy Spirit. I ask You, heavenly Father, to fill me with Your Holy Spirit. In Jesus' name I pray. Amen.

After you have confessed all known sin, pray:

I now confess these sins to You and claim through the blood of the Lord Jesus Christ my forgiveness and cleansing. I cancel all ground that evil spirits have gained through my wilful involvement in sin. I ask this in the wonderful name of my Lord and Saviour Jesus Christ. Amen.

Step 7: Acquiescence Versus Renunciation

Acquiescence is passively agreeing with or giving in to something or someone without conscious consent. For example, to some extent your sexual bondage may be the result of tendencies or curses passed on to you from your ancestors. You did not have a vote in the matter, and likely you have little or no knowledge of such activities. You only reaped the sad results.

The last step to freedom is to renounce the sins of your ancestors and any curses which may have been placed on you. In giving the Ten Commandments God said: 'I, the Lord our God, am a jealous God, visiting the iniquity of the fathers on the children, on the third and fourth generations of those who hate Me' (Ex 20:5 NASB).

Familiar spirits can be passed on from one generation to the next if they are not renounced and if your new spiritual heritage in Christ is not proclaimed. You are not guilty for the sin of any ancestor, but because of their sin, Satan may have gained access to your family. This is not to deny that many problems are transmitted genetically or acquired from an immoral atmosphere. All three conditions can predispose an individual to a particular sin. In addition, deceived people may try to curse you, or satanic groups may try to target you. You have all the authority and protection you need in Christ to stand against such curses and assignments.

In order to walk free from past influences, read the following declaration and prayer to yourself first so that you know exactly what you are declaring and asking. Then claim your position and protection in Christ by humbling yourself before God in prayer and making the declaration aloud.

Declaration

I here and now reject and disown all the sins of my ancestors. As one who has been delivered from the power of darkness and translated into the kingdom of God's dear Son, I cancel out all demonic working that has been passed on to me from my ancestors. As one who has been crucified and raised with Jesus Christ and who sits with Him in heavenly places, I renounce all satanic assignments that are directed toward me and my ministry, and I cancel every curse that Satan and his workers have put on me.

I announce to Satan and all his forces that Christ became a curse for me (Gal 3:13) when He died for my sins on the cross. I reject any and every way in which Satan may claim ownership of me. I belong to the Lord Jesus Christ, who purchased me with His own blood. I reject all other blood sacrifices whereby Satan may claim ownership of me. I declare myself to be eternally and completely signed over and committed to the Lord Jesus Christ. By the authority that I have in Jesus Christ, I now command every familiar spirit and every enemy of the Lord Jesus Christ that is in or around me to leave my presence. I commit myself to my heavenly Father to do His will from this day forward.

Prayer

Dear heavenly Father, I come to You as Your child purchased by the blood of the Lord Jesus Christ. You are the Lord of the universe and the Lord of my life. I submit my body to You as an instrument of righteousness, a living sacrifice, that I may glorify You in my body. I now ask You to fill me with Your Holy Spirit. I commit myself to the renewing of my mind in order to prove that Your will is good, perfect, and acceptable for me. All this I do in the name and authority of the Lord Jesus Christ. Amen.

Once you have secured your freedom by going through these seven steps, you may find demonic influences attempting re-entry days or even months later. One person shared that she heard a spirit say to her mind 'I'm back' two days after she had been set free. 'No, you're not!' she proclaimed aloud. The attack ceased immediately.

One victory does not constitute winning the war. Freedom must be maintained. After completing these steps, one jubilant lady asked, 'Will I always be like this?' I told her that she would stay free as long as she remained in right relationship with God. 'Even if you slip and fall,' I encouraged, 'you know how to get right with God again.'

One victim of incredible atrocities shared this illustration: 'It's like being forced to play a game with an ugly stranger in my own home. I kept losing and wanted to quit, but the ugly stranger wouldn't let me. Finally I called the police (a higher authority), and they came and escorted the stranger out. He knocked on the door trying to regain entry, but this time I recognised his voice and didn't let him in.'

What a beautiful illustration of gaining freedom in Christ! We call upon Jesus, the ultimate authority, and He escorts the enemy out of our lives. Know the truth, stand firm, and resist the evil one. Seek out good Christian fellowship, and commit yourself to regular times of Bible study and prayer. God loves you and will never leave or forsake you.

After Care

Freedom must be maintained. You have won a very important battle in an ongoing war. Freedom is yours as long as you keep choosing truth and standing firm in the strength of the Lord. If new memories should surface or if you become aware of lies that you have believed or other non-

Christian experiences you have had, renounce them and choose the truth. Some people have found it helpful to go through the steps again. As you do, read the instructions carefully.

For your encouragement and further study, read *Victory Over the Darkness* (or the youth version, *Stomping Out the Darkness*), and *The Bondage Breaker* (or *The Bondage Breaker: Youth Edition*). If you are a parent, read *The Seduction of Our Children*. *Walking in the Light* (formerly *Walking through the Darkness*) was written to help people understand God's guidance and discern counterfeit guidance.

Also, to maintain your freedom, we suggest the following:

1. Seek legitimate Christian fellowship where you can walk in the light and speak the truth in love.

2. Study your Bible daily. Memorise key verses. You may want to express the Doctrinal Affirmation daily and look up the verses.

3. Take every thought captive to the obedience of Christ. Assume responsibility for your thought life, reject the lie, choose the truth, and stand firm in your position in Christ.

4. Don't drift away! It is very easy to get lazy in your thoughts and revert back to old habit patterns of thinking. Share your struggles openly with a trusted friend. You need at least one friend who will stand with you.

5. Don't expect another person to fight your battle for you. Others can help but they can't think, pray, read the Bible, or choose the truth for you.

6. Continue to seek your identity and sense of worth in Christ. Read *Living Free in Christ* and the devotional *Daily in Christ*. Renew your mind with the truth that your acceptance, security, and significance is in Christ by saturating

your mind with the statements at the end of this chapter. Read the entire list aloud morning and evening over the next several weeks.

7. Commit yourself to daily prayer. You can pray the following suggested prayers often and with confidence:

Daily Prayer

Dear heavenly Father, I honour You as my sovereign Lord. I acknowledge that You are always present with me. You are the only all powerful and only wise God. You are kind and loving in all Your ways. I love You and I thank You that I am united with Christ and spiritually alive in Him. I choose not to love the world, and I crucify the flesh and all its passions.

I thank You for the life that I now have in Christ, and I ask You to fill me with Your Holy Spirit that I may live my life free from sin. I declare my dependence upon You, and I take my stand against Satan and all his lying ways. I choose to believe the truth, and I refuse to be discouraged. You are the God of all hope, and I am confident that You will meet my needs as I seek to live according to Your Word. I express with confidence that I can live a responsible life through Christ, who strengthens me.

I now take my stand against Satan and command him and all his evil spirits to depart from me. I put on the whole armour of God. I submit my body as a living sacrifice and renew my mind by the living Word of God in order that I may prove that the will of God is good, acceptable, and perfect. I ask these things in the precious name of my Lord and Saviour Jesus Christ. Amen.

Bedtime Prayer

Thank You, Lord, that You have brought me into Your family and have blessed me with every spiritual blessing in the heavenly realms in Christ. Thank You for providing this time of renewal through sleep. I accept it as part of Your perfect plan for Your children, and I trust You to guard my mind and my body during my sleep. As I have meditated on You and Your truth during this day, I choose to let these thoughts continue in my mind while I am asleep. I commit myself to You for Your protection from every attempt of Satan or his emissaries to attack me during sleep. I commit myself to You as my rock, my fortress, and my resting place. I pray in the strong name of the Lord Jesus Christ. Amen.

Cleansing Home

After removing all articles of false worship from your home, pray aloud in every room if necessary.

Heavenly Father, we acknowledge that You are Lord of heaven and earth. In Your sovereign power and love, You have given us all things richly to enjoy. Thank You for this place to live. We claim this home for our family as a place of spiritual safety and protection from all attacks of the enemy. As children of God seated with Christ in the heavenly realm, we command every evil spirit that would claim ground in the structures and furnishings of this place based on the activities of previous occupants to leave and never to return. We renounce all curses and spells utilised against this place. We ask You, heavenly Father, to post guardian angels around this home (flat, room, etc.) to guard it from attempts of the enemy to enter and disturb Your purposes for us. We thank You, Lord, for doing this, and pray in the name of the Lord Jesus Christ. Amen.

Living in a Non-Christian Environment

After removing all articles of false worship from your room, pray aloud in the space allotted to you.

Thank You, heavenly Father, for my place to live and to be renewed by sleep. I ask You to set aside my room (my part of the room) as a place of spiritual safety for me. I renounce any allegiance given to false gods or spirits by other occupants, and I renounce any claim to this room (space) by Satan based on activities of past occupants or myself. On the basis of my position as a child of God and a joint-heir with Christ who has all authority in heaven and on earth, I command all evil spirits to leave this place and never to return. I ask You, heavenly Father, to appoint guardian angels to protect me while I live here. I pray this in the name of the Lord Jesus Christ. Amen.

In Christ I am accepted

- I am God's child (Jn 1:12).

- I am Christ's friend (Jn 15:15).

- I have been justified (Rom 5:1).

- I am united with the Lord, and I am one spirit with Him (1 Cor 6:17).

- I have been bought with a price. I belong to God (1 Cor 6:19,20).

- I am a member of Christ's body (1 Cor 12:27).

- I am a saint (Eph 1:1).

- I have been adopted as God's child (Eph 1:5).

- I have direct access to God through the Holy Spirit (Eph 2:18).

- I have been redeemed and forgiven of all my sins (Col 1:14).

- I am complete in Christ (Col 2:10).

In Christ I am secure

- I am free forever from condemnation (Rom 8:1,2).

- I am assured that all things work together for good (Rom 8:28).

- I am free from any condemning charges against me (Rom 8:31–34).

- I cannot be separated from the love of God (Rom 8:35–39).

- I have been established, anointed, and sealed by God (2 Cor 1:21,22).

- I am hidden with Christ in God (Col 3:3).

- I am confident that the good work that God has begun in me will be perfected (Phil 1:6).

- I am a citizen of heaven (Phil 3:20).

- I have not been given a spirit of fear but of power, love, and a sound mind (2 Tim 1:7).

- I can find grace and mercy in time of need (Heb 4:16).

- I am born of God, and the evil one cannot touch me (1 Jn 5:18).

In Christ I am significant

- I am the salt and light of the earth (Mt 5:13,14).

- I am a branch of the true vine, a channel of His life (Jn 15:1,5).

- I have been chosen and appointed to bear fruit (Jn 15:16).

- I am a personal witness of Christ (Acts 1:8).

- I am God's temple (1 Cor 3:16).

- I am a minister of reconciliation for God (2 Cor 5:17–21).

- I am God's co-worker (1 Cor 3:9; 2 Cor 6:1).

- I am seated with Christ in the heavenly realm (Eph 2:6).

- I am God's workmanship (Eph 2:10).

- I may approach God with freedom and confidence (Eph 3:12).

- I can do all things through Christ, who strengthens me (Phil 4:13).

Taken from *Living Free in Christ* by Neil T. Anderson, published by Regal Books.

APPENDIX
Presenting a Healthy View of Sex and Sexuality to Your Children

Paul says, 'When I was a child, I talked like a child, I thought like a child, I reasoned like a child' (1 Cor 13:11). Children don't think like adults. They live in a convoluted world of feelings and experiences. They can misunderstand messages from authority figures and peers. It would be great if we all had perfect parents who taught us the truth about love and sex, but such is not the case. Most teenagers today have been raised in pagan and/or broken homes, and many of our Christian homes are dysfunctional. Consequently, many children are not afforded the opportunity to develop their sexuality in a God-intended way. And the effect will be felt in succeeding generations.

But however healthy or unhealthy your upbringing may have been, you have the exciting opportunity to positively impact your children and bring them up in the nurture and admonition of the Lord. This includes teaching them God's truth about sex and sexuality. Sexual development should never be seen as isolated from a child's spiritual, emotional, and mental development. We should dedicate our children to the Lord, pray for their protection, and provide the emotional support and sexual education they need to develop.

Incest is double jeopardy not only because the children are sexually violated but because their parents were the offenders. Children of incestuous parents lose their spiritual covering and protection. Nothing can be more disheartening than to be abused by the very ones who are intended by God to protect them from such abuse.

In the Scriptures, sexuality and spirituality were interrelated. The Mosaic Law (Lev 12:2–7) required that a mother present a burnt offering and a sin offering for her cleansing after the birth of her first male child. The boy was to be circumcised on the eighth day, but the mother remained unclean for 33 more days. After Joseph and Mary had completed the days for their purification, they brought Jesus to Jerusalem to present Him to the Lord (Lk 2:22). God desires to be involved in all phases of life, including sex, pregnancy, birth, and development.

Healthy sexual development

Not all children develop exactly the same way, but there are several factors which should be considered essential for a child's healthy sexual development. A sense of trust should be encouraged beginning with infancy. In healthy, stable homes, emotional bonding takes place within the first nine months. Breast-feeding epitomises the closeness of mother and child and fulfills the dependency needs every baby has. The belief that an infant boy may develop into a homosexual from over-exposure to his mother's breasts is a myth. Affectionate touch is a primary means by which a child develops emotionally. Hugs, kisses, and the genuine loving touch of parents should always be perceived by the child as an affirmation of his worth. That is why it is such an incredible violation when a parent touches a child for his or her own sexual pleasure. The child may grow up feeling dirty, and some violated children can't stand to be touched even in an affirming way.

Spanking may be used as a means to shape behaviour. The intention is to shape the will by reinforcing good behaviour and discouraging wrong or wilfully defiant behaviour by spanking. Spanking should not be viewed as punishing children for doing wrong but as discipline to keep them from doing wrong again. Punishment is retroactive, but discipline is done to superintend future choices. Hebrews 12:11 reminds us, 'No discipline seems pleasant at the time, but painful. Later on, however, it produces a harvest of righteousness and peace for those who have been trained by it.' Proper discipline is a proof of a parent's love. Whenever possible, use an instrument other than the hand for spanking. The hand of a parent should be extended in love. Anytime we touch another person it should be for his or her benefit.

The exploratory stage

Children between ages two and four are in an exploratory stage. During this time they should learn to control body eliminations, with the process only understood to be dirty by the child in reference to hygiene. Fondling the genitals, like playing with their toes or curling their hair with a finger, is normal at this stage as children explore their own body parts. Conveying adult sexual taboos and stereotypes to an innocent child will prove counterproductive. It could lead a child to distorted concepts of himself in one of two ways.

First, he could develop sexual inhibitions leading to frigidity. I think we unwittingly do this when we assign silly names to body parts, like parents who say to their child, 'This is your nose, and this is your arm, and this is your waa waa.' Consequently, many adults are embarrassed by words like vagina and penis because they perceive these terms as vulgar or dirty. But why should legitimate names for God-created parts of our anatomy be considered dirty?

Second, being negative during the exploratory stage could prompt a child to respond rebelliously by thinking, 'I want to touch myself here. What's wrong with it?' Out of wilful defiance or curiosity they begin to play with themselves secretly. Parental silence or distortions may contribute to unnatural experimentation and eventually their sexual promiscuity.

If a child is sexually violated during this time, his or her development may be distorted. I have counselled adults who have confided that they have compulsively masturbated since they were three. That is not normal development. There is a good chance someone with this problem has been sexually abused as a child.

The questioning stage

Questions about sex begin between ages four and five. Children at this age neither want, need, nor can they understand a comprehensive sex talk. Start by reinforcing their questions and reviewing what they already know or have heard. Again, don't project adult feelings into a child who is not ready to understand or receive them. No storks! Fantasy answers for real questions are neither healthy nor honest.

The experimental stage

Between ages six and ten, children begin to experiment sexually. Many children during this stage will become involved in opposite-sex exploratory play or experiences. In most cases such play is normal and seldom causes any lasting problems. An over-reaction or response of horror by parents to innocent experimentation may do more damage. Nudity is an important issue at this stage. Modesty should be taught and modelled in a healthy way.

Puberty

Puberty begins between ages eleven and thirteen for most children. Hormone secretion begins three years before puberty. For the female, oestrogen and progesterone are very irregular until a year after puberty, and then the rhythmic monthly pattern of menstruation begins. For the male, testosterone increases at puberty and reaches its maximum at twenty years of age.

Personal touching of the genitals is no longer a soothing or comforting experience, but a means of sexual arousal. A healthy parental discussion should precede this time. A boy needs to understand why he experiences erections and seminal emissions. Otherwise, guilt and shame may be associated with a natural and pleasurable experience. A girl should fully understand what her monthly period is before she experiences her first one. She may be frightened or embarrassed if it occurs before she is prepared for it.

Dating

Your adolescent children must be taught that to treat a date as anything less than a child of God is to defile and defraud him or her. A college student under my ministry years ago was dating a lovely Christian lady. He shared with me a profound thought: 'I treat my girlfriend the way I think her future husband would want her to be treated.' That couple is now happily married.

Years ago I spoke at an outreach meeting to a group of high schoolers about sex. A non-Christian was there with his girlfriend. He asked, 'If I had sex with my girlfriend, would I later regret it?' What a mature question. But I think there is an even more mature one he could ask: 'Would my girlfriend later regret it?' Questions like these need to be lov-

ingly discussed with your teen children before they go out
on their first date.

Discipline and spiritual training

Prior to puberty, responsible behaviour is the major objective of parenting and Christian education. Wrong behaviour should be disciplined and good behaviour reinforced
with praise. Children should be taught what is right and
wrong, and swift, cheerful obedience should be presented as
their only viable option to parental directives. Rules should
be clearly explained, discussed to ensure understanding,
and consistently enforced in love. Rules apart from a loving
relationship lead to rebellion.

Along with the physical changes of puberty, other
changes are occurring in the child. His ability to reason has
become fully developed. Numerous studies by Jean Piaget
and other child development specialists have clearly established that the mind of an average twelve-year-old is able to
understand symbolism and abstract thoughts. It is interest-
ing that the only appearance of Christ other than being an
infant or an adult was when He was twelve. Historically,
Jewish families conduct bar mitzvahs (for boys) and bat
mitzvahs (for girls) at the completion of a child's twelfth
year, believing that he or she is now religiously responsible.
Many liturgical churches conduct confirmation classes and
ceremonies between the ages of twelve and fourteen. This is
also understood by many to be the age of identity.

Dedication to the Lord

It is my firm belief that we should dedicate ourselves as parents and our children to the Lord as soon after their birth.
Then at the earliest opportunity we should lead our children to a saving knowledge of the Lord Jesus Christ. As

they approach their twelfth birthday, they need to know who they are as children of God. As parents we can't go everywhere they go, nor can we totally protect them from the harsh realities of this world. But God can and does go with them wherever they go, and He can and will protect them. This concept is discussed in greater detail in a book I wrote with Steve Russo, *The Seduction of Our Children*. The point I want to make here is that our instruction to our children during this age concerning sex needs to go far beyond behavioural objectives such as 'Don't touch that,' 'Don't show this,' and 'Don't do that.' Simply laying down the law won't do it. Telling them what is wrong does not give them the power to stop doing it. The law is powerless to give life: 'For if a law had been given that could impart life, then righteousness would certainly have come by the law' (Gal 3:21). Our children need to understand their feelings, the nature of their thought life, and the nature of temptation. They must have a biblical understanding of who they are, who God is, and how to relate to the opposite sex.

If our children are going to walk as children of light (Eph 5:8), they must first understand who they are as children of light. Right belief determines right behaviour. If your child knew who he was as a child of God, would it affect the way he lives? The apostle John sure thought so. 'How great is the love the Father has lavished on us, that we should be called children of God! Dear friends, now we are children of God.... Everyone who has this hope in him purifies himself, just as he is pure' (1 Jn 3:1–3). It isn't what your child does that determines who he is; who he is determines what he does. Not only will a true perspective of himself affect our child's behaviour, but how he perceives others greatly determines how he treats them.

Higher Ground

Taking faith to the edge!

Discover:

- The awesome role faith plays in keeping you strong
- Why you are tempted and where to find power to resist
- How to make - and keep - decisions that honour God

You can do it. The choice is yours. Accept the challenge to take the higher ground!

ISBN 1 85424 465 5
£6.99

Radical Image

God can change your life

Discover how to:

- Live a holy life
- Handle difficult situations
- Make decisions God's way
- Surf the waves of change
- Win the battle for your mind

As a Christian you are in the process of being transformed. Get ready to take on your radical new image!

ISBN 1 85424 459 0
£5.99

Righteous Pursuit

A life-changing 40-day devotional; live your Christian life to the max!

To help you:

- Get God's input daily
- Understand what true faith is
- Say no to the negative and yes to the positive
- Make God's Word personal to your life
- Face today's challenges with integrity

ISBN 1 85424 488 4
£6.99

MONARCH
BOOKS

 # Freedom In Christ
In The UK

Church Leaders - can we help you?

Many churches use Neil Anderson's material to help Christians find their freedom in Christ - often with results that amaze them. If you are a church leader and would like to establish your own "freedom ministry", Freedom In Christ is here to help: we run a programme of conferences and training; we can provide opportunities for church leaders to see freedom appointments in action; and we are always more than happy to offer advice.

Send for our Resource Catalogue

Send for our full colour catalogue of Neil Anderson books, videos and audiocassettes. It includes resources for individuals, for churches, and for local freedom ministries as well as for specialist freedom areas such as fear, depression and addiction. It's also crammed with hints and tips.

Join the UK Freedom Fellowship

If you are ministering to your community using Neil Anderson's materials, join our network of like-minded Christians and receive regular news, encouragement and affirmation. Open to anyone involved in a local freedom ministry or considering setting one up.

For details of any of the above write to us at:

Freedom In Christ Ministries (UK), PO Box 2842, READING RG2 9RT

Or e-mail us: ukoffice@ficm.org

You can find the Freedom In Christ worldwide web site at www.ficm.org

"It is for FREEDOM that Christ has set us FREE"
Galatians 5:1

Freedom in Christ is an international, interdenominational ministry whose objective is to
"free Christ's body to advance His kingdom".

Please note that Freedom In Christ Ministries does not generally arrange personal freedom appointments but works by equipping local churches. We may be able to refer you to a local freedom ministry.